D0722326

The people who call themselves Dene Dháa, a group of the Athapaskan-speaking Natives of northwestern Canada known as the Slave or Slavey Indians, now number about one thousand and occupy three reserves in northwestern Alberta. Because their settlements were until recently widely dispersed and isolated, they have maintained their language and traditions more successfully than most other Indian groups. This collection of their stories, recorded in the Dene language with literal interlinear English glosses and in a free English translation, represents a major contribution to the documentation of the Dene language, ethnography, and folklore.

Patrick J. Moore is a linguist with the Yukon Native Language Centre; Angela Wheelock is a freelance writer.

**Studies in the Anthropology
of North American Indians**

Editors
Raymond J. DeMallie
Douglas R. Parks

WOLVERINE MYTHS AND VISIONS
Dene Traditions from Northern Alberta

Compiled by the Dene Wodih Society
Edited by Patrick Moore and Angela Wheelock
Illustrated by Dia Thurston

Published by the University of Nebraska Press,
Lincoln and London
in cooperation with the American Indian
Studies Research Institute,
Indiana University

The paper in this book meets the
minimum requirements of American
National Standard for Information
Sciences—Permanence of Paper
for Printed Library Materials,
ANSI Z39.48–1984.

Library of Congress
Cataloging-in-Publication Data
Wolverine myths and visions:
Dene traditions from northern Alberta /
    edited by Patrick Moore and Angela Wheelock;
    illustrated by Dia Thurston.
        p.   cm.—(Studies in the anthropology
of North American Indians)
    English and Slave.
"In cooperation with the American
Indian Studies Research Institute,
Indiana University."
    Includes bibliographical references.
    ISBN 0-8032-8161-7 (alk. paper)
    1. Slave Indians—Legends. 2. Slave
Indians—Religion and mythology.
3. Wolverines—Alberta—Folklore.
4. Slave language—Texts.
I. Moore, Patrick, 1954–   .
II. Wheelock, Angela, 1953–   .
III. Indiana University. American Indian
Studies Research Institute. IV. Series.
E99.S65W65   1990
398.2'08997207123—dc20
89–29379 CIP

Contents

PART TWO. DENE TEXTS

TRADITIONAL STORIES

ACCOUNTS OF THE PROPHET NÓGHA

Illustrations

Acknowledgments

This collection of Wolverine stories was originally conceived by the late George Ahnassay, who wanted young people in Assumption, Alberta to be proud of their traditions. He translated many of these stories before his tragic death in an automobile accident in 1982. The remaining English translations and Dene language versions of the stories were prepared by the members of the Dene Wodih Society: Josephine Natannah, Lorny Metchooyeah, Gena Kolay, Janice Dahdona, Ricky Seniantha, Laura Dahdona, Baptiste Metchooyeah, and Pat Moore. The collection was illustrated by Dia Ahnassay Thurston and edited by Pat Moore and Angela Wheelock.

Without the cooperation of the Dene Th'a Band and the elders who recorded these stories, this collection would not have been possible. We thank Louison Ahkimnatchie, Elisse Ahnassay, Willie Ahnassay, Sr., Willie Denechoan, Harry Dahdona, Alexis Seniantha, Emile Sutha, and Jean Marie Talley for their patience and wisdom. This project was also facilitated by the continuing friendship and support of Father Camillo, O.M.I, Dr. Jean-Guy Goulet, Associate Professor, University of Calgary, Dr. Pat McCormack, Curator of Ethnology, Provincial Museum of Alberta and Dr. Carl Urion, Associate Professor, University of Alberta. Later work on the project was supported by the Yukon Native Language Centre, whose director, Mr. John Ritter, offered many valuable comments and criticisms. Dr. Keren Rice, Associate Professor, University of Toronto also provided invaluable assistance in revising the final manuscript. Funding for this project was made possible in part by a grant from the Alberta Cultural Heritage Foundation through monies provided by Alberta Lotteries. Support for this project by Alberta Culture and the Alberta Native Secretariat is also greatly appreciated. Documentation of the Tea Dance in northern Alberta was funded by the Boreal Institute for Northern Studies, which support is gratefully acknowledged.

Introduction

The stories are to help people live, that is why people told about these dangerous beings. Yes, old men told these stories. They talked to them, that way, that way, that way.

Harry Dahdona

The Dene of northwestern Alberta, Canada, told the stories brought together in this book. These people, who call themselves *Dene Dháa** 'Ordinary People,' are called Slavey [slévi] by linguists and anthropologists.

Although the Dene Dháa have a rich oral tradition recording many aspects of their life in the bush, all the stories presented here are of one genre, with a particular character, Wolverine,† as the protagonist. Dene, like many native peoples, believe that long ago animals talked and lived like humans. Standing out in these stories are Wolf and Wolverine, animals with the power to help people or destroy them, to be spiritual guides or relentless enemies. Wolf, who often helped people in Dene stories, is respected by many traditional Dene Dháa, who will not trap wolves for fur. Wolverine is a trickster and cultural transformer in Dene tradition, much like Coyote in Navajo or Raven in Northwest Coast traditions. Wolverines may destroy people's traps and furs and ruin their belongings, yet paradoxically in stories Wolverine also has great powers of healing and transformation.

In this century a Dene Dháa prophet called *Nógha* 'Wolverine' became the leader of the messianic Tea Dance religion in northwestern Alberta. His visions and accounts of his life show how historic events have become myth and how myth pervades contemporary Dene worldview. One story-teller said about the animal Wolverine, "His tracks go on and on, back to the time before people were living here." The stories lead the reader back to that time.

---

*This is also spelled *Dene Th'a* by the local band. I have used the term *Dene Dháa* to avoid confusion with other groups such as Dogrib, Kaska, Chipewyan, and others who also call themselves *Dene*. *Dene Dháh* 'Dene Language' is the language spoken by the *Dene Dháa*. The term *Dene* is used to refer to Northern Athabaskans in general.

† The names of specific animals are capitalized when they are used to mean the spirit animal which appears in human form.

A Short History of the Dene Dháa

*Even though there is only one person left to dance you will not be tired,
and you will have the strength to sing for him as he dances. God made this
land, and we should live following God's ways.*

The Prophet Nógha

Approximately one thousand Dene Dháa are presently settled on three
reservations in Alberta: Assumption, Meander River, and Bushie River.
Until the 1950s they lived in small family groups which moved across
northwestern Alberta, northeastern British Columbia, and the southern
Northwest Territories. These areas are still used for trapping and hunting,
but the former settlements and camps at Duck House, Zama Lake, Bistcho
Lake, Habay, Rabbit River, Amber River, and Rainbow Lake are now
abandoned.

During the early trading period, and until the 1950s, this region of
Alberta was relatively isolated in comparison to communities on the Peace
and Mackenzie rivers. Alexandra and Louise Falls on the Hay River
effectively blocked transport up that stream, so that most trade was
conducted at posts beyond the periphery of Dene Dháa territory. Trappers
traveled overland by dogsled and on horseback to trade at Fort Vermilion,
Hay River, Fort Liard, Fort Nelson, and Peace River. When white traders
did enter the area, freight had to be transported overland between Hudson
Bay posts at Fort Vermilion, on the Peace River, and Meander River, on the
Hay River, at considerable expense.

The early missionization of the area by Catholic priests was conducted
from the same peripheral outposts. Missionaries from Fort Vermilion visited
the area regularly after 1860 and referred to all Dene in the area served by
Fort Vermilion as Beaver Indians. In the 1870s Father Emile Petitot, an
Oblate missionary, reached Bistcho Lake from the Mackenzie River. Also
beginning in the 1870s priests from Fort Vermilion visited the Hay Lakes
area each summer, and in 1927 a church was built at Habay where the
priests stayed during these visits. The residential school and mission in
Assumption were not built until 1951.

Even though they remained somewhat inaccessible from the outside,
Dene Dháa were able to travel freely over the vast network of lakes, rivers,
and wetlands that characterizes northwestern Alberta. Through spring
burning they maintained large areas of open meadows and new-growth
forest as bison and moose habitats. There were dependable supplies of fish,
and successful trappers regularly returned with a hundred or more beaver
from the spring hunt. Dene Dháa in the Hay and Zama lakes area may have
avoided some of the epidemics which affected the Beaver Indians living

along the Peace River valley because northwestern Alberta was not on the main trade routes and the native population was widely dispersed.

Partly because initial contact between Dene Dháa and Europeans was not as intense as it was for groups such as the Beaver and Chipewyan living nearer the major trading centers, the Dene Dháa have maintained their own traditions. Children of all ages in Assumption still speak their own language, and most older people continue to speak only the Dene language. Native religious celebrations, called Tea Dances in English, are attended by the whole community, and older people still share traditional Dene Dháa stories, including many tales about Wolverine.

The Dene storytellers represented in this collection were reared traditionally, moving between campsites with their families. One woman described this traditional way of life:

> The tent poles pointed out to the sky, and people decorated the opening at the top with bones. To make camp we simply covered the floor with spruce boughs, set up meat poles, and cut some wood and made a fire. During the winter we lined the inside of the tent with dry grass. When the fire died down we covered up with rabbit skin blankets. They used to slide off—you had to be careful if you slept next to the fire.

Storytellers often describe periods of hardship when they ate lichens or stale tea leaves, and children had to help feed their families. One man said, "If we saw some rabbit tracks we made camp, then waited until the moon was bright to set snares. Early in the morning I used to run off to check them, and if I caught one rabbit I was thankful to have something to eat."

The fur trade had already affected the lives of the Dene Dháa when these storytellers were growing up. Guns and other trade items had been introduced. People used horses as well as dogs to move their camps and transport furs. Formerly only a single dog was used by each woman to assist with moving camp. In the fur trade period some basic ideas of Christianity were well known. The traditional stories themselves, however, are based in the world that preceded contact with fur traders. In that world there are no horses, guns, matches, or flour, and religion centers on dreams and visions received from animal people. Indeed, traditional stories are among the best sources of information on how Dene lived and what they believed before contact with white culture.

The fur trade period did not result in permanent settlements in this area, since most Dene Dháa continued to travel almost continually. It was at this time, however, that Dene ceremonies were transformed to become the Tea Dance religion, which is described in Part Two below. The religious leader

Nógha was active during the end of this period of change, when people were still living year-round in small camps.

In the 1930s Dene began to build log houses at Meander River, Habay, Zama Lake, and elsewhere. Eventually, permanent settlements developed as schools, stores, health facilities, and roads were constructed. Nevertheless, elders still remained the focus of the community throughout this period and kept Dene traditions alive.

Today, as fewer young people live in the bush, they are losing contact with the lifestyle and beliefs of their parents and grandparents, and the Dene Dháa oral tradition is waning. Although young people are still fluent in their native language, few of them are learning the stories well enough to tell them, preferring to watch television instead.

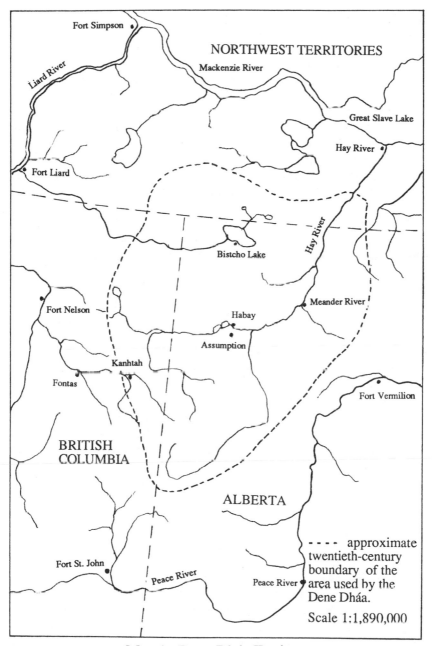

Map 1. Dene Dháa Territory

The Storytellers and Their Stories

I could tell you stories for three or four hours without stopping. Hey! I know lots of stories! I used to tell stories all night until dawn.
Jean Marie Talley

Dene storytellers usually start by naming the people who told them the stories. "These are not my stories, but my father's stories, and those of an old man called Ekucho as well," said one storyteller.

"I remember visiting the old Talley," one woman told me. "He wouldn't start to tell stories until there was a big pile of firewood. When the wood was cut, he cooked all sorts of special foods for us before he started his stories."

The cycle continues back through generations as elders tell about the people they knew. They recall the places where they camped together: Gun Prairie, Rosehip Hill, Big Willow Creek, Goose Blind, and others. The animals come alive from the memories of these places. "My grandfather knew about different animals," one man told me. "We were paddling up the Hay River to hunt for moose when he told me to watch the yellowlegs [a shorebird]. Those birds keep track of the moose near the water and can tell you where the moose are."

Dene Dháa storytellers are part of a well established oral tradition, within which some storytellers are more knowledgeable than others. One may be known for a dramatic style of presentation, another for attention to detail or for explanations of the meanings of stories. To become a storyteller, Dene study as adults with one or more expert storytellers. When they know the stories well themselves, they tell and retell them, developing their own style. The best storytellers were so well known that people would travel long distances to visit and hear their stories.

Although the stories are based on shared traditions, each storyteller has slightly different versions which are usually shared with relatives in the same way as food or shelter. Men also learn stories from older men with whom they regularly hunt and trap.

Stories are so highly valued that anyone who wants to learn them has to treat the elders with respect. One man recalled that he cut wood all winter for his grandfather so he would tell stories. Others brought rabbits, ducks, and moose meat to storytellers. The elders who contributed to this collection have been honored in this way. These storytellers are religious leaders, respected elders, and authorities on Dene tradition. They learned the traditional stories of Wolverine from the foremost storytellers of the preceding generation and listened to the religious leader Nógha's prophecies.

Traditional stories are told to children to prepare them to survive in the bush: that they should work hard, respect animals, and avoid danger. They are prepared to receive a vision of animal people as they travel in the bush. Many Dene stories are clearly accounts of these visions, which are experiences of various kinds with animal spirits in dreams or in the bush. In some stories a person sets out to seek a vision and meets a group of animal people; or children are kidnapped and raised by animal people. In other stories people use magical powers which they have received from animals to cure people or avenge their relatives. In stories about culture heroes, such as *Yamonhdeyi* 'The Man Who Traveled Around The World,' and *Mbetsun Yendéhshéhi* 'The Boy Raised By His Grandmother,' monster animals still eat people. Thus stories establish a variety of relations between humans and animals which are described in visions.

In Dene stories, animals and people still pass between our world and theirs. Animals appear in human form, children are raised by animals, and people assume the powers or forms of animals. The animals in the stories are spirit beings that Dene saw in visions. One man told a story in which wolves came upon a man as he slept:

> They were beautiful. They were wearing bright clothing unmarked by sparks. Two came ahead of the rest, then again they circled around him. An old man was walking behind. "My sons, this man is pitiful; so hungry there is no fat left on him. Go kill some grouse to feed him. What are you waiting for?" The man thought he heard a wolf howl as the young men ran off on snowhoes.

Wolves and even wolverines may have interacted more freely with Dene prior to the arrival of Europeans. Mech (1988) reports being accepted with relative ease as a member of a wolf pack on Ellesmere Island in the high arctic, where they have not been hunted. Wolves may have similarly accepted the Dene, who did not hunt them before Europeans intervened. The explorer Samuel Hearne (1911:339), who traveled with the Chipewyan from 1769 to 1772, observed:

> I have frequently seen the Indians go to their [wolves'] dens, and take out the young ones and play with them. I never knew a Northern Indian to hurt one of them, on the contrary, they always put them carefully into the den again; and I have sometimes seen them paint the faces of the young wolves with vermillion, or red ochre.

In the stories of culture heros, animals are present both as animal people and as ordinary animals. In other stories only animal people are present.

Some Dene feel that these stories of animal people were told to human beings in visions by the animal people themselves, a belief similar to the traditions of their linguistic relatives, the Navajo, concerning the mythological origins of such ceremonies as Blessingway or Coyoteway. Luckert (1979:18-19) records the following tradition for the origin of the Navajo Coyoteway Ceremony:

> Rock Extending Between (Middle Point) is the name of the place. It snowed early in the morning. A man was going out with the intention to hunt. He saw Coyote tracks. He started backtracking. . . . and saw Coyote Human Beings. They were in fact human beings, but they were Coyote People. . . . Toward evening the Coyote People assembled, and he was taught the Coyoteway ceremonial—the songs, the prayers, the procedures, and the prayer-sticks. He was taught everything.

Children were prepared to receive visions by learning the traditions concerning animal people and songs which had been acquired in visions. Experiences with animal people might occur in predictable places—along a game trail, beside a nest, or while resting by a tree split by lightning. They might also happen without prior notice in a dream or while traveling through the bush. In a vision Dene might receive special abilities from animal people, magical abilities that are not obvious from the behavior of the ordinary animal. Frog, for example, is considered to be a powerful animal which can project itself through the frozen ground in the middle of the winter. One man, as another example, spoke thus about Frog's powers:

> People used to carry a frog to help them shoot straight. Even in the winter they carried a bundle with a frog. Wolverine they say—and Frog—those two were on this land. In the very beginning, long, long ago, they helped make people good, they say.

These visions are not generally discussed outside the context of traditional stories, however, since visions of animal people are personal experiences for Dene Dháa and should not be revealed. Hence, stories are important reference points for those seeking a vision, and many of the storytellers repeatedly admonish young people to seek their own visions.

The stories were not meant to help the people sleep behind secure walls of just-so. Those who seek a vision often wake to find that the world has changed. The people who shared a meal of moose meat may turn back into wolves during the night and devour the entire carcass:

The man had been sleeping a long time, when the sky began to grow light as dawn approached. Suddenly he was cold, terribly cold, and each time he moved he could hear hard-packed snow crunching beneath him. The man woke to find himself sleeping surrounded by chewed pieces of bone, the remnants of a moose knee, leftover scraps, and black wolf droppings. He could see where the wolves had run off, and in the distance he thought he heard a wolf howl.

The people who told these stories are curious about the great and small mysteries of life, and carefully reveal the wonder of the stories. Where Dene Dháa once gathered around a fire, only a few signs remain: a depression in the grass, roasting sticks, feathers, charcoal. The stories are likewise spare and mysterious, recording a way of life very different from our comfortable modern existence. The elders lived through difficult times which prepared them to show a new generation how to survive, both in the bush and in life. "In the evenings you should wonder what the old man has to say," one storyteller said, explaining why the stories remain so important and why he tells them to young people today:

Children come to visit me every night, and I tell them stories. Don't think that the elders don't care enough to tell you something. If an elder comes to talk to you, you should be thankful and grab onto the words coming out of his mouth. Then you would be successful: someone like that would be successful.

Performance and Translation

Dene Dháa stories are all classified as *wodih* 'stories, lectures, news,' a category which includes accounts of recent events, hunting stories, moral lectures, and prophecies as well as traditional stories. Almost any extended speech act in Dene Dháh is properly classified as *wodih*. The term itself is composed of the prefix *wo-* 'general' and the stem *-di* or *-dih* 'say.' *Wodih* are used to influence an audience by establishing a common base of belief, by sharing the experiences of others, and by suggesting what will happen in the future. *Wodih* can be contrasted with *shin* 'songs,' which are used primarily to address spirits. Dene Dháa storytellers often mix various types of *wodih* and *shin* in an extended performance.

All traditional stories are called *tonht'onh wodihé* 'stories of long ago.' This subclass of *wodih* includes all the stories about animal people and culture heros. It also includes stories about people who are no longer living or about events which occurred many years ago. All of the stories in this collection are considered to be *tonht' onh wodihé* regardless of whether they describe events in the mythic past or events in the life of a historic figure. They can be further differentiated by identifying a major character, as, for example, *nóghe wodihé* 'wolverine stories,' or stories about the culture hero who was raised by an old woman and performs many incredible feats, *Mbetsun Yendéhshéhi wodihé* 'The Boy Raised By His Grandmother stories.' Since more than one of these readily identifiable characters may appear in a story, there is some overlap in classification. Some of the stories in this collection of *nóghe wodihé* also feature one of the culture heros, although each may not be identified directly. The man who tricks Wolverine in 'Wolverine Is Outsmarted' and who survives the family of murderers in 'The Young Man Who Sought a Wife' is really Yamonhdeyi, the foremost Dene Dháa culture hero. It is possible to distinguish all the traditional stories about animal people by asking specifically for *wolinghedi wodihé* 'animal stories,' but storytellers will also include stories about culture heros with these stories because they all feature animal people. It is difficult to request stories about culture heros as a class without mentioning a specific character, as there is no clear division between animal stories and the stories of culture heros. Similarly, the division between animals and people in stories blurs as animals appear in human form and the culture heros, especially Yamonhdeyi, take the form of animals. Yamonhdeyi may appear as a fish, as in 'The Young Man Who Sought a Wife,' or as a beaver or bear.

This is especially evident when similar stories from related Dene groups are compared. In one Gwich'in story recorded at Fort Good Hope, a hero similar to Yamonhdeyi escapes from wolverine people who impale their victims on overflow ice in the mountains (Voudrach 1965:56-58). In a related Dene Dháa version the hero, Wolverine, escapes from a similar trap set on a hill greased with groundhog fat. In the Dene Dháa story 'Wolverine Steals a Wife,' Wolverine appears to have married into a human family, whereas in a similar Gwich'in version from Chalkyitsik, Alaska (Moses 1972) Wolverine lives with a family of wolves. Some storytellers may actually know the alter identities of the characters in particular stories, but neglect to explain these details fully in a given performance. Similarly, culture heros such as Yamonhdeyi 'The Man Who Traveled Around The Edge' and Mbetsun Yendéhshéhi 'Boy Raised By His Grandmother' are often interchanged in related Dene stories, and even within one community storytellers may disagree as to which particular culture hero performed a certain feat.

Measured by the frequency with which he appears, Wolverine is a very important character in Dene Dháa stories. Most storytellers are familiar with all the narratives in this collection and know at least as many wolf or bear stories. They also know many narratives about the culture heros,

Yamonhdeyi, Mbetsun Yendéhshéhi, Gahtsóné, Dene Mbetthén Ndátse, Ehtsie Gotsínle, Dene Woyon, and others. There are stories about other animals as well, including birds and even insects such as ants and spiders. The repertoires of the best storytellers include nearly a hundred stories, and one ranconteur stated that he had told fifty stories at one sitting to a particularly attentive audience. Each storyteller develops different themes and may emphasize different characters or aspects of a story.

Most of these narratives were told with several other stories, either with ones about Wolverine or ones about animals or themes which are somehow related to Wolverine. There are many obscure relations between animals in stories, which are often only mentioned and not fully explained. Wolverine and Wolf are closely allied, and often appear as in-laws, for example. Wolf and Wolverine are also the animal helpers of the Siamese twin giants who appear in 'Wolverine Steals a Child.' Marten is said to be Wolverine's cousin, *mbechidle* 'younger brother, parallel first cousin,' a belief which is recalled when trappers find a marten that a wolverine has removed from a trap, but not eaten. Complex symbolic associations link almost all the mythological Dene Dháa animals in some way.

The storyteller's comments have been included with the stories whenever possible to indicate what message they were intended to convey to the audience. All but one of these *wodih* were told to children at school, or with children present at home, and the message was often addressed to them. However, stories 3, 5, 6, 8, 9, 10, 13, and 14 were primarily addressed to an adult interviewer. Even though children were present at these performances, the interviewer was seated by the speaker and was addressed directly by the storyteller. The account of the prophet Nógha's prophecies, number 12, was addressed to an assembly of native elders from across North America held in Assumption in 1979. In each performance, the storytellers tailored their commentaries to suit their intended audience, so that students in school received general admonitions to seek visions, respect elders, and behave themselves. In interviews speakers directed their discussion toward topics suggested by the interviewer, but also added more detailed information based on their perception of the interviewer's knowledge of specific topics.

Wodih 'messages' are distinguished from *shin* 'songs' both in function and form. Dene Dháa songs frequently contain vocables or sounds which have no lexical meaning, although words frequently occur as well. Michael Asch (1988:77), in his description of Slavey drum dances at Pe Tseh Kí, Wrigley, Northwest Territories, states that, like Western music, Dene music contains the notions of a melodic scale, melody, and metric rhythm. Dene Dháa songs, like Slavey songs in the Northwest Territories, generally follow a descending pattern, beginning at the highest note in the song and moving downward toward the lowest, or foundation, tone. The Dene Dháa singing voice is quite distinct from a normal speaking voice because it conforms to a regular melody, with each syllable pitched according to the Dene Dháa musical scale and timed according to the metric rhythm of the song.

All Dene Dháa songs are prayers and are often directed toward spirits, which include animals, natural forces, the spirits of people who have died, or God. Thus *shin* are always addressed to a different audience than *wodih,* which are used to inform a human audience. As with *wodih,* there are many types of *shin,** which can be classified in several ways. *Ekezia yiné* 'love songs' are used to pray for a special sweetheart. *Ndáts'e'á yiné* 'gambling songs' are sung when playing hand games. *Dehsine yiné* 'Cree songs' have been borrowed from the Cree and are sung to a double beat on a smaller drum. *Eghasuli yiné* 'prayer songs' are used as opening prayers and offering prayers at Tea Dances. *Kemo yiné* 'mothers' songs' and *ts'ídoa yiné* 'children's songs' are special songs of blessing for mothers and children. *Dawots'ethe yiné* 'Tea Dance songs' are the regular dance songs for the Tea Dance, each associated with a particular style of dancing, including circle dances, line dances, and friendship dances in which everyone links arms and sings without using drums.

There are also songs which are very personal and can only be described in general terms. When people have died, the wailing songs of relatives at the wake and graveside are a special type of prayer and expression of grief. When people are sick or afflicted by spirits, curing songs acquired in visions of animal people, including Wolverine, may be used as part of the curing process. Almost all older Dene Dháa have personal songs of one or more of these types which they acquired in dreams or visions. Nógha, the Dene Dháa prophet described in Part Two below, had many songs of each type, possibly fifty or more in all.†

All *shin* 'songs' are forms of prayer, but not all *eghasuli* 'prayers' take the form of songs. Prayers which are not sung do not follow a melody and are not pitched according to a musical scale or timed according to a metrical rhythm. They nevertheless resemble songs in addressing a request to spirits or God. The storyteller includes one of these prayers in the story 'Wolverine Steals a Child' when the father seeks to revive his son by praying over his bones:

---

* Note that the stem for song is *yin* after a vowel in a compound construction and appears as *shin* in its independent form.

† Western ideas of music as a secular event now strongly influence younger Dene Dháa so that popular music may eventually replace many types of traditional songs, giving rise to concern among some Dene elders that the spiritual meaning of the Tea Dance and Tea Dance songs will be lost in the future.

"Hé sechuen xetleet'ónh lon.
"Hey, my son morning hopefully.

Kíi kandádéhtsed úh sóon sechuen lon.
Just as strong as he was and then my son hopefully.

Xetl'eet'ónh lon, sets'ín gundeh úh.
Morning wishing, to me you will be talking and.

Lon ndute.
Hoping he would sleep.

Gulon ndawoda,"
Hopefully he will be living again,"

kudi éhsán.
he thought then.

This unspoken prayer is presented as a direct quote of the father's thoughts. He starts and ends by praying for his son, talking about him in the third person, and apparently addressing other spirits or God. In the middle of his prayer he addresses the spirit of his dead son directly in the second person. This prayer is also marked by the repetition of the word *lon*, and prayers, like songs, are often repeated. The simplest form of this type of prayer is a request for whatever a person needs, as in 'Nógha's Teachings' where people are directed to offer tobacco on the fire and think, *"Gulon guedeh sayú'áh* 'Hopefully he will give it to me quickly.'"

In this collection prayers are presented with line breaks where the speaker pauses. Some anthropologists and linguists have used this style of transcription to represent all forms of oral narration. Dennis Tedlock discusses his reasons for using this style in the introduction to his influential collection of Zuñi narratives, *Finding the Center* (1978:xix):

It was not until late in 1968, after listening to many oral performances of modern poetry, that I returned to my Zuñi tapes and began to work out the details of the mode of presentation used here, which combines poetic and dramatic features. . . . The results of this effort have convinced me that prose has no real existence outside the written page. . . . What makes written prose unfit for representing spoken narrative is that it rolls on for a whole paragraph at a time without taking a breath: there is no silence in it. To solve this problem I have broken Zuni narratives into lines.

Tedlock feels that line breaks and other dramatic features, such as the use of capitals to represent a loud voice, represent more of the original performance. He encourages his audience to read translations aloud to experience the original sense of performance.

Another reason for using the verse format is advanced by Dell Hymes, who in his use of it makes line breaks on the basis of the "structure" of the native-language narrative rather than at the occurrence of pauses. Hymes (1981:42) defines structure as "the form of repetition and variation, of constants and contrasts, in verbal organization." In the Dene Dháa prayer above Hymes might, for instance, see the repetition of the word *lon* 'hopefully' as a structural device which would require a line break. Although he would not necessarily insist that the break come at the word *lon* itself, he would use the occurrence of this word to break the prayer into a series of requests. Hymes believes (1981:339) that almost all oral narratives are best rendered in poetic lines, although he does not assign primary importance to oral pauses in breaking lines as Tedlock does.

Prose format has been used here in preference to verse format because the Dene Dháa translators find that verse format imposes a very strong break on the flow of thought. When experimenting with verse format they found that the reader might easily be induced to make longer pauses than exist in the original narration, a tendency that negates the purpose of using verse form to direct the reader toward a reading more faithful to the original performance. Similarly, the translators were not comfortable with the extent of analysis used by translators such as Hymes, except for narratives which are specially structured, such as prayers. The Dene Dháa separate *eghasuli* 'prayers,' including *shin* 'songs,' from *wodih* 'messages.' Because they emphasize the message of the narrative, *wodih* seem to parallel English prose narratives, whereas *eghasuli* are structured more like chants and songs and depend on an exact performance to achieve the desired goal. Thus, prose format may be as appropriate for Dene Dhaa narratives as for English.

Although the translators have used a prose format, they have carefully noted both pauses and repetitions of discourse markers, such as *sóon* 'then,' *éhsán* 'must have been,' and *úh sóon* 'and then' in the transcriptions. The first draft translations were prepared directly from tape recorded narratives by Dene Dháa translators and were then revised by the editors using the native-language transcriptions in consultation with the native translators. Special attention was given to punctuating the Dene Dháa transcriptions to indicate both the structure and performance of the original narrative.

Any representation of narratives in written form raises larger questions about the purpose of the narratives and the use of written language. The

Dene Dháa have a fine sense of etiquette concerning traditional narratives and elders. Elders should not be interrupted or disputed, and the audience must listen attentively throughout a series of narratives. It is inappropriate to pretend to know more than the person who is telling the story, unless the storyteller is younger. Even knowledgeable storytellers are reluctant to tell a story as long as older relatives are still living. Extensive analysis of written stories by academics may violate this protocol by placing the original narrator in an inferior position. Therefore, in this collection notes are used sparingly so as not to displace the voice of the Dene Dháa narrators. The written format, moreover, makes it easier for someone to use the stories inappropriately because they no longer have to sit quietly listening to an elder. The real authorities, nevertheless, remain the original narrators who are able to tell a hundred or more traditional stories in their own language— the people who themselves met animal people. They advise listeners to use the stories and songs respectfully:

> I will tell you this story because you have been good to me. You must learn it well and tell it to the children where you live. The songs I have sung, too, can be used whenever you want to give thanks, or if you really want to pray for something. The drum I made you can be used wherever you go, but you cannot give it away, because it was made for you alone.

PART ONE

ENGLISH TEXTS

Traditional Stories

1 Two Sisters

I could tell you stories for three or four hours without stopping. Hey! I know lots of stories! I used to tell stories all night until dawn.

Yamanhdeya* he is called, the first one. He is called Yamanhdeya, but he is really God. He tricked all the animals that lived on this land; he killed all the giant animals. He put things straight on earth. That is the one we call God.

This happened long ago. The mother of two girls was preparing to bring back meat from a moose her husband had killed. "Stay here with your little sister while we go get some meat," she told her oldest daughter. "Don't go anywhere," she cautioned the girls, "there are unknown dangers in the bush," and with these words of warning their mother left.

Evening came and still their parents had not returned. The younger sister began crying as darkness came. "Little sister, what's wrong?" the older sister asked. "Tell me why you are crying."

"Mom and Dad are both gone," the little sister said.

"Hey, little sister," the older sister replied, "I know how you must feel. I'm afraid, too."

Then the two girls got ready to go to sleep, lying between some packsacks. The older sister looked up toward the sky and, trying to keep her sister's mind off her fears, said, "Little sister, that small star will be yours, and that big star will be mine." They pointed one after the other at the two stars, as first one, then the other, fell asleep.

When they awoke the girls found themselves with two strange men. "What's happening?" the older sister thought. "This isn't even our land." She recalled the stars they had claimed as their own the night before, and guessed that the men they were with might be those stars. "We aren't trapped yet," she told her little sister. "There must be a way out, but don't say anything," she cautioned, and they decided to keep quiet.

Now the two star men were always hunting. When they killed moose, the girls would secretly cut the hide into long strips to make rope, but the

---

* *Yamanhdeya* or *Yamonhdeyi* is the Dene culture hero who killed the animal monsters in ancient times. His name means 'He Went Around The Edge' because he traveled all over the earth killing monsters wherever they lived.

3

© Dia Thurston ·87

men didn't suspect what they were doing. The girls then started digging a hole through the sky, and they took turns working on it every day. All day long they were pounding, pounding, digging in that land above us. They dug through the clouds each day until the men returned in the evening.

The girls spread out piles of pemmican, as planned, and when the men asked, "Why do we always hear you pounding?" the younger sister told them she loved pemmican, and to make it, she pounded up dried meat everyday. The two men thought she was telling the truth and so, unconcerned, continued to go off hunting, leaving the girls alone.

And so the girls continued digging, and below them still were clouds. At last they dug through the clouds until they had made a hole just the size of their souls. They dug only that far, and after sunset they covered the hole and went to sleep. In the morning the men left as usual and the girls uncovered the hole.

"Little sister, hang onto this rope as tight as you can, while I let you down," the older sister said. "Pull on the rope when you reach the Earth, then I'll slide down after you."

The little sister started down, dangling at the end of the rope. The moose-hide rope was almost running out when the rope finally slackened. When the younger sister signaled by pulling on the rope, her sister secured the rope and swung down after her.

Again misfortune lay in their way. An eagle was nesting in a large spruce tree in the middle of a big river. The younger sister had been lowered into that nest, and now her sister joined her there. They had almost returned to earth, but happened to land in an eagle's nest,* with no way down. They were high in the tree, and whenever animals passed by the sisters asked for help, but without success. They begged each passing animal person, but none would help.

Now it happened that Wolverine was coming along just then.

"Grandfather, won't you take us down?" the girls pleaded.

"We'll play with you if you take us down,"† they told him.

"Yes, I'll take you down then," Wolverine said.

"Yes," the girls cried excitedly, "take us down! Take us down!" And so Wolverine packed the two girls down from the tree.

When Wolverine had carried both of them to safety, the older sister said, "we only play along the edge of cliffs," and the girls ran off along the river to where there was a steep bank, and sat down on the edge. As Wolverine rushed toward them, they pushed him over the edge; they pushed him down and ran off.

"Whistle! Whistle! Whistle! Whistle!" the girls told the trees as they ran. Then, as Wolverine came after the girls, the trees all said, "Whistle! Whistle! Whistle!" All those trees whistled from different directions, and as Wolverine ran he became confused and couldn't decide where the two girls had gone. One tree after another whistled at him. He really had no idea what had happened to the girls, it is said.

* Eagles used to eat people, as in the story "The Young Man Who Sought a Wife" in this collection.

† Wolverine is really interested in sexual relations with the girls.

Storyteller's Commentary

Do you know? Was it like that? It must have been like that. When someone whistles at you, don't pay any attention; people are trying to fool you.

I could tell stories for hours. That opening in heaven was for the prophets, an opening to God in heaven, it is said. They must have been children like you. Girls, too, can look for a vision. Even children can find their own way. If someone thinks about what might appear to them in the bush, maybe it's not hard. Make something of yourself—that's how you survive to become an elder. Then someday you'll be alive to tell stories about the past, to tell your children to go look for a vision in the bush.

2   Wolf and Wolverine's Revenge

People may think that they know about animals, but it isn't true; a human's powers are insignificant. We are people, we know only a little about animals and their ways. Animals have special abilities which they depend upon to live, giving us only the powers which they no longer need. They hold fast to their secrets until they are used up, and then they throw them away. An animal chooses someone to receive these leftover powers, a person who has treated the animals with respect. My father talked to me. He taught me in many ways, and that is how I have learned these things.

I know the stories so well, although I was not one of the people living at the time these things happened. These are the stories of an old man called Ekucho, and they are my father's stories as well. When the elders told the stories, each in his own way, I tried to understand fully. Perhaps you are looking at me when I tell you that I'm an old man, wondering why I don't get sick. It's because I respected those old men. When we worked together then I took pity on them and helped them. That's the way I lived, and how you should be, too. When elders tell you about someone who is bad, someone who is really rotten, don't be like that.

I know the stories in so many ways. Long ago people told about this.

An old woman was moving camp, pulling her two small children on a toboggan. She stopped and set up camp beside the trail and cared for her children there. That is how things were when—suddenly—the old woman felt a premonition in her breast.* The men had gone ahead hunting while the women were moving camp by themselves, and the old woman was with the young women who were moving camp. Now among the women were two young women who had been married not long before. The old woman spoke to them about her premonition.

"My daughters-in-law," the old woman said, "there is surely some reason for this unusual feeling in my breast. Be careful while we are alone, and all may yet be well."

But the young women ridiculed her. "Grandmother," they said, "it must be constipation that is causing you to have these feelings." Their answer made the old woman sad.

---

* She has a strange feeling in her breast, a common form of premonition for Dene women.

Whenever they made camp after that the old woman knocked snow off the spruce branches to conceal her trail. She camped far off to one side, away from the others, and listened throughout the night to protect her children from danger.

One morning, as the sun was almost coming out, they heard the sounds of people approaching. Then they heard the other children calling, "Dad! Dad!" as they ran out to meet the approaching men, thinking their fathers had returned. Suddenly cries of pain could be heard, when the women and children were killed by these men from a strange band. But the two children with the old woman remained concealed in her camp.

When all was quiet the old woman piled the children onto the toboggan and pulled them onto the main trail. After hiding the children, the old woman ran on alone, following the men who had gone ahead.

The men were sitting together where they had killed a moose. That is how it must have been. Suddenly the old woman ran among them crying, "Perhaps none of your families are alive back there!" Now among them were two young men, the husbands of the young women who had been killed. As they listened to the old woman's story they were both anxious to go back to see what had happened to their wives and small children. These two brothers-in-law prepared to run back, but before they were gone an old man called out to them, saying, "It's no use. Just let them be!" It wasn't the right time yet for revenge.

Then came the time of year when the snow crusts and winter is almost over. Now it was easy to run on the crusted snow. Again the young men talked about revenge. One of the young men said to the other, "My brother-in-law, how is your strength?* Let's take revenge! Let's go in search of the ones who killed our families!"

"How about you, my brother-in-law, how might you be?" the other replied.

"Yes, I am strong," the first said.

"I am also strong," the second answered.

And so they went after those people who had killed their families. One man became Wolverine and the other became Wolf, and together they embarked on their quest. Aaa! They were confused at times, but Wolf knew how to see the murderers' tracks. He didn't miss anything. Together they were always following the murderers, on and on.

Then suddenly they came to a camp, the camp of the ones who had left them childless. Together the in-laws rummaged around this camp, and when Wolverine found snowshoes hanging up, he tore them up. He tore up all the snares and stole the flints the people used to start fires. They did this time and again.

Then finally there was only one source of fire remaining. Yes, it was becoming hard for those people that they were following. They had started to suffer, and some were hungry now. Still, Wolf and Wolverine followed them, destroying their livelihood, their means of survival.

Now Wolf and Wolverine knew that the fire was coming from the place where an old woman was living. Every night they rummaged through her tent, but they couldn't find a flint. Finally, Wolverine used his powers on the old woman, causing her to fall fast asleep. Then during the night he searched through her clothes and on her body, at last finding a small flint between her legs, tied right there, high on her thigh. Putting his mouth there Wolverine snapped at the string, bit it off, and ran away with the flint. Then—sadly—there was no way to make fire.

Now one old man blamed the ones who had murdered the women and children, saying, "You wanted to kill. Now that loss is being revenged, and maybe none of us will be left alive in the future." Having said that, he brought out a stiff piece of dried moose shank which he had been keeping. He propped this piece of dried meat under a log as bait, using his powers to

* He is inquiring about his brother-in-law's animal powers.

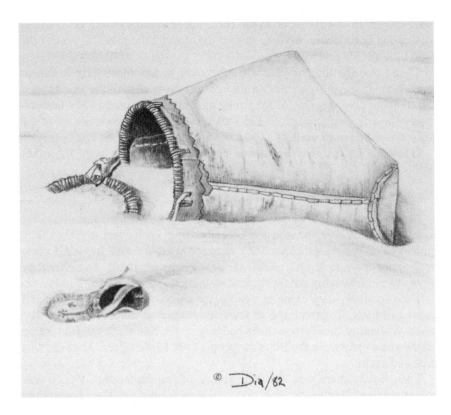

make a huge deadfall trap for Wolverine.

It was hard for Wolverine to resist that trap because of the old man's powers. Wherever Wolf and Wolverine traveled it was always there, just off to the side. It was tempting and its power drew Wolverine to it. Wolf and Wolverine were passing by that trap again when—suddenly!— Wolverine couldn't resist any longer. He glanced to the side a little and ran under the log, causing it to come crashing down.

"Yes! The log fell!" the people said as they heard the crash, and they started running toward where they heard it drop.

"Brother-in-law, roll in the direction of the sun," Wolf cried. Wolverine flexed and flipped himself over, then quickly ran off. Together they ran free. Yes, those two got revenge, and none of those people were left alive.

Storyteller's Commentary

Would we do such things?

I know so many stories. In the evenings you should wonder what the old man has to say. Children come to visit me every night, and I tell them stories. Don't think that the elders don't care enough to tell you what they know. Even a girl can acquire a vision; it is important.

In the bush when you're not in school, look for yourself there in the hills. That's important. Don't put it aside until you are grown up. The people I grew up with were directed to go into the bush. Even if they were frightened their fathers made them go into the bush. Morning and evening they expected the unexpected, even while setting snares at night. Look for something for yourself; act like an animal looking for something—only then can you be like me. Look at my hair! (indicating that he has survived to old age).

If you jump into something without thinking, then you begin to develop your mind in the wrong way. That's bad and it is your main weakness. You can't live that way. Even if you know about something it may not be important. There are two ways that you can know things, but there aren't two ways to live.

Alexis Seniantha is also an elder. I wonder what he tells you. If you don't have a father, you should have faith in something. Even if you are living a good life you still have to have faith; that is the only way to live. Long before our time there were people who wanted to know everything. That was the only kind of people there used to be.

I was once foolish like you. Here, look at my knee. I did that to myself. Although I did foolish things, I never wrestled with a woman when I was in diapers. If I liked her, I still respected her. I might laugh with her and joke with her, but that was all. I wasn't a daredevil. That is how you should live.

All of us living here (in Assumption) are descended from Gadéhtl'un.* It seems that we are all from one man. Besides telling you a story, I'm telling you how people should live. I don't believe in telling only one side of a story. You boys, if you should happen to go hunting and bring me a frozen rabbit, I would gladly take it. Perhaps you're not aware of that. If you went goose hunting with me, I would take the geese, pluck them, and eat them. I'm not telling you this so that I can live depending on you, but so that you can live, depending on yourselves. Sometimes young people are ashamed of what the old people say, but they should really be ashamed of not knowing how to live in the bush and of not having a vision.

---

* The father of the chief who signed Treaty 8 in 1899. He had several wives and many children.

The reason you're going to school is to have a good life. If an elder comes to talk to you, you should be thankful and grab onto the words coming out of his mouth. Then you would be successful: someone like that would be successful.

I'm not always comfortable telling these stories. Why is that? How can I be certain that I am telling the truth about events that happened before my time? That's why it sometimes seems to me like I'm burdening myself with a lie. That's the way it may appear, and I don't want to tell something which I can't be sure is true.

3 Wolverine Steals a Child

They say that once Wolverine stole a child.

Yes, there were three people living in an isolated camp: a young man who had recently married, his wife, and his little mother-in-law. The young wife was expecting a child at any time, and so to occupy himself while his wife was pregnant, the young man hunted and hunted.

"Tripe! I crave tripe!" his wife declared one day. "I want some moose stomach to broil.* Even though you are always hunting, you never bring back any moose stomach! I am hungry for tripe, and if you kill a moose be sure to bring the stomach back for me," she told him, begging him to bring her some moose tripe.

And so to satisfy his wife the young man went hunting again, and as darkness approached he fell asleep beside a fresh moose trail.

At this time the young husband's little mother-in-law was living beside the young couple. She was staying alone in her tent, but every night when she went to sleep a man visited her. He was crawling up to her. Yes! He was crawling up on her!

"It is my son-in-law," the mother-in-law thought to herself. "It must be my son-in-law," she thought in the morning as she got up. "It must be my son-in-law who is coming at night since my daughter is pregnant,"† the mother-in-law thought as she sat beside her daughter. (However, the man who appeared to her each night was really a product of her own imagination.)

Now the daughter's pregnancy was very advanced, and she was about to give birth at any time, since the baby was fully formed. But still the husband didn't stay with her. It was very hot and the sun was shining brightly when, again, the son-in-law left to go hunting, leaving his wife alone with the mother-in-law.

During the day while the daughter was sleeping, the old woman was thinking about her son-in-law who had just left. "It must be my son-in-law who is coming to me," she thought, and then she went to visit her daughter.

---

* Moose stomach is considered a to be a delicacy.

† Traditionally the son-in-law should not have sexual relations with his wife while she is pregnant. Hence the mother-in-law suspects that her son-in-law is interested in her.

13

It was already midday, and the sun was shining white overhead when she went to her daughter's tent. Her daughter usually didn't have much to say when her mother came to visit, but now as the old woman entered the tent she said to her, "Mother, look through my hair for lice!" The daughter rested her head on the old woman's lap and quickly fell asleep, while her mother looked for lice. The old woman held her daughter by the hair, and shaking her daughter's head tried to rouse her, but the girl remained asleep.

"I should do it now," the old woman thought,* while her daughter lay sleeping. She now disliked her child, thinking that the only thing that came between herself and her son-in-law was the girl. She was daydreaming about her son-in-law, imagining how he came to her each night, when her attention returned to her daughter.

The girl was sleeping on her mother's lap while the old woman searched

---

* The long days of summer are thought to bring on insanity. In June the days are so long that there is very little complete darkness, and the sun may be directly overhead for many hours.

her hair for lice. Then the mother took out of her pocket an awl made from the leg bone of a loon, and she placed an axe beside her foot. The old woman was having second thoughts, but she decided that the time was ripe to carry out her plan.

While her daughter slept on her lap the old woman placed the awl in the girl's ear and pounded it with the axe until the girl stiffened. She had killed her own daughter. The old woman had killed her daughter, while the son-in-law was still away hunting.

Then the old woman began to prepare for the return of the son-in-law: she built a shelter for her dog[*] —her little bitch—and after clearing a place to the side, put up a big shade and carefully piled lots of firewood nearby. She tied her dog and sat looking into the fire.

After she tied the dog, she turned to her daughter's body. (Now she made a horrible wig for herself.) The old woman tore off her daughter's scalp, took this gruesome scalp and stretched it to dry by the fire, and when it was finished put it on her own head. Then the woman dragged her daughter's body a short distance away. She spread a hide on the ground, placed her daughter's body on the hide, covered her with a huge tanned moosehide, and piled branches on top of everything. And so the old woman buried her own daughter.

When the young husband returned he wondered what could be troubling his wife when she sat there without greeting him. "I wonder what she has done," he thought. He began to question her, still believing that the woman by the fire was his wife.

"You said that you wanted moose tripe," he said to her, "but now you don't even care that I packed this tripe home for you. What's come over you? Why won't you talk to me?" the man demanded. "That's not like you. Why are you ignoring me?" he shouted, and, grabbing the woman's hair, he pulled on it in frustration, saying, "Turn around toward me!" As he pulled, the wig came off, revealing the old woman's white hair. Now the young man struck the old woman on the head, knocking her into the fire with the nearest burning log. He killed her—beating her to death—and threw her body aside.

The man now planned to return to the site of his recent moose kill and began arranging things carefully in his pack. But then he noticed his wife's scalp where it lay beside his wretched mother-in-law's body. He rolled it up and put it in his jacket.

"Where did it happen?" the man wondered. "Where did the old woman kill my wife?" Then he looked until he saw the tracks where her body had

[*] Dog teams became common with commercial trapping. Before that women kept a single dog to assist in moving camp.

been dragged along. Following the trail, the man discovered the horrible place where the old woman had buried the girl and he uncovered her body. Now the man placed his hand on her stomach, and when he felt the baby, which was still moving inside, he quickly cut his wife open and pulled the baby out. Then he swaddled the baby in rabbit skins and they went on their way.

The man carried the baby everywhere. When he killed grouse, rabbits, moose, or other game, he used the brains of the animals he killed to feed his son. He fed the baby fat mixed with animal brains, and in that way he cared for his son. (Well, in those days where would you find a store? They didn't exist.) The man went along carrying the baby, always carrying him.

At first, since his son was tiny, the man packed him wrapped in sphagnum moss diapers. He took the boy with him everywhere. Even when he went hunting the man was packing him, packing him. As the boy got bigger he started to crawl, moving around a bit on his own.

One day as the young man was packing the baby along he began to feel tired. "Maybe my son is hungry," he thought, taking the boy down off his back.

"My son," he said, "I'm going after some grouse that flew over there. Don't cry if you hear anyone coming along. Wolverine is not always a proper person, and something unexpected might happen.* Don't say,'Dad!' Don't talk to him! Even if you hear a noise don't call out, 'Dad!'"

His father then placed a flat driftwood stump in a large spruce tree and stuffed the boy into the moss growing on the driftwood, using a long pole to lift him up. "Stay there and wait for me," he told his son, concealing the stump and baby among the thick spruce branches. Before starting out he gave his son a piece of fat to chew on. "Suck on this!" he said, putting it in the boy's mouth. Then he told his son one last time, "Don't say 'Dad,' whatever you do!" But as he left the man thought to himself, "Wolverine is not a proper person; I shouldn't leave my son alone."

The man killed two grouse, which had landed together nearby, then quickly headed back to where he had left his son. But there—there—only the pole that he had used to lift the boy up remained. The man trampled the bush looking for the boy, at the spot where the stump had fallen, but it was no use. Wolverine had stolen the child!

Now the man ran after them. Wolverine was avoiding him, always avoiding him, but still the man pursued them. First the man came to a place where Wolverine had slept, leaving behind wet moss from the child's diapers. When again he came to where Wolverine had slept, the man found

---

* This means that Wolverine is not a proper person in two senses: he is an animal person rather than a normal human, and he does things no Dene should do.

wet moss. On the third day, however, the child went off on small snow-shoes which Wolverine had made. He was going with snowshoes.

His father continued after him, after him, wandering about, but Wolverine and the boy were always ahead. Now hunger was defeating the man. After killing some small game—a rabbit or a small grouse—the man would make camp, and when he had eaten he would get dressed and continue on after them again.

The man continued chasing after them, but during the night Wolverine would make another pair of snowshoes, each larger than the ones before.*
At last the man came to a place where his son was using large snowshoes, zigzagging back and forth beside Wolverine as they hunted for grouse among the trees. Both Wolverine and the boy had toboggans, and wherever Wolverine dragged his toboggan, the boy pulled his alongside it.

The boy was now wandering about here and there looking for grouse, and where the tracks were running along beside a grouse trail his father followed. He thought this might be his son's trail and so pressed on, using his own large snowshoes. Then he came to a place where his son had plucked a grouse.

"Maybe I will see my son soon," the man thought, and yes, now he was continually finding fresh signs: places where the boy had plucked grouse, and even places where there was fresh blood. His father went along with

_____
* Wolverine is using his powers to raise the child in a few days.

only his son in mind, and there—at last—they met. Now the man told his son what had happened and that he was the boy's real father.

"My son," the man said, "these things have happened to you because of what your grandmother did to your mother," the father told him. "Because she killed your mother I was forced to raise you under the most difficult conditions. I had to pack you around everywhere, and once when you became too heavy I lifted you up into a tree—but then Wolverine came along. I told you not to say anything. I said, 'If you cry out, 'Dad! Dad!' then Wolverine might steal you,' and that is what he did. That's what happened to you," his father told him.

"No!" the boy said. "Wolverine told me that he is my father, that I am his son. That's what he told me," the son replied. Then the boy left, following after grouse again, and his father also went hunting but then circled back to his son. "My son," he said, "I am your real father. How many days have I traveled over these hills—one hill, two hills—walking, walking, looking for you? Where you slept, time after time Wolverine made you go on, using larger and larger snowshoes. Twice I found wet moss from your diapers, but you were always taken away from me. Yes, I am your father," the man said to his son. "Even if I was already hungry, I walked after you all day until I was almost starved."

The next time the boy met his father, he gave him some grouse to eat and then traveled on.* (He had believed his father's story, it seems.)

The boy eventually caught up with Wolverine and pretended that nothing had happened, but of course Wolverine already suspected that the boy had seen his real father. Now the boy gave Wolverine some grouse, saying, "Dad, I only killed these few grouse. I didn't do well, and I'm afraid that they're all frozen."

He placed a few of the small grouse he had killed beside Wolverine, who inspected them and then threw them aside. (Wolverine knew that the boy had given his father the choicer spruce grouse, which are preferred because they have larger gizzards.) "Give the grouse to someone's father!" Wolverine told the boy angrily, implying that the boy's real father was unknown and that the boy was a bastard.

"You are the one who said you were my father," the boy replied angrily. "Don't talk to me like that or I'll destroy you! Don't talk to me about my father! Why are you telling me that I'm not your son? What is all this foolishness that you are telling me?"

Wolverine didn't like what the boy said and told him to cook the grouse, attempting to end the conversation. "That was the only kind of grouse I saw," the boy continued, unwilling to let Wolverine avoid the issue. The

---

* By giving the man a grouse, the son indicates that he recognizes him as his father.

boy skewered a grouse, then put it beside the fire to cook, wishing that it would fall. He used his own thoughts to make it drop, and as the grouse breast was barbecuing it moved slightly and fell into the fire. The boy then reached just short of the grouse, which had fallen across the fire, and told Wolverine, "You pick it up! What are you afraid of? Pick it up!"

When Wolverine reached to pick up the grouse, the boy struck him on the head with a burning log, and Wolverine fell headfirst into the fire. The boy now kindled the fire higher, then threw Wolverine's coat into the fire after him, the horrible dark grease from Wolverine creating billowing clouds of smoke as he burned. The boy also burned Wolverine's toboggan and snowshoes, completely destroying everything.

This all happened in the morning, and so the son sat waiting for his real father to arrive. The boy waited until finally he heard his father approaching; then he sat watching for him to appear. At last they were united, and the boy gave his father some grouse. "My son," the man said, "I am your father. I am truly your father."

After they had eaten, they camped where the man had finally found his son. The next morning the two dressed and set out again, traveling on and on. They camped once more, then set out again going toward their land, as the older man directed his thoughts along the familiar trails leading to his homeland. "Yes, our land is in that direction," the man thought. "Soon we will be there."

Meanwhile, the young man had gone on a little ways ahead to look for grouse. "Father, I'll go ahead to look for grouse," the son said, and his father followed right behind, right behind him. The man was afraid that Wolverine would try to harm his son again, and so he pursued the boy with all his strength. But being younger, the son soon outdistanced the older man.

"Father!" the son called out in the distance.

"Yes!" his father shouted in reply.

"My grandparents have passed this way dragging their toboggan. I'm going after them," the boy called.

Now the tracks the boy saw had actually been made by two horrible giants, joined together at the back and facing in opposite directions. These monstrous Siamese twins had recently passed by there, pulling a huge toboggan, and it was these tracks that the boy imagined had been made by the grandparents he had never known.

"I'm going after my grandparents!" the boy called out, and was gone.

"No!" his father cried out in despair, as he ran chasing the boy through a clearing. "My son, they are giant Siamese twins," the man called. "They are the beings called giants, and they are dangerous."

It was getting late, and still his son's tracks continued on ahead in the darkness. Soon the boy had completely outdistanced his father. The older man now hunted for grouse as he walked, looking for a place to sleep. After killing a grouse he at last made camp, laid his head on a little pair of gloves, and fell asleep.

The next morning the father got up and resumed his chase. At midday he found the place where the giants had camped the night before, leaving behind some meat scraps. The man was so hungry that he was tempted to make camp himself, but thought, "I will get to their camp soon," and continued on. Meanwhile, the boy had already been killed in his quest to locate his grandparents. The Siamese giants had cooked the boy and scattered his bones. When the man arrived at the place where they had eaten his son, he gathered together all of his son's bones, including his skull. Then, preparing a place to sleep, he prayed for his son. He concentrated completely on prayer.

> *I wish my son would live again.*
> *I wish I could talk to him in the morning.*
> *I wish he would be restored just as strong as ever come morning.*
> *I wish he would live again.*

Then he slept, placing his son's bones beside him under his blanket, falling asleep facing away from his son's bones.

In the morning the man heard the sound of someone making a fire, and there was his son! He had become a person again. Now the boy was rekindling the fire to warm things. "My son," the father said, "cook those small grouse that are in my pack." Then, pausing, he began lecturing his son. "Don't ever go off ahead of me again," the man warned him. "If you go ahead again, those giants may kill you, and if they kill you what will I do? You have completely exhausted me. I can't chase after you again."

Perhaps the boy was troubled and drawn to his own destruction, because his father had killed the boy's little grandmother, the little mother-in-law.* Whatever the reason, bad luck seemed to be in their way. The next morning they set off together again, making camp at night and eating together when they woke in the morning. But before long misfortune overtook them as the son went in search of his grandparents again.

"Father, my grandparents have passed by again," the boy said. "I'm going after them!" he yelled from the distance, as he ran ahead again, forgetting his father's warning.

Oh my, how that boy wore his father out! Hey, his father had warned the boy, but the father now found himself going after his son again, traveling

---

* Possibly also because the son had killed Wolverine. In some stories Wolverine is a pet of giants who wander around killing people.

endlessly, until he must have fallen asleep.

The next day he came to the place where the giants had camped, but as before, it was too late. Again the giants had devoured the boy by the time the man stumbled onto their camp. They must have cooked him there, as it was there that the father found his son's crushed bones. The giants had thrown his bones away, then drawing on the boy's skull, had raised it on a pole. In despair, the man gathered all of his son's bones and slept by them three times as before. This time, however, the boy did not come back to life. Yes, his father prayed in vain, and when his attempt to restore his son failed, the man set out in pursuit of the giants.

"My son," the man said, "I'll kill them, just as they killed you." Darkness approached as the man pursued the giants. It was dark when he arrived at where they were camped and saw their fire glowing red in the darkness. The giants had dragged their huge toboggan behind them, behind the wall of their shelter. Now the man crept up to those grown-together monsters trying to get a closer look. "What could I do to take them by surprise?" the man wondered. Then he crawled under cover of their toboggan and waited close to the giants.

"Ker-thwack!" Suddenly the man sent an arrow ripping through their huge blanket, seizing this opportunity to grab one giant by the hair. Now the giants fought each other, each thinking he had been attacked by his Siamese twin. They broke each other's necks, killing each other. Yes, they killed each other then. Now the man did to them as his son had done to Wolverine. He put the giants into the fire along with all of their belongings, including their huge toboggan. He destroyed everything.

Hey, then the man wandered about, always thinking of his son, crying now and again. Hey, he was always sad, it is said. That poor boy! Wolverine raised him on milk, it is said. Wolverine was bad then—he was once a person, they say. He was always going along, going along. Yes, it is said.

4 The Children Raised on Fat

A long time ago there were people on this earth, and in those days the animals that lived in the bush were people, too, it is said. Even in those days these animal people could see into the future.

You who are listening are to be pitied. Wolverine—Wolverine they call him. When he was on this earth he stole and destroyed things, and whatever he wanted, he stole. He existed before there were people, it is said. He stole three children and raised them. That is the way it must have been.

This Wolverine story is known to people today. In the very beginning Wolverine raised two people—he stole two children and he was raising them. He kept them in a tree cache and below them, in another cache, he stored his food. He stored all types of food in his cache, enough to survive for one year on this land. He kept the children above and watched them, feeding them only on fat, and because of this they also began to get fat, and they didn't like this. They were tired of fat.

Now the children began to wonder where Wolverine was going. They observed the path he took, and one little boy looked to see where Wolverine entered the cache. "Let's look below there," the little boy said to the other child.

Then they went, following Wolverine, and they discovered his food cache. Hey, they found all sorts of food in Wolverine's cache—whatever a person might want to eat. But Wolverine had only fed them fat. (Many people steal today, children. That is the way of Wolverine.)

Now the children went inside Wolverine's cache while he was gone and prepared meat for themselves. They only prepared a small amount of meat and then went back to the upper cache. When Wolverine returned in the evening, he discovered that the boys had been in his food cache. "Why did you wander from my house?" Wolverine demanded.

"And why did you only give us fat," the children answered, "when you were hoarding other types of food below? Why didn't you share with us?"

Then Wolverine tried to kill them, but he couldn't because he had raised them, and they knew his ways. "All I did was for your benefit," Wolverine told them. "It was for the future when you will be on your own, but you betrayed me. If you survive you will be thieves and liars," he told them.Wolverine was a person before, it is said.

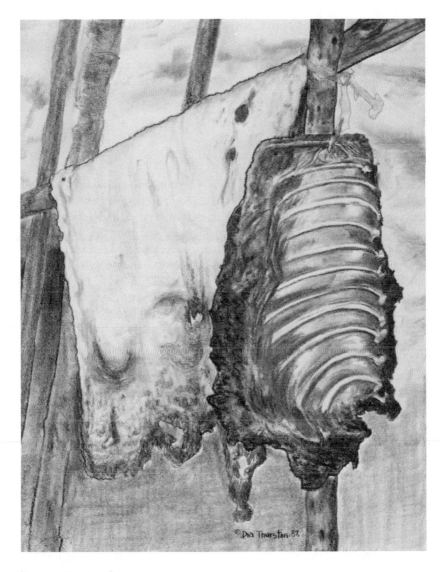

Storyteller's Commentary

Wolverine, they say, and Frog—those two were on this land in the very beginning. Long, long ago they made people good. Frog was able to shoot straight, and for that reason people carried a frog with them to help them shoot straight. Even in the winter people carried frogs on their backs to help them.

5 Wolverine, Giant Skunk, and Mountain Lion

Many people tell stories, each a little differently as they tell and retell them. I know only some of these stories, ones grandfather told me, stories about Wolverine and those times long past.

Part One

A long time ago there were people, and Wolverine was also a person and that big cat Mountain Lion was a person, too. The people saw Mountain Lion's tracks and everyone cried about it, everyone cried, and they moved a long ways to get away. But Mountain Lion sensed that the people had crossed his trail and he backtracked, chasing after them, after them. At last Mountain Lion caught up with them and he killed all the people. Mountain lions killed people in those days.

Now at that time there was also Giant Skunk.* The people saw this Giant Skunk's tracks and they cried. Hey, they already imagined themselves dead when they saw his tracks! The people moved far away to live. They fled, yes, crying as they went.

Now there were many people in those days, and there were also beaver, too, and the people went to hunt beaver in the winter, cutting open beaver caches and beaver dens with an axe. They were looking for beaver when they saw Wolverine's tracks. Then it happened! "Come here!" one of the people called. There in the distance they could see Wolverine coming, and following him was a huge animal. It was Giant Skunk! They were coming toward the people. Closer and closer they came. "Hey!" the terrified people cried then.

"Brother-in-law!" Wolverine called to Skunk. "Brother-in-law, let's look for beaver here." Now they had almost arrived at the beaver house when Skunk turned around to spray the people, it is said. Skunk's stinky spray would have killed the people. He raised his tail and was ready to spray. "T'ong!" The spraying sound was already coming from Skunk's spray

---

* The storyteller indicated that the first part of this story may have come from the Cree.

hole, when Wolverine bit it shut. Wolverine bit it really hard. He bit it, saying, "Oo, oo, oo!"

Quickly the people all ran toward Wolverine and Skunk, grabbing spears, long knives, and arrows—as there were no guns at that time. Wolverine was already killing Giant Skunk, biting him, saying, "Oo, oo, oo," fighting to keep his grip as he faced into the wind, and Giant Skunk struggled to get free. But some of Skunk's spray escaped and made the yellow streaks wolverines have on their sides today.

Not all of the animal people* helped kill Skunk. The cowardly Groundhog ran away, but the other animal people wanted to destroy Giant Skunk because he had killed so many of them in the past. "Let's cut him up," they said when Giant Skunk was dead. Then the animal people all got knives; they cut Giant Skunk up into small pieces with knives and scattered the pieces all around to become the small skunks we know today. Giant Skunk no longer existed.

Part Two

Now the people saw Giant Mountain Lion's tracks, and Wolverine decided to follow Mountain Lion.† He followed the tracks until he came to Mountain Lion's strange snowshoes, one made out of a moose antler and one out of a caribou antler. Wolverine arrived at a beaver house where Mountain Lion had cut through the ice in front of the house just as the sun was setting. Mountain Lion was under the ice, having left his snowshoes, arrows, and pack behind. Now Wolverine began looking through Mountain Lion's pack, and he discovered a child's small hand, bitten off and dried to be used as a soup spoon. He also discovered a dried breast from a nursing woman, and he became very frightened.

Suddenly! Suddenly! There was movement in the water. "Here, here, take this!" Mountain Lion called out, handing Wolverine the rope he had used to catch the beaver. Wolverine pulled on the rope, and out came a large beaver all wrapped up. Mountain Lion leapt out of the water, shook himself, rolled in the snow, and then began piling the beavers he had killed on the bank.

"Let's eat some beaver and camp here," Mountain Lion said. Now this is how it happened. Wolverine was watching Mountain Lion's shadow, afraid

---

* The people in this camp are animal people.

† The main character in this story is simply called "the man," but the storyteller said this refers to Wolverine at the time when he was a person. This may also be one of the forms of Yamonhdeyi.

that Mountain Lion would pounce on him, when Mountain Lion said, "Carry one beaver in your pack and go in front of me!"

Wolverine took one beaver, and Mountain Lion began putting the rest of the beavers into his pack. They traveled until they came to some trees, where they planned to make camp for the night. Suddenly Mountain Lion moved. "This is what I've been watching for," Wolverine thought as he saw Mountain Lion's shadow moving toward him. Then Mountain Lion feinted a pounce in Wolverine's direction, and Wolverine jumped.

"Well!" Wolverine said, "what's the matter with you?"

"My snowshoes got caught," Mountain Lion said. "They get caught like this. That's all." Then he feinted toward Wolverine again and then began chasing him in earnest. They were almost in the woods now, and Mountain Lion began chasing Wolverine through the trees. He threw his pack away and began closing on Wolverine. Mountain Lion chased Wolverine from treetop to treetop to treetop, both of them wearing snowshoes. They bounded on their snowshoes, and every time Wolverine turned there was Mountain Lion right behind him, mimicking exactly his every move as he followed on his antler snowshoes. Mountain Lion effortlessly jumped from treetop to treetop, until at last Wolverine jumped with all of his strength, leaping through the fork of a tall tree. Mountain Lion followed, but his snowshoes hooked on the sides and he was left hanging in the tree upside down.

Now Wolverine got ready to cook a beaver.

"Get me down, get me down," Mountain Lion begged him, hanging from the tree, but Wolverine ignored him and began building a fire. In those days there were no matches, and so Wolverine had to use dried grass to start the fire. He carefully arranged wood shavings and dried grass, thinking fire, fire, fire. He struck a spark using a flint, the fire started, and soon flames lit up the night.

Meanwhile, Mountain Lion was still hanging from the tree, wearing his two snowshoes, hanging upside down. "I'm cold," he moaned over and over. Ignoring Mountain Lion, Wolverine made a fire at the base of the tree, and taking one beaver out of his pack, he butchered it and cooked some beaver meat for himself. While Wolverine was eating, Mountain Lion cried out suddenly and quit moving. He was dead, it seems. As his body went limp, he urinated and the urine dripped down onto Wolverine's head. Mountain Lion had frozen to death.

Wolverine was watching then. Yes, he was watching. "Maybe his brothers will come looking for him," he thought. "Yes, Mountain Lion is really frozen." Wolverine poked Mountain Lion's body and snowshoes down with a long stick, and then he cut him up into small pieces and scattered the pieces as the people had done with Giant Skunk.

Then Wolverine ran away. He ran away and started singing and dancing on the snow with all his might. "Oo wee!" he sang. Soon it began to snow and before long the snow had become a blizzard, and where Mountain Lion had passed with his snowshoes there were no longer any tracks. Then Wolverine ran away; he ran away.

That Mountain Lion died, and snow drifted over his tracks. The blizzard covered his tracks and they were no longer visible. His relatives searched for him but they never found a trace. He was gone.

Wolverine made the giant mountain lions small and they weren't dangerous anymore. In the beginning mountain lions ate people. They are called "the trackers" by Dene, it is said.

6 The Man Who Sought a Song

There was once a man who told his son to seek a vision. "Go look for a song," the man said. This song, this vision, is what Dene use to help each other survive,* and this is what the father told his son to seek. The young man's beard was already black and full when his father told him to seek a song alone in the bush. And so he did as his father told him. Then the father went traveling himself, returning at last to be with his wife and son.

"My son, is it really you?" his father asked.

"Yes," the son replied.

"And what have you seen?" the father asked.

"I'm not sure," the son answered. "Nothing—nothing has appeared to me. There was nothing at all."

"What is the problem?" the father asked, then gave his son some advice. "Go and sleep by the entrance to our tent where your mother gave birth, at the place where you were born," he told him. "Sleep there on your mother's ragged old moccasins."

And so the young man slept with his parents again. He laid his head on his mother's moccasins; they made him lay his head on his mother's moccasins at the place where he was born.

"Go to sleep," his father told him, and the son laid his head on his mother's small ragged moccasins and fell asleep.

"My son, suck from your mother's breasts again," his father told the young man when he woke. "Then return to the bush again. If you remain just as you are, you will be as helpless as a torn-out liver. What would your life be like then?" his father said.

"Yes," the young man said, agreeing.

Now the young man sucked from his mother's old shriveled breasts, and then returned to the bush. But again there was nothing. When he returned his father told him to sleep another night on his mother's moccasins. And so he slept another night at the place where he was born.

"My son," his father said, "go into the bush again, then tell me what happens."

Again the young man went back into the bush, but before he had gone far

* A song used in curing is often acquired as part of a vision.

© Dia Thurston, 87.

he returned.

"What happened?" the father asked his son.

It seems that the young man had been traveling in the bush, expecting to see someone or something. It was getting late as he walked along—almost midnight—and he was looking for a place to sleep when suddenly two huge stumps loomed up in front of him. The young man lay down between the stumps, wanting to go to sleep. He ate, then he prepared to go to sleep. Yes, he snapped off several spruce branches and then placed his small mitts on the branches, and as the sun was going down, he fell asleep at the base of the stumps.

"Here! Up here!" the stumps called out to the young man as he woke up in the morning.* He started toward the fire, but then he stopped breathing, fainted, and fell down. Before long he woke up.

"Father told me something like this might happen in a vision," he thought when he woke, and he thanked the stumps. "I'll visit Father," he thought. "It's not far to where I left him. He told me to look carefully for something in the bush; this must be what he meant." And so the young man ate and returned to his parents' camp.

"I was frightened and went to sleep between two huge stumps," the man told his father. "As the sun was coming up one stump spoke to me and I stopped breathing. You told me a vision might be like that."

"Hey, my son, don't say any more. Don't tell me anything about what happened," his father told him. "Go back into the bush and look for a purpose! Look for a vison! There is more than one place where you might see something."

And so the young man went back into the bush, wandering, traveling everywhere. He came to where a large group of people had passed. Then, deciding to follow their trail, he soon came upon their camp. As he watched the people from a distance he noticed that they were smaller than his own people. Now he went into their camp and sat down to visit.

"That person is pitiful," one old man said, referring to the young man. "Give him something to eat!" One young woman liked the young man, and cooked meat for him, and brought him hardened moose grease.

"Eat all the food you are given, and don't store any of it away," they told him when he had finished eating. "Don't go around visiting; stay right here!" they added. And so he slept with them, and in the morning they gave him more to eat.

Now another man joined these people. "Whatever he is, he is certainly pitiful," the people told this new visitor. "He was barely able to sit up before, the poor thing!"†

"I wonder what he was before?" said the visitor. "Cut him open then and urinate on him: when you go to the bathroom, go to him."

They cut the young man open on the path from the camp to the river.††

---

   * Some Dene believe that large spruce trees protect them from dangerous spirits as well as from the elements when they sleep beside them. The stumps of these trees also have the same powers, as in this case, where the stumps speak to the man.

   † The young man had nearly starved, either because he was fasting or because he had abandoned himself to death. The term translated as "pitiful" also means "adorable" when applied to babies or anything that brings out tender sentiments. This may indicate why the animals take pity on both children and people in need.

   †† They are at a winter fish camp by a river or lake.

There inside him, and all around him, it was icy where the people went to him. This was also part of the young man's vision, that he should learn through suffering. That is why the people cut him open.

The people remained camped there for almost a month, then prepared to move camp, leaving the young man where he was. The girl who had fed him went to see him one last time before they left because she thought he might yet be healed. She held a beautiful pair of moccasins embroidered with porcupine quills in her hand, and cutting a branch from a tree that stood beside him, she tied the moccasin laces to the branch and hung them up. She had also made a jacket of tanned moosehide, and she hung this beside the young man, too. Then she sat there with him for a long time.

At last the rest of the people had begun to leave, after she had been sitting there for a long time. "I'm afraid the others will outdistance me," the girl thought as she heard the people from her camp moving off. Then she realized she must follow them. But she was sad to leave the young man behind. "He is pitiful," she thought. She was thinking about him even though she knew she must follow the rest of her people. Finally she hung the jacket and moccasins beside him, and then—yes—she went.

It was getting dark when suddenly—pitter-patter, pitter-patter—came the sound of someone running along quickly nearby! The young man heard this pattering sound as he lay there. At that time Wolverine was a person, and when he came close the young man spoke to him. "Like me, you take in filthy things," he said. "You are able to put strange things in your stomach." He heard Wolverine run around him singing. Yes, he ran around him singing; he ran around him. Then suddenly Wolverine was gnawing the frozen urine in the young man's chest. He licked inside the young man's stomach, inside his heart. "What will you do now?" Wolverine asked. Then Wolf joined Wolverine and put the young man's ribs back together. He sealed the wound with his saliva, then blew on the wounds in a magical way.

The young man sat up; they pushed him up; then he stood up. "Put on the moccasins!" Wolf and Wolverine told him. They helped him put on the moccasins and jacket, and then they dressed him. "Just stay here for a while," they said. "Just sit here. Then come after us later. Our children will prepare some food for you. Follow when you have rested." Wolf and Wolverine went on ahead of the young man, then he camped there that night before following them. The next day after traveling a fair distance he came to their campsite and went to sleep across the fire from Wolverine.

A large tipi stood nearby and there were broken marrow bones scattered around the camp. "They left some meat for you," Wolf said, "but—well— the children are not really proper people. Put the food up in a tree so they won't bother it. Then when you get hungry take down as much as you want." Wolf now broke a marrow bone for the young man to eat later, and they placed it up in the tree. (Not long before, it seems, several moose had passed by the Wolves' old camp, and they had pursued them, killing three large moose. Then they had moved camp to the site of the moose kill, where now only the bones remained.)

The Wolves were staying in a big tent across from where the man slept, and now they gave the young man some moose meat, told him to put it up in a tree, then left while he slept.

When the young man woke he discovered the meat still suspended above their trail, started a fire, skewered and roasted a piece of meat, then stayed there eating when he felt hungry.

Soon Wolverine came back. "Those people who left you are camped nearby," he told the man, "you must go after them. Go along the edge of the trees toward the sunrise, and there you will find a place where a fisher came to a big bent-over spruce and chased a marten. Follow where the fisher ran off."

The young man traveled along the banks of a river until he came to a big spruce that had fallen over. There a fisher had run under the tree, then came out again and retraced his path. The young man looked around where the tracks disappeared, but he sensed that something was watching him, and as he moved his head around, something under the roots followed his movements. He pulled out an arrow and shot, killing the huge bear which had its den under the tree; he shot it with an arrow. The young man managed to pull out a paw, but the bear was so heavy he finally just cut the paw off, tucked it into his pack, and continued on.

Yes, the young man went after them then and soon came to a camp of spruce branch lean-tos where the small people were living. The old man who welcomed him before was living at the far end of the camp. He was glad to see the young man and invited him to stay with him. "I don't like being alone," the old man said. He couldn't believe that the young man had come back, and now he was sorry that they had mistreated him.

"Grandfather, cook this bear paw," the young man said as he took it out of his pack. "I wanted to take the whole bear out, but it was too heavy." He gave the paw to the old man, and soon it was cooked. But the young man didn't eat any because Wolf and Wolverine had told him not to eat anything except the meat they left for him.

"Someone has killed a bear," the people cried, running off toward where the young man had left the bear. They broke open its huge den, then dragged the bear out, pulled it out, and singed its hair off. After it was singed they cut it up, brought it back, and spread it out to be cooked. They got ready to cook that big bear. The people hung pieces of bear meat over the fire and, taking turns with a birch bark cup, drank lots of bright bear grease. They feasted that night on bear meat and bear fat.

In the morning when the sun came up, the young man was sleeping beside the old man. "I wonder why nobody is up yet?" he thought. "It's getting light. I better rekindle the fire." Now when he turned to look at the old man, there was grease frozen around his mouth and grease was oozing out of his lips. Another man who had slept with them was also smeared with frozen grease. "Hey, they are both dead!" the young man thought. "People will think I killed them." In shock the young man started a fire, then sat puzzling over what had happened.

There were twelve lean-tos in the camp, and from the corner of his eye the young man observed a little smoke coming out of one lean-to near the edge of the woods. "I'll look over there last," he thought, and went to each of the campsites. No one was left alive. All the people had bear grease frozen around their mouths from the feast of the previous night. They had been killed by the being that healed the man—by Wolverine. At one place, however, a little smoke was rising. The man now opened this tent flap and saw a girl sitting inside.

"She must be the one who cared for me," he thought. The young man looked at her, then went back to his fire. He still had a little moose meat left that the Wolves had given him, and he cooked it and ate it. "I'll go kill some grouse," he thought. "I have to go somewhere or maybe I'll be discovered."* The young man was frightened about what had happened there and wanted to leave that place, and so when he had finished eating he got dressed and put on the moccasins that the girl had given him.

Now the young man went into the bush again, wandering, traveling on and on. He had traveled a long way when finally, as the sun was setting, he reached his destination: a place where patches of ice showed through the snow on a small muskeg lake. "I hope the snow drifts over my trail," he thought, and crossed the lake to cover his trail. Crossing the middle of the lake, he headed along a trail that led into some thick spruce. "I might be able to survive here," he thought. He was tired and made a lean-to, but before going to sleep he killed several grouse and, cooking one, kept the rest for later. He was sitting there asleep as the sun came up.

"Hey, the fire must have looked bright while I was sleeping," he worried. The young man got up and rekindled the fire, expecting someone to be coming after him. Then he moved his camp on ahead a short distance before sleeping again. Meanwhile, a fox covered with frost was following along behind him. It ran along until it became confused crossing the lake, but finally it was able to find his scent and ran off after him again. The fox came into the young man's camp, lay down across the fire from him, and slept there unnoticed.

---

* The young man is afraid that the relatives of the people who died will come to kill him to avenge their deaths.

Then he saw it. "Oh my, there's that animal!" he thought. "I'd like to kill it," he thought, but then he changed his mind. Really, he wasn't sure what he should do.

Every day he traveled on. Again and again the fox caught up to him. The snow fell and drifted over his trail, but the fox still followed, frosted from the cold. After crossing another icy muskeg lake the young man camped beside a clearing.

"I'll just sleep here and try to understand clearly what the fox wants," the young man thought as he settled in, and, making a rough shelter, went to sleep. As he expected, the fox was not far behind. Again, it sat down across the fire from him. The man reached for his jacket, thinking he might put the unburned ends of the logs in the fire.

"I have no clothes. I have nothing to wear," the fox suddenly said, as the man put on his jacket. "I'm always following you. Why are you always running away from me?"

"The fox must be the girl that left the moccasins and jacket for me," the young man thought. He thought about this, and then he knew why she had been following him. Now he and Fox Girl fell asleep, side by side. Yes, the young man slept and slept.

When he finally woke the young man peeled the bark from straight, smooth trees and made a perfect dwelling for the girl, without even a speck of dust on it anywhere.

Now the young man slept for three days: every day he slept and every night he slept. At last he woke up; finally he woke up. Then he woke up and wanted a drink, and lifted his head.

Oh my! Scored fish fillets blanketed the spruce bough floor. There were many fish, and piles of groundhogs, singed, gutted, and skinned, piled beside where Fox Girl sat. The young man rose to put a fish back on a pole, but he didn't ask where Fox Girl had gotten the fish, and she didn't say anything. The young man was thinking about what Fox Girl had told him— that she had nothing to wear—but he didn't say anything. "Would you like to eat this?" Fox Girl finally asked him softly, serving him with a decorated birch bark plate. The man was so hungry he ate one large fish by himself.

"Now I'm going to provide food for you," the young man told her. "Just wait here."

The next morning before the sun came up the young man went hunting. "That girl once helped me and now she is pitiful," he thought. Returning just before dark, he gave her a moose head and choice pieces of moose fat.

"Tomorrow let's go to where I killed the moose and pack the meat back," he said, and so in the morning they traveled to the kill and back, packing the meat with packstraps. When they returned the young man told Fox Girl to make dried meat. Then she proceeded to cut thin pieces of meat from the four moose. "Prepare the meat for drying," the young man told the girl, "and I will go hunting." She sat there by the meat as it dried, waiting for her husband to return.

7 Wolverine Is Outsmarted

I survived many hardships. My father died when I was young. Do you think you could have survived? I was only this big [indicates with hands] when my father died but, yes, I found a way to survive. Hey, we were poor! We lived in a tipi and we could only get around with snowshoes. We made snowshoes ourselves and looked for a way to survive. I had no traps in those days but I watched my uncle set a log trap, then set a log trap myself and trapped martens. Yes, I was a poor orphan but I survived. I hope your elders will talk to you and teach you everything you need to know to survive.

Wolverine was bad, they always say. For some reason Wolverine was looking to cause mischief. In those days people used flints to make fire, and they carefully hid the flints before they went to sleep. But Wolverine searched and found the flints, taking the means of making fire that they depended on. Now what could they start a fire with? Yes, long ago Wolverine was bad, they say.

Now one time Wolverine was camping in the bush, and, hey, he came upon someone's camp! Wolverine went toward this man's camp and camped across the fire from him, near where the man's wet moccasins were hanging by the fire.

Now it seems that the man was suspicious of Wolverine and so he was watching him. Some time passed and then Wolverine got up, roused himself, and looking carefully at the man—who pretended to be asleep—he took a pole and knocked the man's moccasins into the fire, stirring the embers first and then throwing them in. After stirring up the embers again Wolverine went back to sleep. Well, while Wolverine was sleeping, the man took Wolverine's moccasins, threw them into the fire, stirred up the embers, then went back to bed.

Now it seems that the man had two pairs of moccasins. In the morning he got up, put on his extra pair of moccasins, and left. Well, when Wolverine woke up he looked for his moccasins, but they were gone. The man had outsmarted Wolverine, leaving him without moccasins. Wolverine ran off without moccasins and his feet froze, and then he froze to death, they always say.

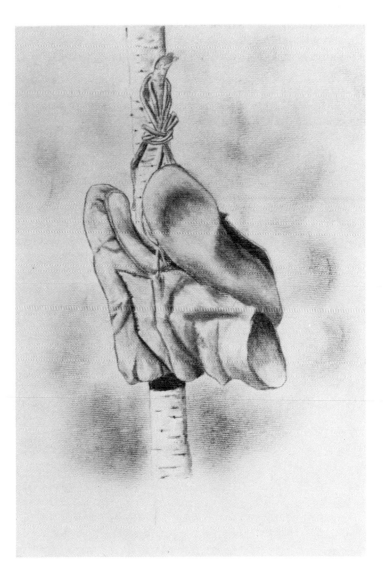

Storyteller's Commentary

Yes, Wolverine was always looking for trouble, it is said. Yes, people even used to hide their flints from him. Hey, Wolverine would even chew up snowshoes that someone was making. The people always moved around in the past, and without flints how could they start a fire? Wolverine was not good, it is always said. Wolverine was always wanting to cause mischief, it is said.

Now some people are that way, it seems to me. They are always going to High Level [a nearby town] for no good reason. They go and leave their children behind. Yes, it makes me sad.

8   Wolverine Steals a Wife

My Grandmother told me about Wolverine long ago when I was a child. "Grandmother, tell me a story," I said, and she spoke with me.

Wolverine stole someone's wife. In the days when Wolverine was a person he stole someone's wife and lived with her in-laws. His little mother-in-law lived next to Wolverine's house, and when her sons were off hunting she depended on Wolverine to hunt for her.

Now Wolverine had a child who also lived with them, and this young boy often visited his grandmother. He observed that although Wolverine was killing beaver, he didn't feed his grandmother, and the old woman was dying of hunger.

To get food for his grandmother, the boy would cry loudly, and when they cooked something for him to eat, he chewed his food, then spit it into his coat when no one was looking. He did this many times and then said, "I'll go visit grandmother," and if they didn't let him go he started crying again. Yes, he would go to his grandmother's and enter her house.

"Grandmother, lift up your cup," he said, then emptied his coat into her cup, and his grandmother finally ate.

Meanwhile, Wolverine was hunting for beaver, eventually bringing back several. He urinated into the stomach of one of the beavers, then gave it to his mother-in-law. The old woman cooked the beaver, then ate it, and threw up. Wolverine continually did this, giving the old woman contaminated food.

Finally the old woman's sons came back and found her still living there without them. Then they moved camp during the night, taking their old mother with them. They moved up ahead and made camp, and here she told them what Wolverine had done to her.

The sons had killed a fat moose near where they were camped. Now they hung the intestines over the embers of their campfire to broil.

Early in the morning, Wolverine was coming along their trail and saw the intestines hanging over the fire. "We have already planned what we will do," the brothers-in-law thought to themselves.

"In-laws!" Wolverine called. "I see you have killed a nice moose. I'm hungry and I fed your mother well."

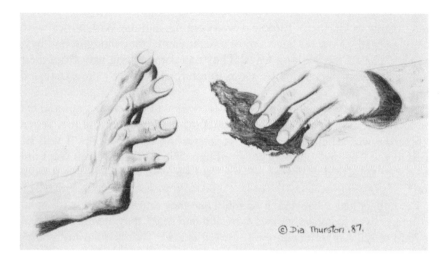

© Dia Thurston .87.

then lift their breechcloths and shut their eyes. Only then can we give them something to eat."

And so Wolverine sat down by the fire, lifted his breechcloth, and spread his legs in expectation of being fed. The brothers took the fat from the intestines, poked it into the hot embers, and then shoved it between Wolverine's legs. As Wolverine jumped in pain they clubbed him to death, and then hid his body in the snow.

Soon afterwards Wolverine's wife was coming. She was about to give birth to Wolverine's baby and pulled her other child on a toboggan. Now she arrived at her brothers' camp as they were preparing dried meat and pounding pemmican. Yes, it was tasty, but then her brothers urinated into the food. Then it was truly tasty! They gave some meat to eat to Wolverine's wife and Wolverine's child, who became sick and vomited. Then the men killed them both. But they saw that the woman's stomach was still moving, so they cut into her and took the baby Wolverines out of her womb.

But they were unable to hold them, and the two Wolverines ran away with the men in pursuit. The brothers chased the young Wolverines up trees and set fires under them, but again they escaped.

"In the future," said one Wolverine, "if this land still exists, we will not destroy your traps or eat your bait. But you must leave us alone."

Then the brothers started to return home, but when they were still in sight, the Wolverines came down from the tree.

"Until the end of this land we will destroy your traps, your bait, and your caches," the Wolverines said. "Nothing will be left for you."

Again the men chased the Wolverines up a tree and piled branches below to set fire to the tree. The Wolverines urinated into the fire, and so the men were unable to kill them. Darkness was coming, and the Wolverines were running ahead. "Now we have almost caught them," they thought, but, hey, they had chased them a long ways! They had come a long way from their camp and it was impossible for them to return since they were exhausted from hunger.

Now, because of what happened, wolverines will take your traps and eat the food you store in caches. That is what my grandmother told me. When Wolverine was a person he was always stealing from people. "I will be good to you," he said, but they bothered him. "Now I'll steal from you until the end of the world," Wolverine said. "If I see your food, I'll take it from you."

But hunger had exhausted those men, and they returned home with great difficulty. Even today wolverines exist and they steal; they are clever. It will be hard to kill wolverines in the future, it is said. That is what my grandmother said.

9 The Young Man Who Sought a Wife

In the past when Wolverine was hungry, he stuck his hand into the snow as he was running along, running along. He would feel a tingling in the tips of his fingers while he was running along, if there was an animal under the snow. If he couldn't feel anything while traveling one way, he would turn and set off in another direction. He kept traveling on until he felt a tingling in his fingers, until he found something to eat. That is what they said long ago.

In the very beginning of this world there were no knives or axes. Wolverine chewed rocks, gnawing them to make knives, they say. He was the only one who made knives long ago, they say.

Wolverine used to steal things; whatever he liked he stole. Wolverines are still like that. If a wolverine passes by a snared lynx it will tear it up. Hey, they're strong, really strong! A wolverine can run off with the front quarter of a moose, just bite it in the middle and carry it without putting it down. Their tracks go on and on, back to the time before people were living here.

Wolverine was not the one who made the arrow in this story; it was someone else that made this Wolverine tooth arrowhead.* It was Yamonhdeyi. Once, Yamonhdeyi was traveling with his family, and his father said, "Your poor mother is almost blind and she still has to make moccasins and mitts for you. Go look for a man who will give you his daughter. Then she can make you moccasins and mitts."

"Yes," Yamonhdeyi said, and he packed and left to look for a wife. At last he came upon an old man and woman who had an only daughter, who was sitting across from them. "I'm happy to see you," the old man said. "Since there is nobody to hunt for us, I'll give you my daughter."

Now the daughter was already married, and the old man wanted to trick the stranger. But Yamonhdeyi was clever and noticed that there were fine wood shavings among the spruce boughs, where someone had been making a pair of snowshoes beside the girl. "She must be married," he thought, but pretended to believe her father.

"I'm going hunting," Yamonhdeyi said, then packed a few things and left. It was summer, and he walked and walked. Meanwhile the girl's

---

* Wolverine does not appear directly in this story, but he is said to have made all of the flint arrow points, knives, and fire strikers used by the Dene. In this way Wolverine helped make people human. Wolverine is also one of the animal helpers of Yamonhdeyi.

husband, the man who had made the shavings, was killing people somewhere in the bush.

Yamonhdeyi had been walking a long time when he treed two bears and killed them. He skinned one bear and put the meat from both bears into its hide, since he was planning to roast it over the fire. Then he traveled on, and as the sun set he was splashing through a muskeg. The branches snapped with each step—"snap! snap! snap!"—and the water slurped at his feet as he walked slowly through the muskeg. Beyond the muskeg he put up a lean-to and made a small fire. He piled spruce branches in the light of this small fire, put the bearskin over them, then covered everything with his blanket. It looked like a person sleeping by the fire with a bit of black hair showing beneath the blanket in the flickering light.

As Yamonhdeyi got ready behind the lean-to, he heard the sound of someone else walking through the muskeg. Then from behind the lean-to he moved the bearskin form with a pole as the sound from the muskeg continued. "Snap! Slurp, slurp, slurp." Yamonhdeyi took out a stone arrow point, a Wolverine tooth, which he tied to an arrow shaft, and as the stranger approached in the dark Yamonhdeyi drew his bow and shot. There was a loud "ker-thwack!" as the arrow hit. Yamonhdeyi thought he saw someone holding an arrow where it had entered his chest. He piled wood on the fire to see, but there was nothing, and so he ate and fell asleep beside the fire.

In the morning he went to look in the direction where he had shot and found a man in a beaverskin coat covered with frost, with that Wolverine's tooth arrowhead sticking in his heart and out his back. The dead man was the young woman's husband who had killed many people while they slept. While they were sleeping he killed and killed. He had killed many people that way.

Now Yamonhdeyi started back toward the camp of the young woman and her parents, taking the bear meat with him into their camp. The young woman was sitting outside working as he approached and called out to her father, "That young man who went off hunting has returned." She took some bear meat inside to her parents and said, "He must have killed that man we depend on because he has returned alive."

"Where does your father get the eagle wing feathers for his arrows?" Yamonhdeyi asked the girl when she came out, and she directed him into the bush. He soon left and came upon a huge nest with two giant eaglechildren sitting in it. Yamonhdeyi climbed the tree and tunneled up, making a hole part way through the bottom of the nest. When he had tunneled through into the nest, the boy eagle spoke to him, warning him about the mother eagle.

"When Mother is coming back it rains a little," the boy eagle said, "and then you know Mom is coming back."

Now the boy eagle's sister was angry because he had warned Yamonh-deyi about their mother. "When Mother comes back I'll tell on you," she said. This was in the days when animals ate people.

Still the boy eagle continued to warn Yamonhdeyi. "If Mom is coming back it rains a little," he said, "and if Dad is coming it snows a little." Just then it started to rain a little, and the boy eagle cried out saying, "Yes, Mom is coming," and Yamonhdeyi hid himself in the nest.

The mother eagle arrived carrying half a person. "Here," she said to the boy eagle, handing him the person. "Where is your little sister? I'm going below to rest because my head hurts." (Now it seems that Yamonhdeyi had killed the girl eagle.)

"Hey, Mom, I'm hungry. Give me some food," the boy eagle cried, trying to lure his mother back to the nest.

"What are you crying for?" the mother eagle asked. "I brought you a person." As she prepared to feed her son, Yamonhdeyi pulled her down into the nest and killed her.

Soon after this it began to snow and the father eagle arrived. "Son, where is that smell of people coming from?" he asked.

"It must be from that person you killed," the son replied. Just then Yamonhdeyi grabbed the father eagle and pulled him into the nest, where he removed his wing feathers.

Yamonhdeyi tunneled to the top of the nest again and spoke to the young eagle. "A person should not eat human beings," he told him. "You should live on rabbits, fish, grouse, and ducks—not people. I'll teach you how to fish," he told the eagle.

Now just then there was a fish in the clear water down below. "I'll help you to see the fish," Yamonhdeyi said, and he took ashes and rubbed his hands in them, then passed them in front of the young eagle's eyes. "Do you see the fish?" Yamonhdeyi asked. The fish was still not clear to the eagle, so he passed his hands over the eagle boy's eyes once more.

"Yes, I can see him," the eagle said.

"Attack it then," Yamonhdeyi said, and with a splash the eagle grabbed the fish. "Eat it," Yamonhdeyi said.

"This is tasty," the eagle said. "Fish taste better than people."

From that day on eagles have killed only grouse, ducks and fish (not people). They kill, they kill, they kill—yes, bald eagles. Even now around Bistcho Lake the bald eagles nest where fish are plentiful.

Yamonhdeyi returned then to the girl's camp with the eagle wing feathers. "Where does your father get the sinew he uses to tie his arrows together with?" he asked the girl. She didn't say anything, but when her father returned she told him, "That young man brought back the bald eagle wing feathers."

"My daughter," the old man replied, "he is taking away everything: our land—everything we depend on. Yes, it is all gone."

"That man we depended on is gone," the girl said. "And just now he asked me where you get your sinew."

"Yes, everything is lost," the old man said.

When Yamonhdeyi again inquired about the sinew, the young woman said, "There—he goes over there."

Yamonhdeyi went to a meadow where he saw a huge animal sleeping.* A yellowlegs was nesting on top of its head, and when anything approached it would call out, "Dunh, dunh, dunh, dunh." But as Yamonhdeyi drew closer, it remained quiet.

"You skinny legs, what do you see up there?" the monster said.

"The grass is blowing so I can't see," the yellowlegs answered, lying.

Yamonhdeyi crawled through the grass thinking, "I wish a mouse would run by," and just then a mouse ran by. "Go to the monster and gnaw an opening over its heart," he told it, "and one day I'll help you in return." The mouse climbed up on the monster and began chewing its hide.

"Why are you nibbling away at my fur, mouse?" the giant animal demanded.

"My children are cold and I need fur for their clothes," the mouse replied.

---

*·This animal is said to have been a wooly mammoth or mastodon.

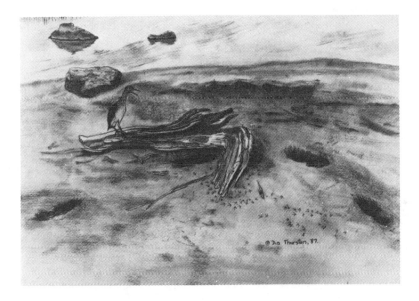

Now Yamonhdeyi pulled his bow back as far as he could and shot at the monster's heart. The monster thrashed about, calling out as he was hit.

"You twig-legs, you said the grass blew in front of your eyes! Agh!" he cried out, falling dead. Yamonhdeyi cut out a pile of the monster's pure white sinew with his knife. Yes, he killed this monster, too.

He returned to the camp of the girl and her parents. "Those wolverine teeth—those arrowpoints—where do you get them?" he asked.

"Over there," the girl said, pointing in another direction. Then Yamonhdeyi traveled until he came to a place where black stones—arrowpoints—could be heard whistling through the air like arrows in flight. "Tl'eng, tl'eng, tl'eng, tl'eng!" As they landed he picked them up, then started home with his bag of arrowpoints. Yes, he brought those back, too.

"My daughter," the old man said, "that man is taking everything away from us; he is taking away our world. You will have to turn into a bear and chase him. He has only small game arrows, the ones with thick wooden ends."

When Yamonhdeyi approached, the girl turned into a bear and almost caught him as her parents watched. While she chased him Yamonhdeyi assembled a game arrow, carefully attaching the point and feathers with sinew, and then he wheeled and shot the bear. He killed it then.

"Hey, my daughter!" the old man cried out, and the old woman joined him, wailing for their daughter. Together they chased Yamonhdeyi, and they chased him until they reached a beaver pond where Yamonhdeyi leaped in, and with a splash he became a fish. He escaped them by hiding at the bottom of the pond.

Now the old man called two giant pelicans to land on the pond to help them catch the man. Together the pelicans drank all the water from the pond, but the fish was still treading water under a tiny piece of wood. The old woman went to the middle of the pond, searching in the shallow water. She killed everything, even the insects. "So you think you are the only smart one! You think you're the only smart one, don't you?" the old woman said.

While the old man and woman were killing all the insects, a yellowlegs was walking nearby in the mud.

"The water is almost gone and my skin is drying out," the tiny fish called to the yellowlegs. "Pierce the pelican's pouch with your bill," he requested.

The yellowlegs now walked nearer the pelican.

"You spindly legs, stay away from my pouch," the pelican said.

"I'm just looking for insect skulls," the yellowlegs said, and when it was right beside the pelican, it fluttered its wings and darted into the pelican's pouch. The pouch burst open, and Yamonhdeyi was able to escape while the old man and woman drowned. Yes, all of them were killed.

Storyteller's Commentary

Before there were people on earth long, long ago, there were dangerous beings, animals that were like people, it is said. These stories are about those beings.

Dene have religious leaders like the white priests, people who pray. People like Alexis Seniantha pray for people and sing. It was like that long ago, they say.

These traditional stories are really true, although people today don't know about these things. Long ago people talked to the elders; they had no schools, just the animals in the bush. They had to search for food—a rabbit—anything to eat. The stories are to help people live. That is why people told about those dangerous beings. Yes, old men told these stories. They talked then, that way, that way, that way.

10 The Man Who Received a Vision in Old Age

Yes, long ago when I was a child Grandmother told me this story.

Yes, in the days when people used only bows and arrows there lived a young man, and one morning he was in a hurry to go somewhere. He had a moosehide belt, and as he was in a hurry he grabbed the first belt he saw, thinking, "That's my belt." Meanwhile his mother was working nearby, not paying attention to him. Yes, he took his mother's belt by mistake and started to put it on, when his mother looked up.

"My son!" she called out "That's my belt!" The young man threw the belt away without saying anything.*

He was only a child when this happened, and afterwards he wandered in the bush seeking a vision, but no vision appeared to him. One day he came to a little creek, and being thirsty, he stooped to drink. Now he saw that his beard was becoming full as he grew older and he was very unhappy. "No vision will appear to me because I put on my mother's belt," he thought. "What's the use of living? I don't even care if I'm eaten alive." (Now really listen to me children!)

The man continued wandering while his beard was growing, but he still had not seen a vision. One day he was walking along a river bank when he came to a game trail, where the snow was packed down. "It doesn't matter if I'm eaten alive," the man thought, "since I have not received a vision." Saying this, he went to sleep near the trail. He had been sleeping a long time, and it was exactly the middle of the night when he heard someone talking, a sound coming. He had not expected to meet people, and now he heard chattering as someone was talking back and forth, coming closer and closer.

"I don't care," the man thought, "since I haven't received a vision and my beard is grown. It doesn't matter what's coming. I don't care if I'm eaten. So what if something kills me. It wouldn't matter."

Suddenly! Hey, the man was surrounded by a large group of young men, who walked around him, followed by an older man with grizzled hair. Yes, the man felt their presence but said nothing. These strange young men

* Men could not contact women or their clothing inappropriately, or animals would avoid them.

49

gathered at his feet, then the large old man walked to the middle of the group.

"My sons," the old man said, "your uncle is coming. We can't help this poor person, but a way exists. When bad things like this happen, your uncle, the one who is coming, may be able to help." Then they left, and as the man peeked out from under his blanket, he saw wolves running away. That old man, the old wolf, had no canine teeth left from gnawing bones.

Some time passed and the man heard someone else coming. He must have fallen asleep again, when he sensed someone approaching. A large stocky man was walking toward him, then walking around him.

"Stranger, what has happened to you?" the newcomer asked.*

But the man didn't answer.

"You're pitiful. Get up!" Wolverine said. "Get up, get up!" he said, walking around the man. "Stand facing away from me," he told the man, then put his mouth on him. "Now look at me!" Wolverine commanded. Wolverine placed his mouth on the man and sucked away everything, including his mother's dirty belt.†

"This is why you haven't received a vision," Wolverine said. "Now what shall I do with this belt?"

"Do whatever you want with it," the man replied. Then he began weeping, crying and crying, as Wolverine ran off.

After Wolverine was gone the man began traveling again. He walked and slept and walked again, continuing walking through the winter. One day he was walking and, hey, it became dark, and he made a fire and kept it going without making any sparks! Hey, then he slept and slept! Again a chattering sound was coming toward him as he was looking for a vision. These were not the people he had seen before, however, but a different group of people, all dressed beautifully, without even a spark from the fire marking their clothes. Two elegant people came upon him, ahead of the rest. Then the others followed, running around and around him, followed by a large man who came walking behind.

"My sons," the old man said, "this person is pitiful and hungry, without anything to eat. Go kill some grouse for him, then feed him," he said. "Go on! What are you waiting for?"

"They must be wolves," the man thought, and he saw that they were traveling on snowshoes. "That old man must be their father," the man

---

* The storyteller says this newcomer is Wolverine. The man has nearly starved after abandoning himself to die.

† His mother's belt had left a mark on him. Wolverine removes the mark by sucking, a traditional method of curing.

thought, "that big old man." Then that large old man sat down across the fire from him.

"Let's go," the old wolf man said, "and we'll follow them (his wolf sons)." And so the man began walking after the old man, after him, using snowshoes, walking after him. Not far ahead they came to a place where several moose were roaming around, and the wolves' snowshoe tracks were following close behind. Then the moose had run off. Oh my, they ran through the woods and over tangled deadfalls, farther and farther, until at last they came to a place where the snowshoe tracks were close together, and they saw signs where the moose had frantically tried to get away. The wolves had followed on snowshoes and not far ahead, up on a rise, the wolves were camped, sitting across from each other cheerfully eating together. (They must have killed the moose.)

They approached with the old man in the lead. Then the young wolves all ran away. That is how it must have been. There were some wolf droppings on the ground, and the old man picked them up and put them in his pocket, saying, "I use these to make my sons' arrows."* Then they walked on after

---

* The old wolf picks up the droppings because they contain something magical which wolves use to kill moose, something like reloading shotgun shells.

the wolves. At last they rejoined the young wolf men and cooked some meat.

Yes, they finally went to sleep, settling down with only animal fur blankets, each person sleeping across from each other, with the large old man sleeping on the side of the lean-to away from the fire. "You sleep here by me," he said to the man, and the man lay down alongside him and prepared to go to sleep.

"Your brothers usually eat everything up," the old man warned him. "Put your share of food up a bit, somewhere where they won't take it." And so the man cached a small piece of meat up in a safe place and then went to sleep.

The man had been sleeping a long time when the sky began to grow light as dawn approached. Suddenly he was cold, terribly cold, and each time he moved he could hear hard-packed snow crunching beneath him. When at last there was enough light to see, he adjusted his blanket, and in the distance he heard a wolf howl. The man woke to find himself surrounded by chewed pieces of bone, the remnants of a moose knee, leftover scraps, and black wolf droppings. The only thing left uneaten was the small piece of meat he had cached. As he looked, he could see where the wolves had run off.

"What will I do now?" the man thought. He took the meat down, crossed the trail, cleared a place for a fire, built a fire, and cooked and ate the meat. Finally in his old age he had received a vision. He had been alone in the bush for a long time without meeting any other people, without receiving a vision. But now he truly knew something and was becoming powerful.

He didn't know where his father was, and now he began thinking about this. It was winter and he made snowshoes for himself to walk with, and he was always thinking about where his parents might be. He knew where he had left them many years before, then started off toward his former home, searching for his parents. At last he came upon the trail of an old woman and an old man. He looked carefully and, remembering that his mother was left-handed, observed that one of the old people was left-handed by the way in which they had been chopping brush. Now he followed this trail until he came to the place where they were living.

At first the old couple didn't recognize their son. "Hey, I wish this would be my son," the old man said to his wife as he hung his bedroll outside and then entered the tipi, looking carefully around but saying nothing.

"Mother, it's me," the man said. "Where have you put my clothes?"

"Hey, my son, I carried your clothing around and carried it around until I couldn't wait any longer for you to return," his mother said. "Then I left it behind."

The son didn't say a word but, not liking what he had heard, returned to the bush and began wandering again. The man who received a vision in old age became young again as he traveled, and just as he became young enough to marry he met an old man.

"Be my son-in-law," the old man said to him, but the young man was suspicious because he saw wood shavings among the spruce boughs where the man's young daughter was sitting (as if a man had been making snow-shoes).

"He asked me to be his son-in-law," the man thought, but he was hesitant and wondered why there were shavings around where the girl was staying.

Soon it was time to go to sleep, but the young man had left his pack outside. "Father-in-law," he said, "I've decided to stay here with you, but for now I'll make camp somewhere close by." Then he went outside and made a lean-to far away in a clearing in the woods.

Now he knew that the girl's real husband would probably follow him and try to kill him when night came, and so he only pretended to be sleeping. He stayed awake, and keeping watch from under his blanket, he turned into a wolf and ran away when the girl's husband came close. The girl's husband looked all around, but all he could find was a firepit. Even the man's blanket was gone, as he had run off taking the form of a wolf.

Now the young man became a person again and continued walking, expecting to see no one among the trees. Suddenly someone passed, and the young man came upon bear tracks.* He passed the tracks now and then and carefully followed them, staying a few feet off to one side, periodically stepping on logs whenever there was a clearing to hide his own tracks. Suddenly there was another set of tracks—human tracks—of a man who had passed before, tracking the bear as he was doing. Now he saw where the bear had crashed through the woods and chased the other man. The young man was very careful now and went along the edge of some spruce where the other man must have made camp. He could see the signs where the bear had crashed through the woods, and he suspected that when the other man was sleeping the bear had jumped on him, killed him, and eaten him.

Now the young man moved cautiously through the snow-covered spruce until, as evening passed, he arrived at the other man's camp. He looked around very carefully, thinking that the man had been eaten. There he saw that someone's snowshoes were standing propped up against a tree, and some arrows had also been left there. The young man thought that the bear must have eaten him. He was afraid then, very afraid, that he would suffer the same fate and he felt weary. He took off his snowshoes. Then, going

* The man whose tracks he finds is being pursued by a bear that eventually pounces on him.

back over his own trail, he knocked the light fluffy snow off the trees. It made a quiet sound, "di-di-di," as he walked along covering his trail. It was already dark as the man walked along the edge of a muskeg and made camp in a clearing among the trees.

The next day he built a lean-to using two large spruce trees, cleverly placing them so he could stand concealed behind them. Then he went into the muskeg, where he found some small cone-laden spruce, and cut some and took them back to his camp. There he fixed the spruce branches to look like a man sleeping under a blanket, then hid himself behind the lean-to. He placed his snowshoes nearby, all ready to jump into, one snowshoe ahead of the other. He also prepared some arrows of the right size and sat waiting, gripping the arrows. He waited a long time, far into the night.

Finally the man sensed something approaching. Yes, that bear was approaching carefully along the edge of the woods. The man pushed the unburned portions of wood into the fire, making a small fire just barely bright enough to see. Then he put a stump on the fire, and he could see the bear close by, crawling up to his camp. Now the bear detoured, trying to approach downwind.

The bear continued to crawl toward the man, until at last he was right across the fire from the man, watching him. Now the man moved the spruce branches, so that it looked as though someone was moving under the blanket. The bear stood up on his hind legs and pounced on the sleeping form, biting down on the spruce branches, chewing the spruce branches.

The man hit the unsuspecting bear on the back of his neck, striking him again and again until he quit moving. The man killed the bear and carried him out of his camp. The next morning he gutted the bear and found human hair in its stomach. He left the bear where he had killed it, taking only a paw. "So that is what happened to that man," he thought.

The next day he woke and began wondering where the man the bear ate was from, and he wanted to find out. He came to the main trail and traveled a little ways, continuing to check for the tracks of the other man. He traveled a long time and came at last to a place where people were living in a log lean-to, but he didn't enter, going off instead in another direction.

"I'll go and visit them," the man thought as evening came and darkness fell. He hid his belongings in the woods, and, yes, as it became dark he went to visit those people. He placed the bear paw in his pack and then went into the lean-to. An old man and old woman were sitting there.

"Hey, stranger! Where did you come from?" the old man said. "My son said, 'I'll go look for grouse,' three days ago and he hasn't returned. Where did you come from and where is my son?" the old man asked.

"So that must be who the man was," the young man thought, but said nothing.

"Yes," the old man continued, "my son planned to sleep one night in the bush, then return."

Now the young man went back out and got the bear paw. "Grandfather, what can I say? I think this will explain," the young man said, placing the bear paw on the spruce boughs near the old man. Then the old man began crying; that's what the elders said.

PART ONE

ENGLISH TEXTS

Accounts of the Prophet Nógha

Introduction to the Dene Prophets

After this I looked, and there before my eyes was a door opened in Heaven.

Revelation 4:1

Prophets

As long as the Dene Dháa can remember there have been prophets called *ndátin* 'dreamers' living among them. As children, the prophets, both male and female, were trained by listening to stories of animal people and culture heros. They were taught to pray, singing the songs of the prophets who had come before them, until they were ready to seek a vision of their own.

This early training strengthened their ability to see things that are not apparent to ordinary perception. All the prophets received visions of animal people or animal spirits, visions which could occur either in the bush or in dreams. Most of the traditional Dene Dháa stories, including the Wolverine stories in the first part of this collection, are accounts of such visions. Some of these occur in dreams, as in "The Two Sisters," although in other accounts Dene encounter animal people while traveling in the bush and may perceive the animal people as normal humans. Thus the children who later became prophets were trained as visionaries by listening to accounts of visions.

For the Dene Dháa prophets, stories provided the landscape in which visions could occur, and the songs provided the trail through that landscape. Dene Dháa describe a vision as *mendayeh wodekéh* 'something appearing in front of someone' or *mba' awodi* 'something talking to or sounding for someone.' A person who receives a vision may also receive a song, and a young person is often told, "*Shin kaneya* 'Go for a song!'" Just as listening to stories prepares children to seek a vision, singing the prophet songs prepares them to acquire their own songs. One prophet explained, "Grandmother used to tell me, 'Why don't you pray with the Bistcho Lake prophet's song?' After that I always sang his song."

People who receive a vision further strengthen their abilities with special powers from the animal people they meet in their visions. Once a child receives one vision, he or she is likely to learn from other animals later in life. Visions or significant dreams are very common experiences for Dene Dháa. Almost all older Dene Dháa, both men and women, have their own songs. Some individuals who develop their minds by learning songs and acquiring visions can locate moose in the bush by dreaming. They travel long distances as they sleep, and their dreams about the future are said to come true. The special ability to direct one's dreaming originally distinguished a *ndátin* 'dreamer' from other people.

Robin Ridington (1978) has described the early development of the prophet religion among the Beaver near Fort St. John, British Columbia. He suggests that Beaver dreamers "are now, or were at one time, seen to be simply people with swan medicine" (Ridington 1978:19). The Beaver believe that swan people live in a separate land above the earth which might be compared to heaven. Dene Dháa also believe that swans have a special homeland above the earth and may appear to people in visions, but this is also true of seagulls, snow geese, and celestial objects such as the stars and northern lights. In the "Two Sisters" story, two girls travel to the land of stars and return in the same way prophets journey to heaven. Other animals may also live in these lands above the earth; for example, in some stories Spider Woman returns people to earth on a web. The rainbow, *kéleetl'unhén*, is literally 'spiderweb' in the Dene language. For Dene Dháa, visions of any animal may help prepare a prophet to travel to heaven. All animals have special magical powers that they can share with people, and a vision of Swans is not a requirement for traveling to heaven.

The first Dene Dháa *ndátin* who traveled to heaven may have been Gochee 'Brother,' who was active at the turn of the century. Earlier religious leaders are remembered, but it is not known whether they also traveled to heaven. The prophets described by Leslie Spier (1935) went to heaven and received visions. Gochee lived later than many of the earliest prophets who were active among neighboring groups (Ridington 1978:30-31; Spier 1935:25,62), and it is possible Dene Dháa had known about prophets from other groups who had gone to heaven even before Gochee received his vision. Dene Dháa have met together with other prophets from as far away as Ross River in the Yukon and Fort Norman in the Northwest Territories to discuss their visions. They are also aware of the philosophies of the earlier Dene Dháa prophets.

After Gochee there was a series of prophets from the Bistcho Lake area. Gochee's successor was called *Mbek'ádhi* 'He Is Recovered,' and then *Nógha* 'Wolverine' became the head prophet. Nógha may have received his name from his animal helper, Wolverine; he is listed under the name Wolverine in the 1891 census of the Fort Vermilion District. People still talk about the dances he directed and his prophecies, all of which they feel are coming true. In the 1930s, when the Dene Dháa were still living off the land in small groups of one or two families, Nógha foresaw that they would be forced onto a reservation, that welfare would erode their ability to control their children, and that the land would be sectioned by cutlines used to provide access for oil companies.

The ascension of the Dene Dháa prophets can be compared with the developments described in the Christian New Testament. In both cases there is an older religious tradition to which new beliefs were added. The most ancient beliefs of the Dene Dháa include animal spirits which appear in Dene Dháa visions. The traditional Dene Dhaá stories of Wolverine, the animal person, are from this older tradition. Although the focus of Dene Dháa prophet visions became heaven, the prophets still learned from animals in the same way Jesus and his disciples knew the older Judaic traditions. The importance of animal spirits for Dene Dháa is difficult to assess because visions of animal people and their use in curing are strictly private, whereas visions of heaven are discussed openly. The large number of stories and traditions associated with animal people or spirits suggests that these beliefs are still very important for Dene Dháa.

Tea Dance

The Dene Dháa prophets direct a religious celebration which is called a *Dawots' ethe* 'Dance,' called a Tea Dance in English.* The purpose of each Tea Dance is revealed to the prophets through their dreams; they may be held for people who have died, to bring warm weather, to prevent misfortunes, to give thanks for moose that have been killed, or even to increase the number of game animals.

In an open area a large circle is made, bounded by a fence of short log posts supporting a top rail. Special flags bearing symbols from the prophets' dreams are put up on poles near the entrances. A fire is kindled in the center of the circle, where the prophets and singers gather facing around it, the ribbons from their drums floating in the breeze. Offerings of tobacco and food are placed in the fire by the prophets, who kneel to place the offerings and then cross themselves. The prophets may tell the people what will happen, where they will find game, what the winter will be like, or what dangers must be avoided. Then the singers drum and sing while everyone dances. Meat, fat, and tea are served to each family, and then the dancing resumes. People dance until late at night, illuminated by the central

---

* The English name apparently comes from the tea which is served at these dances, although the tea is not of special significance, except to keep people awake. This name was also used to describe similar dances by other native groups farther south. Like many terms derived from verbs, *dawots' ethe* is morphologically complex, consisting of a thematic prefix *da-*, a prefix *wo-* 'general conditions,' *ts'e-* 'indefinite subject,' and *-the,* one of the stems for dancing

fire. Each extended family sits around separate small fires, arrayed just within the larger circle of the Tea Dance ring.

No one knows when the first Tea Dance was held, but the Dene Dháa say they have always danced and sang. In the last century the Dene Dháa also added elements of Christian ritual to the Tea Dance ceremony, some of which may have come from Catholic missionaries. The rosaries worn by many prophets, for instance, were acquired directly from priests. But Dene Dháa did not always use or interpret the symbols of Christianity in the same way as priests. The prophets borrowed Christian forms and gave them Dene Dháa meanings. An elder might place a rosary on the upwind side of a gathering to part and clear away approaching rain clouds. One prophet explained what the rosary beads meant to him: "Each large bead represents a place where the Son of God came to earth. He walked along on earth and then went back to heaven. He did this many times, and each of the small beads represents his tracks on earth."

Some Christian beliefs, such as the conviction that prophets can travel to heaven or the belief in angels, may have spread from other native peoples. Leslie Spier (1934) documented a widespread religious movement, which he called the Prophet Dance, among native people in the northwestern United States and British Columbia. Spier believed that many of its characteristics were indigenous to the core of this area and spread to other native groups, including Dene in Alberta, by traveling native religious leaders or prophets, well in advance of the arrival of missionaries. He cites many examples of these prophets, including Beeny [bini] 'His Mind,' who was active in the 1820s among the Carrier in Central British Columbia two decades before Catholic missionaries first visited the area in 1847 (Spier 1935:62-63).

Spier believed that the Prophet Dance developed in the Pacific Northwest and was spread by native prophets to Fort Chipewyan, Alberta and the Northwest Territories as early as 1812 (Spier 1935:25). More recent descriptions of the ceremonies of Northern Athabaskans show that the prophet religion was based as well on traditional beliefs indigenous to this area.

Dene Ceremonies

Comparison of the religious ceremonies among numerous Dene groups indicates that some elements of the Prophet Dance, or Tea Dance, were shared by many groups, almost certainly not introduced from other native groups farther south, nor were they responses to European influences. The main public ceremonies of Dene groups in Alaska, the Yukon, and British Columbia are called potlatches. Like Tea Dances, they may be held for a

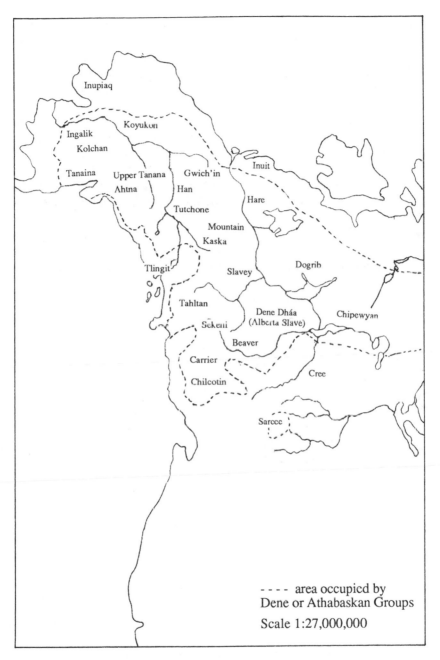

Map 2. Native Groups of the Western Subarctic

Within the map:

Inupiaq

Koyukon

Ingalik
Kolchan

Tanaina

Upper Tanana
Ahtna

Gwich'in

Han

Inuit

Hare

Tutchone

Mountain

Kaska

Tlingit

Slavey

Dogrib

Tahltan

Sekeni

Dene Dháa
(Alberta Slave)

Chipewyan

Beaver

Carrier

Chilcotin

Cree

Sarcee

- - - - area occupied by
Dene or Athabaskan Groups

Scale 1:27,000,000

variety of purposes, including celebration following a successful hunt, to mark the change of seasons, or to commemorate a death.* Potlatches have been distinguished from Tea Dances because potlatches feature gift giving. This characteristic has been cited to link Dene potlatches with those of Pacific Coast groups such as the Tlingit, Haida, and Bella Coola (Honigman 1981:442). However, gift giving was much less extensive in Dene potlatches than in those held by coastal people like the Bella Coola (Tobey 1981:423). Further, this characteristic alone cannot be used to distinguish potlatches from Tea Dances, because accounts of Chipewyan and Cree Tea Dances also mention extensive gift giving much like that found among the Carrier and Upper Tanana today. John Marten, a leading Cree Tea Dance singer, recalled the Tea Dances he attended in Fort Chipewyan (Marten 1988:6):

> They used to give something like a stick to stand for a stove or a dog, or a dog harness. No matter what the cost, they had to give. As they were dancing around they would hold the things they were given until the song stops. Even if they didn't have any big things they would give money.

Boniface Trippe De Roches, a Chipewyan singer from Fort Chipewyan, also mentions gift giving at Chipewyan Tea Dances (1988:3-4):

> Alright, but you wouldn't get up and dance with empty hands, you had to have something in your hand. There were lots of people and they each had something different to give. . . . The others have to give you something, maybe a blanket or maybe some other things, only then you go to dance.

Dene potlatches are commonly held for the souls of people who have died, following a waiting period of at least one year. Dene Dháa, Chipewyan, and Cree Tea Dances are also held for this purpose. The prayers at these Tea Dances are dedicated to the people who have died, and at Dene Dháa Tea Dances the relatives of the deceased place the offerings in the Tea Dance fire.

Even the style of dancing used at these ceremonies may have been the same across the entire territory occupied by Dene in Alaska and Canada

---

* Some or all of these functions of potlatches are mentioned for the Carrier (Tobey 1981: 423), Kutchin (Slobodin 1981: 527), and for the Upper Tanana (Guédon 1981:577). Catherine Bird (personal communication) has confirmed that Carrier potlatches are still held for the dead. According to John Dixon, Kaska formerly held potlatches after successful hunts as well as for the dead.

prior to the introduction of round dances from the Cree. The stationary style of dancing which is used in Upper Tanana potlatches and by other Alaskan and Yukon Dene today is virtually identical to that described for Chipewyan Tea Dances. Samuel Hearne, who lived with Chipewyan for four years between 1769 and 1772, observed this style of dancing. His description is similar to accounts of modern Chipewyan Tea Dances (Hearne 1911:318):

> They always endeavor to imitate either the Dogribbed or Southern Indians, but more commonly the former. The Dogribbed method is not very difficult to learn, as it only consists in lifting the feet alternately from the ground, and as high as possible, without moving the body; the hands at the same time being closed, and held close to the breast, and the head inclining forward.

Chipewyans still used this style of stationary dancing in Fort Chipewyan, until they adopted the Cree style round dance in the 1950s (C. Marten 1988:7).

> The Chipewyan used to dance differently before they came together with the Cree in Fort Chipewyan. I saw them dancing; they danced in the same place. They moved their arms in different ways. It was not a circle dance. That was before they joined the Cree.

Although most Dene Dháa now dance moving in a circle, some older women occasionally still dance in place, a style of dancing known to the Dogrib and Mountain Slavey as well.

The sequence of events in Dene Dháa Tea Dances is similar to that of Upper Tanana potlatches described by Guédon (1981:578-80) and still practiced today. There are opening periods of oratory and prayer by religious and secular leaders, followed by meals, singing and dancing, ritual purification with incense, addresses by guests, and intense singing and dancing lasting late into the night. This cycle may be repeated for several days.

The remarkable similarity of these ceremonies between such widely separated groups as the Upper Tanana and Chipewyan makes it likely that the basic characteristics of these ceremonies and associated beliefs, such as concern for the spirits of the dead, were not introduced from elsewhere or in response to Europeans. Against this shared base of ceremonial practice and religious belief, however, certain characteristics of modern Dene Dháa Tea Dances do appear to be innovations or borrowings from other groups. The style of dancing in a circle may have spread from the Cree to the Beaver, Slavey, Dogrib, and recently to the Chipewyan and Carrier. Cree songs sung to a double beat are also performed along with traditional Dene songs by these same groups. It is doubtful, however, that the Cree were the source of the belief in prophets who experience visions of heaven. The Dene Dháa religious leaders who direct the Tea Dance travel to heaven when they are near death. This does not appear to be a Cree tradition, and like the Tea Dance ceremony itself, this belief is based on widely shared Dene traditions.

The Dene Dháa prophets are called *ndátin* 'dreamers' because they can perceive the spiritual world in their dreams. Similar religious leaders are widely described for other Dene groups. Kaska, for instance, call curers *nedetē* 'dreamers' and believe they have similar powers to foresee the future and work with spirits. Traditionally, Kaska *nedetē* did not travel to heaven, but recently one woman has experienced visions similar to those of the Dene Dháa prophets. The extension of the realm of prophets' experience into heaven is natural given their traditional concern for every aspect of the spiritual world. If this particular aspect of the prophets' abilities was spread from the plateau area as suggested by Spier (1935), it was a logical addition to their established prerogatives.

Similarly, Dene Dháa women did not drum or experience visions of heaven at the turn of the century, but within the last forty years women prophets have begun to do both. Again, this represents merely an extension of established beliefs, since women traditionally acquired songs in visions and foretold the future through dreams.

Prophets and Priests

The relations between native and white religious leaders have been the subject of numerous historical studies. The analyses provided by Kerry Abel (1986) and by Christopher Miller (1981) are particularly relevant to the Dene Dháa. Abel, who deals specifically with the relations between Dene prophets and Catholic priests in northwestern Canada, believes that the Dene prophet religion was firmly based in traditional beliefs which preceded contact with Europeans (1986:212):

> A lifetime was experienced simultaneously in both the physical and spiritual worlds. A skilled person could travel at will between the worlds, and communicate with all of it, including animals, other human souls, and unnamed spirits. Those spirits were of constant concern. They affected all areas of life from success in the hunt to illness or the weather.

This reconstruction is similar to one derived from comparisons above between widely separated Dene groups. Abel documents Dene prophets, beginning with the first records in the journal of Sir John Franklin in 1812, and details numerous accounts between 1849 and 1880 by Catholic priests from La Loche in Chipewyan territory to Fort Good Hope in Slavey territory. Curiously, Abel (1986:218) asserts that "most of these prophet episodes were shortlived with little evidence for any widespread or organized response lasting more than a season or two." The accounts of the Dene Dháa prophets in this collection, however, reveal that their movement developed continuously over the last century.

One of the problems in reconstructing the religious beliefs of the prophets in any area is that almost all the written records come from whites. They provide considerable information about the worldview of priests, explorers, and fur traders, but only tantalizing fragments of the worldview of native religious leaders. Abel does not balance the priests' descriptions of the native prophets with accounts by the prophets themselves. He asserts (1986:222) that "many of these prophets appear to have been engaged in a pure and simple power struggle [with priests] rather than attempting to reorganize a culture." This perception reflects the priests' view of the native prophets; the prophets' own teachings are not directed against the priests. Nógha and other prophets were concerned with the future well-being of the Dene, but their ceremonies were performed for the benefit of all people, including whites. As Nógha said:

> This earth is large, but we pray for the whole earth. When we go into the Tea Dance circle, then we pray, just like the priest offers communion. The prophets talk about the future and then come to God's land. This message is not just for this one place, but for the whole world. I hope it will help you all.

The priests who missionized northern Alberta, and most of western Canada, were well educated and were usually fluent in the native languages, and yet they did not deal with Dene religious leaders as equals. Some of them, such as Father Isadore Clut at Fort Chipewyan (1861), actually came to blows with these prophets:

> The Indian that I wrote about previously listened to confessions of women in the manner of a priest. This was not enough for this demon who had them sleep with him to hear their confession. . . . He wanted to have a conference with me in the spring to prove with the help of the angels and devils (he claims to communicate with both) that he was more knowledgeable than I was. . . . On coming into the great hall of the residence I heard screaming and

then a sound like the residence was being shaken to its foundation. The great prophet opened and closed the door so furiously that he had the cement falling from the frame. . . . I grabbed a piece of wood and struck my adversary on the shoulder. . . . One more blow and he was down.

The accounts of Dene prophets by Catholic priests give the impression that they were dangerous charlatans determined to lead the native population astray. They do not recognize them as having a lasting, well-developed religious philosophy. In fact, the accounts of the Dene Dháa prophets in this collection show that the prophets were well-known religious leaders who performed ceremonies throughout their lives, usually after working for many years with other prophets who shared their religious philosophy. Because this practice probably occurred historically as well, the written accounts by the priests do not adequately portray Dene religion.

Father Emile Petitot wrote prolifically about Dene languages, mythology, and material culture. In the 1870s Petitot visited the Bistcho Lake area, which became the home of most of the Dene Dháa prophets. Many of his books were published in France and were used to recruit young priests as missionaries. With a flair for the dramatic, Petitot (1893) described many hardships he endured in the north, creating an image of native people in need of missionization who also curiously preserved supposed characteristics of Old World mythology. He drew many parallels between Dene cultures and Old World civilizations at the time of the Old Testament (1878:59,60,62,63), and in the process identified Catholic missionaries to the Dene with the Biblical prophets and apostles.

> Further this word of the Prophet Jeremiah teaches and proves to us that there really exist Israelites among those *who dwell in the deserts and woods*, that is among the Indians. Besides, another prophet informs us that the remnant of Israel shall be dispersed toward the northern regions, for it is written: "Go and proclaim these words toward the North, and say, 'Return thou backsliding Israel.'"

Petitot conveniently derived Dene beliefs from the Old World, rather than suggesting that the Dene may have originated some worthwhile ideas themselves.

Christopher Miller (1985) has described religious relations between natives and whites on the Columbia Plateau, the area that Spier believed was the source of the Prophet Dance. Miller links the activities of Northwest prophets to stresses caused by warfare, epidemics, declining food resources, and finally a climatic catastrophe in the form of volcanic ashfall.

He depicts the prophet religion in the Plateau region as a radical departure from previous beliefs (Miller 1985:43). The Dene Dháa prophet religion, however, does not apparently involve any radical departure from precontact Dene beliefs, as the Christian image of heaven was simply integrated into their accounts of visions. Dene ceremonies, which were traditionally used to avert disease, starvation, bad weather, and other afflictions, were not abandoned with the coming of the Europeans.

Jacqueline Peterson (1988) has questioned many of the conclusions Miller draws concerning the origins of the prophet movement in the Columbia Plateau. She rightly disputes many of his conclusions and recognizes the value of carefully examining the ideologies of early-nineteenth-century natives and whites. An intensive study of the ideologies of whites and Dene in northern Canada is even more revealing because Dene prophets are still active and thus their beliefs are more accessible.

The predictions of the Columbia Plateau prophets as described by Miller (1985:43-45) depict a happy outcome associated with the coming of whites, when "All the people will live together. . . .Things will be made right and there will be much happiness." Miller believes the Plateau prophets waited in hopeful anticipation for the coming of white missionaries. The prophet Nógha's messages recounted in Part Two of this collection, in contrast, describe the destructive onrush of white society. The Dene Dháa prophets prepared people to take a more pessimistic, if not cynical, approach to the encroaching white society. Nógha described the coming horrors of life on a reservation:

In the future something black will be hanging over us, over that way near the hill. Your lives will be difficult. Perhaps your dogs will clamp onto you and drag you off, growling. What will you do then? You will all be pitiful. People will do bad things to each other when they are drinking. Winter will be especially dangerous. These things will happen when you live near the hill.

Although Nógha died in the 1930s, before many of the changes he prophesied came about, he and other Dene Dháa prophets appear to have made an accurate assessment of the effects of white society on native culture. They believed that the Dene Dháa should retain their own traditions, praying for all people in the traditional way. He told people they must retain the hand games, songs, dances, and the custom of making offerings.

Today the Tea Dance religion is still active in Assumption and Meander River, Alberta. In Assumption, there are three living male prophets who are assisted by a number of singers, including many young people trained within the last several years. Nógha's nephew, Alexis Seniantha, is now the head prophet there, and Nógha's teachings remain a vital part of Dene Dháa beliefs. There is also one female prophet, who lives in Meander River, and she has also trained a group of young women singers.

11 Nógha's Song

Hey, this is the land.
Hey hey hia hia.
It is God's land.
Hey hey hia hia.
Mother! la hia hia hia.

It is my father's land.
Hey hey hia hia.
It is my mother's land.
Hey hey hia hia.
It is my father's land.
Ha ha hia hia.
Hey hey hey.

It is my father's land.*
Hia haa hia hia.
It is my mother's land.
Hey hia.
Hey hey hey.

It is my father's land.
It is my mother's land.
Ha hia hia hia.
It is my father's land.
It is my mother's land.
Hey hio hey.

---

* This song is a prayer for the land which also expresses some of the sadness Nógha feels for his departed parents. Nógha twice uses the address form *ane* 'mom' instead of the referent form *semó* 'my mother' possibly to express greater closeness. He does not appear to be addressing his parents directly or the earth as mother and father because he uses the third person form *elin* 'it is' rather than the general form *wónlin* or *gúnlin* 'it exists,' the latter being more commonly used in reference to something extensive, such as the land. The phrases 'It is my father's land' and 'It is my mother's land' might also be translated 'My father is the land' and 'My mother is the land' because the specific verb *elin* is used and is more appropriate for a specific subject such as father or mother.

12 Nógha's Teachings

Long ago Weasel jumped up to that cloud land and made a passage to heaven. That is why they talk about the top of the clouds. Weasel went there because he wanted to see God. Long ago people used to be that way—traveling to heaven—and some still carry on those beliefs. Dene people pray, just as priests pray. Heaven appears to the prophets.

There is a lake called *Ts'u K'edhe* 'Girl's Place'* in the Dene language. A long time ago two teenaged girls lived there alone all winter until March, when it began to get warm. That was where the first prophet died. "The prophet is buried right here," my dad said to me at that place. That was the first prophet. This prophet's name was Gochee 'Brother,' and his father was from near Fort Nelson, British Columbia. It was his father who named him Gochee.

Long ago, they say, long before us, there lived some people who were pitiful. They had lost the use of their legs and had to be pulled around in a toboggan. Even in the summer they had to be packed around. That prophet Gochee had two daughters, and he became weak and was unable to walk like those long-ago people at the lake called Girl's Place. The girls had nothing to eat and there were no other people with them. They were on their own, as their father was very sick and something bad had happened to him. And so they made a lean-to and fished all winter. Inside they started a fire and cooked some fish to eat. Fish was all they had to eat. Now one person knew they were there, and he wondered how they were doing and came to see. He saw that the girls had grown larger and nothing had happened to them; they had survived. That is the place called Girl's Place, which is on my trapline. That was where the prophet Gochee died.

Later, Paul Metchooyeah's father, Mbek'ádhi 'He Is Recovered,' was the head prophet, and a little later Nógha 'Wolverine' became the head prophet. Yes, there were several prophets, Paul Metchooyeah's father and then later Nógha. Altogether there were four head prophets, including Gochee's father, who was Jean Marie Talley's wife's grandfather.

---

* July Lake in northeastern British Columbia.

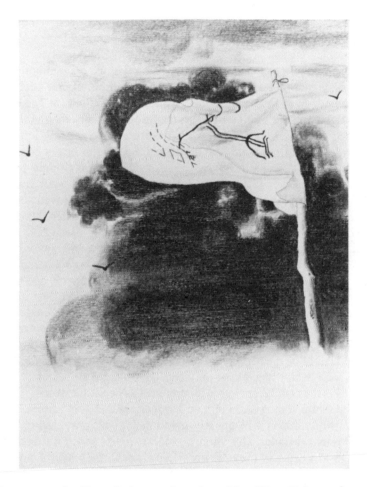

There were also Dene living on the other side of Fort Nelson who spoke Fort St. John Beaver. They had a prophet, and people used to travel by horse to Rainbow Lake for Tea Dances. Hey, those Beaver people from Fort St. John could really sing well, Jean Marie Talley's father said. Hey, they sang well, and in this way helped each other long ago. Harry Dahdona's father was also a prophet and he helped the head prophet. Talley helped as well. They both helped Nógha, praying together. Yes, they told the truth when they talked to us long ago. They told the truth when they told us all would be well if we lived properly.

Nógha told us, "Even though there is only one person left to dance, you will not be tired, and you will have the strength to sing for him as he dances. God made this land, and we should live following God's ways. Do not throw away your traditions. Continue to offer tobacco on the fire. In the future we may be confused, and we may not know who the prophet will be. It could be that way, and this is why I am telling you this," Nógha said. Hey, a long time ago he talked about how people should live. Nógha told this to people long ago.

He told us, "Whoever is the singer will sing without becoming tired, and a place of prayer will appear before him. He will be reborn, becoming a new person. You must all place tobacco on the fire and pray at Tea Dance," Nógha told us. "Don't let go of these traditions, as only then will you be truly good. If you are not like this then there will be nothing left on this great earth—nothing. It will all be destroyed. I carry this heavy burden," he said. "There are strong winds," Nógha said, "but if you all pray properly, and with all your strength, perhaps nothing will happen to you. Something terrible is coming, but if you pray well perhaps we will be saved and we all may avoid destruction. This will happen in the future. Listen, all of you!" he said. Well, I listened, and now I'm wiser for having listened.

Finally God said to Nógha, "There will be two messages with your drum." No one knows what was on that paper. Long ago a person might receive a message about what would happen in the future, and one morning at dawn two such messages appeared in Nógha's drumcase. Hey! He was a good person and he always told the truth. After this happened God spoke to Nógha again because he was a prophet. "The future has already been determined," Nógha told us. "God wants me. Alexis Seniantha is like my son, and he will be the head prophet in the future. God has told me that my life will soon be finished. I have only five days left before the end," he said. "Yes, this is the end." Afterwards it happened as he said it would.

"In the future some people will be hardheaded and won't listen," Nógha told us, "while others will quickly go to dance and pray, living straight lives. We may wonder why we are singers, given songs by God. Some people go to sleep and they dream. Then—hey!—they hear a song, they hear something good with their ears. They wake up and they remember, yes, then they sing and it becomes a song." (This is the truth.) "You must all help the singer," Nógha told us. I think he told the truth.

"This is my father's drum," he told me. "If you take it after I am gone, all will be well for you. Everyone is not good, but you are good and I like you," he said to me, and gave me his drum. I thought he was pitiful, although before that I hadn't sung at Tea Dances. Now because of what he said to me I became like them, drumming and singing at Tea Dances. I know the songs well, and I pray as I'm falling asleep and then I dream. Yes, they told the truth about Tea Dance, and because of this I have become a good person even though it was difficult. I followed after many other people.

Long ago people lived in the bush. In those days, in order to become a prophet or to gain medicine power, fathers would tell their children to sleep beside a tree that had been split by thunder.* They slept there to learn something, something powerful. Now because they had gained knowledge they were able to find a way to survive, even when things became difficult. They became good people.

Long ago there were no doctors, and people who had visions were like doctors. In the past life was hard. Then these people would cure others, making them well. Now all of this training is being wasted, and children are growing up who don't want to dream or seek a vision. They are bad, but still there are some who dream and become good.

"Other people—not just Dene—can also dream and have a vision. All visions are useful," my father said. "When such a person wants something he will be able to go his own way even though it is difficult."

My father talked to me about many things. "You must treat women properly," he told me. "You must seek a vision in the bush. Men who spend all of their time chasing women won't be able to kill moose. Then animals will avoid them," he told us. He talked to us about all sorts of things relating to how Dene lived long ago.

Nógha also talked to the people. "When there is a Tea Dance and four people start drumming and the singer sings, that is God's way," Nógha said. "God knows us all," he said. "We may think He doesn't, but He sees us all. He knows all of us living on this earth. He made people and He knows us all. Hopefully He will help us; God will help us. If you really want something, place tobacco on the fire and pray three times. Even if you are in the bush, you can place tobacco on the fire and pray. You should pray, then sleep, and you will be helped," Nógha said. "Even if you want beaver fur, put tobacco on the fire. Someone could pray using these words. 'Hopefully God will give it to me,' they could say. 'Quickly, quickly He will give me many beaver,' he could pray."

Nógha spoke to us. "Whether you are sick or strong you must all pray," he said. "Pray three times, hopefully, expecting something. You must all try," he said. "In the future the people may be confused and won't know which way to turn; it will be confusing for us. What will happen will happen, but don't ignore my warnings about the future. I pray and I won't stop praying until I am exhausted," he told us. "Even if there are only three people left alive to dance, I will still pray," he said as he talked to us.

"The Cree songs are also important,"† he told us. "Use the small drum, the handgame drum, when you sing them," he said. I was there when he

---

* Dene Dháa believe thunder is the active agent in lightning.

† Nógha tells people to use the smaller handgame drum for Cree songs, both because this is the size drum Crees themselves use and to prevent Cree songs from displacing traditional Dene Dháa songs.

told the people this. "There are two kinds of drums," Nógha said, "the Tea Dance drum and a smaller drum used for Cree songs and handgames. You must not let go of these two things, the songs and handgames. When others tire from playing handgames you must continue on, and when the people are watching don't let go."

"In the future, perhaps, it will be like this," he said. "It is foggy," he said, "and it is difficult for me to see, but there will be blood," he said. "I don't know why. Think about this! All of you listen carefully!"

We didn't understand what he meant then, but he must have been talking about drinking, and how people can become crazy when they drink. Today many people have been killed in bloody accidents. Nógha knew this would happen, as he could see far into the future. Suddenly it may become clear to someone what he meant, and then they will realize why Nógha was praying and why we must continue praying through Tea Dance today.

"Maybe you don't know anyone who is like this," he said then, but now all of this is happening, the things he talked about long ago.

"Nothing will happen to this land," Nógha said, "because the earth is tremendous. Anything can happen on the surface of the earth. There may be bad things happening, but if you yourself are a good person, you shouldn't worry about these things," he often told us. "Sometimes far off there may be a huge wind," he said, "but it avoids us as long as even one person prays." He prayed for us, for the future, I think.

"This earth is large," he said, "but we pray for the whole earth. When we go into the Tea Dance circle we pray, just like the priest offers communion. They talk about the future then and come to God's land. This message is not just for this one place," Nógha said, "but for the whole world. I hope it will help you all." Then he put tobacco on the fire and filled a clean cup with moose fat and poured it on the fire. When the Tea Dance was finished everyone moved out into the bush.

Everyone was making hay and then the people scattered into the bush toward Zama Lake, toward the Mega River, toward Rainbow Lake, and toward the Chinchaga River. They all traveled in small groups of about ten, packing everything on horses. They made hay in September, then they returned to Hay Lakes, and continued traveling on foot. After making hay they went hunting moose in the bush, and after killing a moose they dried the meat. They killed one moose, or two moose, and then dried lots of meat. Afterwards they went home and cut firewood and mixed mud and chinked their houses for the winter. There were no lamps in those days, but if you lit a fire it was bright in the house. Meat was always cooking, ready to eat. Well, in those days perhaps I would do something for you; help chink your house, or make a fire—any small thing, it didn't matter what. People helped each other, yes, it was like that in the past, and my father told us all about it. Hey, he always told us stories. Long ago my father,

Ahkimnatchie, traveled to Fort Providence and Bistcho Lake on snowshoes to visit people. He told us everything he knew. He told us stories and shared everything with us that his father had told to him.

My wife's father prayed with Nógha, and there is his drum hanging there. I saw a leaf and a house on Nógha's drum. Hey, it was a good drum, but I don't know what happened to it. There was also a star on it. Nógha wanted those symbols on his drum to help him pray.

"Tobacco has many uses," Nógha said. "If a person wants to pray, he smokes tobacco. Tea also has many uses and two people can offer it. Pray before you go to sleep and then smoke. When someone goes to sleep, while they're sleeping, they will be helped (by God). After they awaken they will remember their dreams," he told us. "People should offer tobacco and feed the fire with it, even if they are alone. Hold onto the rosary, too," he said, "and pray with the rosary before you go to sleep, and then danger won't come near. In the future, perhaps, you will understand what I am talking about. You have all heard," he said. He was standing in a crowd when he said that. He lectured the people while I listened.

"People are like the dishes you use to eat from," Nógha said. "You eat from them and they become dirty; they have served a useful purpose. There is a place where you will be purified. They will know all about each of you at that place overhead. It will happen that sometimes they will take impurities out from a person's nose or mouth. Just like dishes must be washed, they will help purify you there. You all listen!" he said.

"In our house don't use dirty dishes. People must be reborn. Hey, a person will appear on this land who will look like a white person with red hair. They will put water on his head, and he will be reborn as a white person. A person such as myself may go to heaven and then be sent back. 'You can't go in yet,' they told me there. 'In the future you can come in, but now you can only look,' they said." This is what Nógha said.

They called that prophet Nógha 'Wolverine.' He was called Wolverine. Long ago he was married to Dóamo. My dad was married to her sister, so they were in-laws. Wolverine, the animal, is smart. Even if you hide something while he is sleeping, he will know and steal it he is so smart. The prophet knew Wolverine and that is how he came to be called Nógha 'Wolverine.' He really knew about Wolverine, and that is why something happened to him.

Yes, he couldn't eat groundhog meat. He was called Wolverine, and he knew about Wolverine. He knew many things, and he knew Wolverine was powerful. He knew these things and because of it, because he had Wolverine power, he couldn't eat groundhog meat. Nógha died because he ate groundhog meat. That is the way it must have been. When a person is like Nógha, having animal power, he musn't eat certain foods, they say, because it can be very dangerous. But Nógha ate groundhog meat and he died. That is what happened. There was a sickness that came upon him, a sickness in his chest. He asked my dad to go with him to Bistcho Lake. "Come with me," he said to my dad.

Nógha could really laugh and always prayed for people. While he was talking to you he would start drumming. "That's the way I am," he said. "As long as people are enjoying themselves, it doesn't matter whether they are in the Tea Dance circle or not," he said. When he wasn't singing he would stand beside the drummers or dance himself. "Tell me when you've danced enough," he would say. Then they would say, "Hey, that's good. That's enough then." Yes, he was a good man, and he liked to laugh. The head prophet now is just the same, he likes to joke around with people.

The last time Nógha prayed was at a Tea Dance on the prairie between the bends of the river south of Habay, near the willows this way from Danais' Creek. Here he prayed for the last time.

"I am already exhausted," he said, "finished. Perhaps I am finished. It is the end, I think," he said, and so he went to sleep. He was called Nógha 'Wolverine,' and he was a good person and prayed well.

13 Nógha's Prophecies

My father's brother, Nógha 'Wolverine,' was one of the leading prophets of our people. He was once directed to draw the north star and the sun on a new drum that was being prepared for him. Why did the north star and sun appear to him in that way? Those symbols were revealed for his use; they were like a signature. There was also a house drawn on his drum. "That is my land," God said. We are living on his world and Nógha was telling us what will happen in the future.

"When only two people are left on earth—one to sing and another to dance for him—this song will not become old, but will remain fresh," Nógha was told. I still live according to my uncle's words, according to the knowledge he was given by God.

My uncle said to me, "You may live to see these things happen. Strange people will lie to us with a yellow paper. That paper [welfare checks] will cause you all to forget about your children. Perhaps you will live to see this," he told me. That day is here now. He told me everything that God said concerning that prophecy.* He told many people about this prophecy. I was not the only one. His prophecies and way of praying were consistent with what others have said at this meeting.

My uncle told us what will happen on this earth in the future. "If you all forget to pray, then there will be no sun for a month," he said. That message was also from heaven. "In the morning the sun will rise, followed by the moon, and as they climb higher they will eclipse each other at noon. The sun will stop there, midway in its path, for one hour," he told me. "Why will it happen like that?" he asked. "Together the sun and moon will set and there will be darkness." That was his message. My uncle shared that prophecy with our people. He was a prophet and many people here know about the message he was given; it is not my story.

He once said to me, "I'm always watching, observing everything. I live fully aware." It has been a long time—almost fifty years—since my uncle died, but I still remember his words and that is why I speak to you. This message was not written down; I keep it in my mind and that is why I

---

* He was told that strangers would introduce different colors of welfare checks in succession which would alienate children from their parents.

speak. I hope that we can all understand these prophecies and work together for the future of our children. I hope that everyone, especially those with children, will remember my uncle's words. That is all I have to say. I thank you, my brothers.

14   The Dene Prophets

The prophet they call Mbek'ádhi was my mother's father, my grandfather. His trail is still good even though it was made long ago. He used to speak at Tea Dances, praying for the people's well-being during the year to come. When all the people gathered, then he prayed. My mother said her father was a prophet.

"Maybe there will be no game, nothing left on this land," he told the people. "Perhaps there will be no rabbits, only ducks," he said. And then he prayed for the people in the coming year, before they returned to the bush in the fall. He prayed for his relatives as well. "Maybe this is what will happen in the year ahead," he told the people, and his predictions came true.

He prayed in the Tea Dance circle. Then at dawn he put up a pole stripped of its bark beside the circle. He then tied to the pole a long white ribbon, which fluttered in the breeze. "With this we buy the land," he said, "and in this way we will prevent misfortune." Then all of the people did the same, tying ribbons to the pole to help them in the future when they returned to the bush. In that way they wouldn't suffer from hunger, sickness, or cold, while they traveled around. That was Paul Metchooyeah's father, Mbek'ádhi, my grandfather. "Something may happen in the future," he warned the people. "Perhaps during the winter something (bad) may happen."

Dahdona was another of the prophets. He was married to my mother's sister. He assisted Nógha 'Wolverine,' who was the head prophet at that time. Yahtl'uhimo's father also prayed with the prophets, making offerings on the Tea Dance fire. On his drum there were two moose with their antlers locked together in combat. He would pray for game, making offerings on the fire, and afterwards the people returned to the bush and killed the same type of animal he asked for in his prayers. I still pray, using the song he sang during the offering ceremony.

After Mbek'ádhi, Nógha became the head prophet and prayed for this land. He was truly a good person, with always a kind word for everyone. He talked about angels and heaven. He went there when he died and continues to work for us who are still on the earth.

I had gone hunting, and when I returned to Zama Lake [an abandoned settlement] in the summer they told me that Nógha was very sick. They had

81

taken him to Habay, and before I had returned most of the people had already left Zama Lake; everyone was gone. I was exhausted from traveling and carrying my furs. Yes, the grass was already getting tall when I returned in the early summer.

The head prophet was very sick. I left right away to visit him, even though it was dark and I hadn't eaten. "Jean-Marie will visit me when he returns," the prophet told the people. Three of us went to visit him as he lay dying, and he held my hand. Today I still remember what he said to me then.

"Shondi, Joe Didzena, and you, your names are known by the angels," he said. "Your names are white (pure), and nothing bad will happen to you." I have tried not to make mistakes, to live up to the prophet's expectations. I was with him as he was dying. I was very sad and started to cry, but he told me to stop. "It doesn't matter if something happens to me," he said, "and so why are you crying for me? Don't cry for me. You're all crying, but you should pray. Now I will finally give you my prophecies for this land," he told us.

"If you are unable to kill any moose," he said, "then go toward where the sun comes up. If you kill a moose, then they will put me inside the Tea Dance circle so that I can speak to the people."

Four of us left to hunt then, and just as we crossed the prairie where we used to make hay, we saw signs of moose. We tied the horses near water and ate. Afterwards we carefully circled from both sides, and I went ahead.

There, near where the poplar trees begin, I watched as a moose and two yearlings walked toward me. I got ready and, standing sideways, shot three times. Then I shot twice more at the yearlings, altogether shooting five times. All of the moose fell. It was only noon, and we butchered the moose and made offerings, making the sign of the cross. Then we quickly returned, bringing meat to the prophet. Yes, he made offerings on the fire, and even though he was nearly exhausted he sang for the people.

When all of the elders were gathered around him, he spoke about the future. "In the future," Nógha said, "people will lie to you with four colors of paper. One will be blue and one will be white. After the white paper there will be a blue paper, then a yellow paper, and finally a pink paper. They will lie to you with these four colors of paper," he told us. Afterwards he died. He must have been talking about family allowance checks and other checks from the government. The government gave out blue checks, then white checks, then yellow checks. "They will lie to you with these," he told us. "In the future strange people will lie to you," he said. Yes, what he told us has come true.

"Your land—all of it—will be mapped in the future," he said. "Then not long after, you will be huddled together (on a reservation)," he told us. That time has come now. Today our children don't listen to us, and we are concerned about how they are living. Long ago Nógha knew about these things and he warned us about them. Today the things he told us about have happened.

15 The Death of Nógha

The prophet Nógha was a great prophet, and when they held a Tea Dance for him everyone would come. No one has replaced him since. Songs appeared to him as though they had been written down. In this way the songs came to him and afterwards he sang them. He didn't lie, I'm telling you. Yes, really, you could look at it and see for yourself. He never attended school but he could sing those songs.

"God is watching us living on this land," Nógha told us. "These songs were given to us to ask for something. Pray with them and clean your plate and place it on a clean white cloth for God. If there is blood on your plate, God will give you something when you hunt. If there is no blood, sing the song and you will be sure to kill something," he said.

Nógha received songs for many purposes. He had a song for hot weather, one for children, and also one for mothers. He had many good prophecies that he shared with us, but perhaps no one really listened to him. Now you are asking me about it and I will tell you.

"In the future something black will be hanging over us, over that way near that hill," Nógha said, telling us about the future. "Your lives will be difficult. Perhaps your dogs will clamp onto you and drag you off, growling. What will you do then?" he said. "You will all be pitiful. People will do bad things to each other when they are drinking," he said. "Winter will be especially dangerous. These things will happen when you live near the hill." *

Here at Assumption there was no Tea Dance circle at that time, so they didn't pray or have Tea Dances here. They held Tea Dances in those days at Zama Lake, at Duck House, at the Mega River, and at the Willow River. Everyone gathered at all those places to attend his Tea Dances. In those days people would gather up their children and, placing them securely on the back of a toboggan, would mush the dogs, calling out, "Ready dogs!" and so travel to the Tea Dance.

The Tea Dance ring was laid out like a clock, with the opening at noon, with the boys and men sitting on the east side, and the girls and women

---

* The present reservation at Assumption is located next to the hill which runs along the valley containing Hay and Zama Lakes. Nógha warned people not to live there.

84

sitting on the west side. In the days when we lived in Habay there was a dance for Nógha there and he told us more about the future. "Maybe this will happen," he said. "There will be lots of metal [oil wells and pipes].* Don't live there [on the reserve], because people will be roaming around like packs of dogs," he told us. "This prayer is for your survival. Even if you have to live two, even five, families in one house, stay where you are living now. Don't settle there! Don't live there!" His wife was one of the first people who moved here to Assumption near the school after he died. Her mother was unable to travel because her legs were always sore.

Today I still remember when he died. He had his hand behind my head, and his wife was sitting beside him as he told us all that would happen in the future. He breathed deeply and said, "I'm going to die soon," and then suddenly his hand dropped as he stopped breathing. His prophecies have since come true. "Drinking is bad," he told us. "I have worked hard to keep you all good. Don't settle over there," he said and then he died. Nógha had a picture of Jesus, a piece of soap, and a small piece of moose fat from God. I don't know what happened to them after he died. They may be in the bush somewhere.

Nógha told us that they [the government] would give out papers. I think he was talking about child allowance payments. He said there would be a little window on the letter. He also told us they would give out another type of welfare in the spring. "Give thanks to God as you take the money," he said, "but be careful because the white man may try to fool you."

I saw Nógha's drum. He would hang it up at night, but during the night it made a noise he said. When he took the drum down there would be a message for him from God. But I never saw the messages myself.

He died in a tent at Habay. In those days they used to live in tents all year, not in houses like today. In the fall they put up tents then moved to check their traps. They put hay around the edge of the tents, which were kept smoky to discourage mosquitoes. Nógha died near where the old forestry building was located. The trees at the edge of the woods were turning red with the setting sun when he asked for me. He held my hand and put it on his heart saying, "You are a good person. You will survive on this land. If my son needs something after I am gone—snowshoes, gloves, or moccasins—don't mourn for me. Go ahead and make it for for him. That's all I ask. Now I am going to die." He asked me to help Alexis, who was like a son to him. I sat with him as the sun went down and he died.

We washed him and dressed him in new clothes. There were no coffins but they got one ready. In those days they took down the tent after someone

---

* Assumption is in the middle of a large oil field. Today there are oil wells, access roads, seismic lines, and oil pipelines throughout the area.

died and put it up in a new location; then they asked an elder to pray for the dead person before anyone could go inside. Today we don't observe those old ways. We are becoming like white people. We are in a bad spot, and I am afraid our children are slipping away from us. We talk to them, but they don't listen. When I was a girl I used to pick berries and wild rhubarb with Edanmo. We went picking red berries. It was a long time ago and it seems far away now.

PART TWO

DENE TEXTS

Traditional Stories

The Dene Dháh (Alberta Slave) Alphabet

Dene Dháh [dɛnɛ ðáh] is the designation that Alberta Slave use for their own language and is the name employed here. For writing the language in this collection of narratives, a phonetically based alphabet is used and is described here in three parts. The first presents the vowel and consonant systems, the second deals with dialect differences, and the third describes the history of writing the language.

Description of Vowels and Consonants

Vowels

There are six oral vowels in Dene Dháh:

	Front	Mid	Back
High	i		u
Mid-High	ee		
Mid-Low	e		o
Low		a	

Phonetic Characteristics of Vowels

/i/ is generally a tense vowel [i].

> *jih* [jih] 'mittens'
> *mbetthí* [mbɛtthí'] 'his head'

When /i/ is followed by another syllable, it is lax [ɩ] in stems.

> *mbechidle* [mbɛchɩdlɛ] 'his younger brother'
> *mbeyiné* [mbɛyɩnɛ́'] 'his song'

89

/ee/ is a tense mid-high vowel [e] in stems.

> *łééh* [łéh] 'dust'
> *tthee* [tthe] 'rock'
> *beeh* [beh] 'knife'

/e/ is a lax vowel [ε] in stems.

> *mbeké* [mbεkέ'] 'his feet'
> *téh* [tέh] 'cane'
> *mebé* [mεbέ'] 'his stomach'

/e/ varies between [ə], [ε], and [e] in prefixes.

> *mendajine* [məndajιnέ'] 'his relatives'
> *ndedzeé* [ndεdzě'] 'your heart'
> *netthi* [nεtthi'] or [netthi'] 'you eat'

/a/ is a low back unrounded vowel.

> *gah* [gah] 'rabbit'
> *tsá* [tsá'] 'beaver'
> *sah* [sah] 'bear'

/o/ is a mid-low back rounded vowel.

> *-cho* [cho] 'big'
> *xoh* [xoh] 'thorn'

/u/ is a high back rounded vowel.

> *tu* [tu] 'water'
> *ługe* [ługe] 'fish'
> *du* [du] 'island'

 In Dene Dháh there are five nasalized vowels which are derived by a rule of nasalization, whereby a vowel followed by *n* becomes a nasalized vowel. This rule is a historical process which occurred before a consonant or at the end of a word, and applied both in prefixes and stems. It is revealed in alternations between V̨ and *Vn* in stems which still exist in the language. When a stem is followed by a vocalic suffix, such as the possesive suffix *-é*, the stem ends in *n*.

kón [kǫ'] 'fire'   *mbekóné* [mbɛkónέ'] 'his fire'
thén [thέ'] 'star'   *mbedhéné* [mbɛðénέ'] 'his star'
tsón [tsǫ'] 'excrement'   *mbetsóné* [mbɛtsónέ'] 'his excrement'

The application of nasalization is variable, depending on the dialect of the speaker, with some conservative speakers retaining word final *n* in some words. The process is discussed further in the description of Dene Dháh dialects below.

/ı̨/ is the nasalized counterpart of /i/.

tlin [tlı̨'] 'dog'
shin [shı̨] 'song'
ndéhtin [ndέhtı̨'] 'he went to sleep'

/ę/ is the nasalized counterpart of /e/.

men [mę] 'who'
thén [thέ'] 'star'
nelen [nɛlę'] 'you urinate'

/ǫ/ is the nasalized counterpart of /o/.

thegon [thɛgǫ'] 'dried'
non [nǫ'] 'here (handing)'
kón [kǫ'] 'fire'

/ą/ is rare because historically *a· and *a changed to /o/ before a nasal in Dene Dháh as in all Slave dialects. This is evident from comparison with related languages such as the Ross River dialect of Kaska, which retains /a·/ where Dene Dháh merged *a· with /o/.

Dene Dháh		Kaska		
chon [chǫ]		*chą̄* [chą·]		'rain'
mbegóné [mbɛgónέ']		*megáné* [mɛga·nέ']		'his arm'
dínk'ón [dı̨k'ǫ]		*dénk'ą̄* [dénk'ą·]		'you start fire'

There are some words in which speakers have retained /ą/, as in, for example, *memanh* 'its edge' and *éhsán* 'it must have been.'

/ų/ is the nasalized counterpart of /u/.

> *tl'unh* [tl'ųh] 'rope'
>
> *dluen* [dlųɛ̨] 'mouse'

Before a vowel, /ų/ is phonetically [w]. In this environment it merges with /ǫ/, which is also phonetically [w] before a vowel. The underlying vowels are written even though they have merged as [w] because the underlying vowel is apparent from other examples of the same morpheme, as in the examples below:

Underlying form	Written form	Phonetic form	Gloss
kún (archaic)	*kún*	[kų́']	'house'
kún-áa (modern)	*kúan*	[kʷą̨́]	'house'
me-kún-é'	*mbekúén*	[mbɛkʷɛ̨́']	'his house'
kón	*kón*	[kǫ́']	'fire'
kón-áa	*kóan*	[kʷą̨́]	'small fire'
me-kón-é'	*mekóné*	[mbɛkónɛ́']	'his fire'
me-chun-é'	*mbechuén*	[mbɛchʷɛ̨́']	'his son'
me-chun-áa	*mbechúan*	[mbɛchʷą̨́]	'his small son'
chon	*chon*	[chǫ]	'rain'
chon-áa	*chóan*	[chʷą̨́]	'light rain'

Consonants

	labial	dental	alveolar	lateral	alveopalatal	velar	glottal
Stops							
unaspirated	b		d			g	
aspirated			t			k	
glottalized			t'			k'	'
prenasalized	mb		nd				
Affricates							
unaspirated		ddh	dz	dl	j		
aspirated		tth	ts	tl	ch		
glottalized		tth'	ts'	tl'	ch'		
Fricatives							
voiceless		th	s	ł	sh	x	h
voiced		dh	z	l	y	gh	
Resonants							
oral	w		y				
nasal	m		n				

Phonetic Characteristics of Consonants

There are three series of stops and affricates: unaspirated, aspirated, and glottalized. For stops there is also a prenasalized series. Unaspirated stops and affricates are sometimes weakly voiced; for example, *bilíh* [bilíh] 'hammock' and *netsédle* [nɛtsédlɛ] 'small.' Aspirated consonants are voiceless and strongly aspirated. The glottalized consonants or ejectives are usually strongly glottalized, although intervocalically in some words they may be voiced so that *wots'ín* 'to there' varies between [wots'į'] and [wodzį'] and *tat'i* 'three' varies between [tat'i] and [tadi].

Alveolar consonants are articulated with the tongue far forward, and interdentals are articulated with the tongue against the upper teeth. The velar stops *k* and *g* are pronounced with fronted, or prevelar, allophones before front vowels and with mediovelar allophones elsewhere. The velar fricatives *x* and *gh* also have prevelar allophones before back vowels. Before rounded vowels *(u, o)* velar fricatives are labialized. Examples of prevelar allophones of *k* and *g* are: *ke* [ḳɛ] 'foot,' *géh* [ǵéh] 'roasting stick.'

Examples of the mediovelar allophones of *k* and *g* are *kólaa* [kóla] 'old man' and *gomba* [gomba] 'dawn.' Labialized allophones of *k*, *g*, and *gh* are the following: *kúan* [kʷą̂] 'house,' *guets'ín* [gʷɛts'į̂'] 'to them,' and *mbeghú* [mbɛghʷú'] 'his tooth.'

Dialects

Dene Dháh dialects reflect former settlement and marriage patterns in Northern Alberta. Speakers name three of them, based on common types of variation within the language, and classify them as variants of Dene Dháh, their name for their own language. The names they use for these three dialects, *Xewónst'e* [xɛwǫ́st'ɛ], *Xewónht'e* [xɛwǫ́ht'ɛ], and *Kegúnht'u* [kɛgʏ́ht'u], mean 'It's like that' and identify common types of variation within these communities. In response to the question *Dáwonhtin Dene Dháh wonedeh?* 'What kind of Dene Dháh do you speak?' an older person might say, *Gáa, xewónht'e Dene Dháh wohdeh.* 'Well, I speak that kind of Dene language.'

There are three communities of Dene Dháh speakers in Alberta: Assumption/Habay, Meander River, and Bushie River. Each of them has developed relatively recently as the Dene Dháh have moved to be near such facilities as schools, stores, and nursing stations. These settlements all show some form of dialect variation within them. Assumption is the largest community, with approximately eight hundred Dene Dháh speakers, and Habay, which is only nine miles from it, is now largely deserted because of recurrent flooding. Dene Dháh is the first language of all age groups in Assumption. Although older speakers of all three dialects live there, younger speakers now use the Xewónht'e dialect almost exclusively. Meander River has approximately three hundred residents, most of whom speak the language, although English is also spoken there by younger people. The Kegúnht'u dialect predominates among middle-aged and younger speakers, but among older speakers the other dialects are represented too. Most of the residents of Bushie River, which is located next to the town of High Level, Alberta, have moved to this reserve since 1960. Younger people in Bushie River use English, but there are also a few older speakers who use Dene Dháh almost exclusively.

The classification of dialects which speakers themselves use does not reflect the current settlement pattern. The identification of a person as a speaker of the Xewónht'e, Xewóst'e, or Kegúnht'u dialect reflects an earlier pattern of settlement and intermarriage between regions. Before 1940 there was a high rate of intermarriage between Dene Dháh (Slave) speaking men and Tsát'in (Beaver) speaking women from the Eleske and Fort

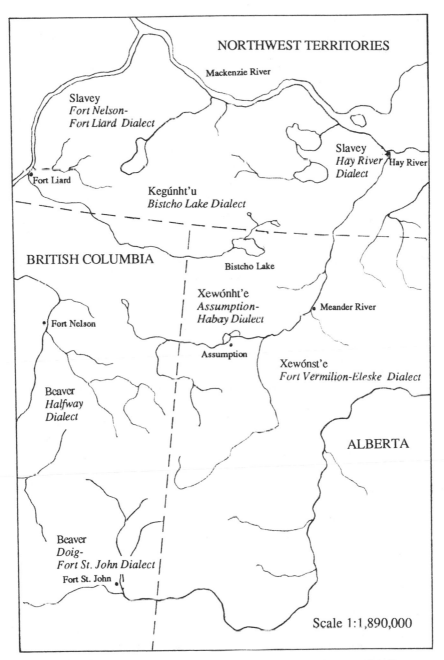

Map 3. Historic Sources of the Dialects of Dene Dháh

Vermilion area. Several factors may have encouraged this pattern of inter-marriage. An important one was the development of trapping in this region, which led to a patrilocal settlement pattern and partially explains why Beaver women, but not men, married into the area. Epidemics that reduced the population of both Beaver and Slave in Alberta (Clut 1864, 1888) may also have encouraged marriages outside the local community. Moreover, many Dene Dháa who lived in the Bistcho Lake region gradually moved to the Hay Lakes and Meander River areas to be nearer trading posts.

The designation of a speaker as either Xewónst'e, Xewónht'e, or Ke-gúnht'u served to identify the language of the speaker's parents as well as his or her own dialect. The Xewónst'e dialect, for example, identified a person who was reared speaking Eleske Beaver or whose mother was a speaker of Eleske Beaver. In discussions of which dialect a person speaks, the language of the mother is often given as evidence for determining which one it is. If someone asks, *Alexi la Kegúnht'u wodeha?* 'Alexis speaks Kegúnht'u, doesn't he?' the person might be corrected, *Endúé, memo la Tsát'in Dháh woindé.* 'No, his mother spoke Beaver.' The Xewónht'e dialect identified speakers whose mothers or grandmothers spoke Eleske Beaver but who used fewer of the conservative features of Beaver. The mothers of those who used the Kegúnht'u dialect spoke Bistcho Lake Slave.

All of the storytellers represented in this collection are from Assumption. Two of them speak the Kegúnht'u dialect and the rest use the Xewónht'e dialect. The short stories "The Children Raised on Fat" and "Wolverine is Outsmarted" were told by Kegúnht'u speakers. Some conservative features are found in the speech of storytellers who use the Xewónht'e dialect, including examples of word-final consonants, but these features are far more common in the speech of those who use the Xewónst'e dialect.

All three dialects—Xewónst'e, Xewónht'e, and Kegúnht'u—are dialects of Slave. They show the same development of stem-initial consonants as the South Slavey* dialect of Slave spoken in the southern part of the Northwest Territories (Rice 1983:85), except that for the Xewónht'e and Xewónst'e dialects *w and *n develop differently. In these two dialects *w becomes *b* before an oral vowel. In the South Slavey dialect spoken in the Northwest Territories, *w becomes *mb* in stems before an oral vowel. Similarly *n became *d* before an oral vowel in these dialects, but became *nd* in South

---

* Keren Rice uses the term Slavey exclusively in reference to the dialect of Slave spoken in the southern part of the Northwest Territories. She refers to the entire language including dialects such as Mountain, Bear Lake, and Alberta Slave as Slave. I have adopted her usage here.

Slavey.* These developments in the Xewónht'e and Xewónst'e dialects of
Dene Dháh can be symbolized as follows:

*w -> b ___ / V   *n -> d ___ / V
    -> m ___ / V̨ or VN   -> n ___ / V̨ or VN

Examples of the development of stem-initial *w in Slave dialects are the
following:

South Slavey*	Kegúnht'u	Xewónht'e	Xewónst'e	Gloss
-mbé	-mbé	-bé	-bé	'belly'
mę́	mén	mén	mén	'lean-to'
mbeh	mbeh	beeh	bees	'knife'

Examples of the development of stem-initial *n in Slave dialects are the
following:

South Slavey	Kegúnht'u	Xewónht'c	Xewónst'e	Gloss
ndu	ndu	du	du	'island'
sendaá	sendaá	sedee	sedee	'my eye'

In prefixes, *w is a nasal with homorganic stop, mb, in the Xewónht'e
and Xewónst'e dialects. In the Kegúnht'u dialect *w is a nasal stop, m.
Similarly *n is a nasal with homorganic stop, nd, in the Xewónht'e and
Xewónst'e dialects, and a nasal stop, n, in the Kegúnht'u dialect. Examples
below show the development of *w and *n in prefixes:

South Slave	Xewónht'e and Xewónst'e	Kegúnht'u	Gloss
nétị	ndéhtin	néhtin	'he went to sleep'
nágoyeh	ndáwoyeh	nágoyeh	'he's playing'
yenéhsheh	yendéhsheh	yenéhsheh	'he is growing it'

In prefixes, *G developed differently in the Xewónht'e and Xewónst'e
dialects from the way it did in the Kegúnht'u dialect and the Slave dialect
spoken in the Northwest Territories. These differences are evident from the
names of the dialects themselves. In the Xewónht'e and Xewónst'e dialects

---

* Keren Rice (personal communication) indicates that some speakers of South Slavey
in the Northwest Territories also use m and n before oral vowels.

*G developed into /w/, but in the Kegúnht'u dialect it developed into /g/. The development of *G in prefixes is illustrated by the following examples:

Xewónht'e and Xewónst'e	Kegúnht'u	Gloss
wots'ín	gots'ín	'to there'
wok'eh	gok'éh	'after them'
wokón	gokón	'it's hot out'
wonjon	gonezun	'it's good (general)'
wohdeh	gohde	'I speak'
ndáwoyeh	nágoyeh	'he is playing'

The Xewónht'e and Xewónst'e dialects also show a different development of *e· in stems from that in the Kegúnht'u dialect and the South Slavey dialect spoken in the Northwest Territories. In the Xewónht'e and Xewónst'e dialects *e· is retained as a mid-high tense vowel, [e], represented orthographically as *ee*, which is distinct from the mid-low vowel *e* [ɛ]. In the Kegúnht'u dialect *e· merged with the mid vowel [ɛ], derived from *ə, which is represented orthographically as *e*. The development of *e· is illustrated by the following examples:

Xewónht'e	Kegúnht'u and South Slavey	Gloss
tthee	the	'rock'
t'ééh	t'éh	'charcoal'
łééh	łéh	'ashes'
mbedéédzé	medédzé	'his younger sister'

The most distinctive characteristic of the Xewónst'e dialect, which is not represented in this collection, is the failure of the first person singular subject prefix *s-* to change to *h-* as it has in the other two dialects. In other dialects of Slave, word-final consonants are generally neutralized to *h* or lost in all environments. When the stem-final consonant is followed by a vocalic suffix, the consonant may be retained in some dialects. In both the Xewónht'e and Xewónst'e dialects final consonants commonly appear in relative and possessed forms; for example, *wohbeedzin* 'boiled,' *dzíinxeli* 'the one he clubbed to death,' and *dihts'inch'ili* 'the one which was torn off.' Conservative speakers of the Xewónht'e and Xewónst'e dialects also retain word-final consonants in some words when no vocalic suffix is present.

Examples of word-final consonants retained by Xewónht'e speakers:

ejin	'he is singing'
ndátset	'it is strong'
ghetl'eł	'he is going along'
xáint'ath	'he cut out'
echitth	'awl'

Systematic differences in the sound systems of the three dialects generally group the Xewónht'e and Xewónst'e dialects together in opposition to the Kegúnht'u dialect and the South Slavey dialect of Slave, which is spoken in the southern part of the Northwest Territories. There are also many differences in common vocabulary, such as the use of *xeda* 'moose' by Xewónht'e and Xewónst'e speakers in contrast to *gulon* used by Kegúnht'u and South Slavey speakers. These lexical differences are very common and make it difficult for younger speakers of the Xewónht'e dialect to understand Slave speakers from the Northwest Territories. Kegúnht'u speakers, however, have little difficulty understanding South Slavey. Although Dene Dháh generally shows many of the same developments of consonants and vowels as found in other dialects of Slave, in terms of mutual intelligibility, the Xewónht'e and Xewónst'e dialects can also be grouped with the Beaver dialects spoken in Eleske. Due to the high frequency of intermarriage between the two groups over the last one hundred years, the Beaver dialect of Eleske shows, as expected, a significant degree of convergence with Slave. Interestingly, the Oblate missionaries who first prepared descriptions of the Dene languages in northern Alberta grouped all three dialects of Dene Dháh with Beaver.[*] Certainly there is a dialect continuum, with the dialects of Dene Dháh representing intermediate forms between Slave in the Northwest Territories and Beaver in Alberta.

Moreover, even within the recognized dialects of Dene Dháh there is variation between individual speakers. Some of this variation reflects sound changes which are currently occurring in the modern dialects. Some changes, such as the loss of word-final consonants, are almost complete for all younger speakers, but less complete for older speakers. Others, such as

---

[*] 1891 Census, Government of Canada, Fort Vermilion District, Public Archives of Canada. Information was apparently taken from baptismal records of the Roman Catholic Church to establish both the ages of native people as well as their 'tribal' affiliation. The prophet Nógha, who was a Kegúnht'u speaker, for instance, is listed under his native name and as a Beaver Indian, age 18.

the use of *wo-* or *go-* 'general conditions,' still show variation in the speech of younger people, but appear to be standardizing differently in Meander River and Assumption, which will eventually lead to dialects reflecting the current settlement pattern.

Development of the Dene Dháh Orthography

The Dene languages in Alberta and the Northwest Territories were first written by Oblate priests over one hundred years ago. The Oblates used two types of writing systems. One was an alphabet based on French, and the other was a syllabary which used symbols to represent complete syllables. The syllabic system was originally developed for Ojibwa by the Reverend James Evans and later modified for use with Chipewyan, Beaver, and Slave (McLean 1890; Rhodes and Todd 1981:63).

In Alberta, syllabaries were more commonly used by native people. A large number of Cree and Chipewyan speakers were able to read and write in their own language, and a few people also learned to read and write using Beaver and Slave syllabics. There are still native speakers literate in Cree and Chipewyan syllabics, and some Slave speakers in the Northwest Territories are familiar with the system. All of the older people who were literate in Slave syllabics in Meander River and Assumption have died within the last decade, although George Providence of Meander River formerly corresponded with his brother, Johnny Providence of Assumption, using syllabics. When asked in 1980 if he still remembered how to write it, he transcribed, *Ye edawondíh kudindi gha?* 'What would you like to know?' in syllabics as follows:

[yɛ   ɛ   da   wǫ   díh   ku   dį   di   gha]
Ye edawondíh kudindi gha? 'What would you like to know?'

Phonetic transcriptions have been added beneath his. Note that the same symbol is used for [wǫ], [gha], and [ku] because the syllabic system does not represent all the contrastive sounds in the language.

Alphabetic systems were also used by several priests for writing the Hay Lakes (Xewónht'e) dialect of Slave. These systems were not widely used by the people in Assumption, however, and are not in use today.

Beginning in the 1950s the Slave dialects in the Northwest Territories were written by missionary linguists using an alphabet based on a phonemic analysis of the language (Howard 1963:42-47). From then until the 1970s, major work on literacy was carried out by missionaries, with some of their work being published by the government of the Northwest Territories (Monus 1974). More recently, the standardization of the writing system for Slave in the Northwest Territories has been a priority of the territorial government. Standardization of the Dene languages in the Northwest Territories has been discussed by the Athabaskan Languages Steering Committee (1976), by the Task Force on Aboriginal Languages (1985), and by the orthography standardization committees established for each of the languages in 1987. While some aspects of the South Slavey orthography are still under discussion, the basic system has been established by the work of these groups.

The system used for writing Dene Dháh differs from the writing system for South Slavey in two respects, both because the language varies slightly and because a pragmatic consideration determined the final orthography. The primary linguistic difference is variation in the vowel systems: an extra vowel is retained in Alberta that is represented by *ee* in Dene Dháh. But perhaps the most significant difference between the two writing systems is the use of a nasal hook under the vowel to represent nasalization in the Northwest Territories, as in *ko̧* 'fire,' where in Alberta a vowel followed by *n* is used, as in *kón* 'fire.' The use of *n* after a vowel reflects the earlier French-based alphabetic system used for writing Dene Dháh in Alberta, and since some speakers are familiar with that earlier French-based system they have expessed a preference for using *n* rather than the nasalization diacritic. The nasal vowels in words like *kón* 'fire' actually appear as a sequence of a vowel followed by the consonant *n* when a suffix is added, as in *mbekóné* 'his fire.' The decision to use *n* rather than a nasalization diacritic is thus primarily pragmatic, since native speakers most concerned with writing have expressed a preference for this convention. To avoid possible confusion between *n* representing nasalization and the consonantal *n* or *nd*, the consonantal *n* is underlined in words where the two might be confused. Since syllable-final *n* has generally changed to nasalization in Dene Dháh, instances where confusion could occur with the nasalization *n* which follows the vowel are rare.

Consonants are written the same way in Dene Dháh as in South Slavey in the Northwest Territories except that in Dene Dháh glottal stop is not written word initially.

1 Two Sisters

Storyteller's Introduction

Dient'i sadzee egóhó tat'i sadzee guh ndahxéhwohdeh
Four   hours   or   three hours then I talk to you all

ghádé.   Héé! wodih netlon edahdíha. Xetl'i ghádé
continuously. Hey! stories lots   I know.   Night during

ndahxéwoghideh   úh* wodeh ndawodígíi, ndawodígá
I talked to you all and stories dawn,   dawn

ddheni ghádé ndahxéwoghideh   úh. Wodeh ndawodígíi
day   all   I talked to you all and. Stories dawn

wots'ín ndahxéhwohdeh éhsín edu, edu mbelonh wole
until   I talk to you   maybe not, not its end will be

éhsín. Eyi ét'i   óon.
maybe. That the same then.

   Di Yamanhdeya ets'edi yaxattheeh ets'edi di. Eyóon
This Yamanhdeya he's called first   called this. That is

Yamanhdeya, eyóon Ndahxetá,   eyóon Ndahxetá.
Yamanhdeya, that is Our Father [God], that is Our Father [God].

Wonlin nde'áh, wonlin ni'á   di díeh k'eh łínt'ónh.
Animals He tricks, animals He tricked this land on   all.

Wonlin,   wonlin ndáhtheghon, wonlin nechi, łínt'ónh.
Animals, animals He killed them, animals giant, all.

Eyi újon níoni'on,   eyi wodah. Ndahxetá   eyi.
That good He put things, that for that. Our Father [God] that.

---

* The conjunction *úh* is usually part of the pause group which includes the preceding verb or noun. For this reason when a comma is used between conjoined words in a list, or between conjoined sentences, the comma follows the word *úh*. For example in the following sentence *úh* is grouped with the preceding nouns *gah* 'rabbits,' *chi* 'ducks,' and *tuge* 'fish': *Gah úh, chi úh, tuge úh, xónht'e etthi.* 'He eats rabbits, ducks, and fish and things like that.'

Eyóon Ndahxetá edídi la.* Eyóon onht'e, eyóon.
That is Our Father [God] we call Him. That is it is, that is Him.

Two Sisters

Úh tígé ju ndéét'i ts'ídoa, mo eghaghedéhde
And one also like you children, mother they went for something

úh mo eghaghedéhde éhsán. "Setúé,
and mother they went for something it must have been. "My daughter,

jon ndedíáa ghamonh ndahda theneda;
here your little sister influence her for us you stay;

eghagúdhi. Gondeji, edulin godahtthi," sóon
we'll go get [some food]. Danger, nothing anywhere," then

di. "Edulin daht'áh," mo guyéhdi.
she said. "Nowhere you two go," mother she said to them.

Xeda ghinghon sóon kaghedéhde, ínyá memo
Moose they killed then they went for it, then her mother

gáa tíónh úh sóon. Gáa tíónh sóon mo
already all and then. Already all then mother

ghendúé. Éé! i mbedéédzáa tígíáa netsédláa
gone. Hey! that her little sister little one small

sóon etse Xoniá wuzen uh, "Hín! hín!"
then she was crying. Suddenly dark and, "Sob! sob!"

éhdi úh etse.
she said and she cried.

"Éé! edíáa, danet'in-a adindi, danet'in-a
"Hey! little sister, how are you you're crying out, how are you

adindi dindi."
you're crying out you tell [me]."

"Éé! ane guxúle úh sadzá'agúnht'e adehsi,"
"Hey! Mom they're gone and I'm sad I say,"

yéhdi.
she said to her.

"Éé! edíáa, ju xónht'i édé ndegoji úh."
"Hey! little sister, also like that then it's scary and."

---

* The word *la* has no simple lexical meaning and its grammatical function is difficult to specify. No translation is given for this particle.

Xeh'inh kegeze   **sóon níghenide sóon, wonlin**
Packsack   between them   then   they were   then,   something

ghaghendéhta.
they were occupied with it.

   "**Sedíaa,**   **eyi aitseláa ndedhéné wole**   **úh eyi**
   "My little sister,   that little one   your star   will be   and that

nechá sedhéné wole   úh."
big one my star   will be   and."

   Ghehtin úh eyi, eyi ghahtlah   **tadedeh úh**
   They slept and that, that one after another   pointing and

sóon, łín mbade   **ju sóon, mo**   **eghadéhde**
then,   one her older sister   also   then,   mother   they went for

wotl'onh ghe_ndéhteh.
after   they went to sleep.

   Jon ts'eghenidhe ínyá, jon dene edu edawodíhicho.
   Here they woke up then, these people not known horrible.

Eyi gáh ts'ín ghehtin, ts'eghenidhe. "Dáwónht'e
Those with to   they slept, they woke up.   "What is it

awónht'e?" kudi,   **mbade**   **kudi úh. Edu**
it is?"   she thought,   her older sister   she thought and. Not

gudíeh k'eh awónht'e kudi.   **Úh yedzíin thén**
their land on   it is   she thought. And that   star

eyi, "Ndedhéné wole,"   **łéghededi**   **íin**
that, "Your star will be," they were telling each other before

úh godzíin thén gáh ts'ín éhsán aghet'in éhsín.
and that   star with to   must be they are   maybe.

Gots'ín éhsán thén, thén gáh ts'ín. . . .
Toward must be star, star with to. . . .

   "**Éé! edíaa, ka edu ahthíde'a kéhéh gúnlin.**"
   "Hey! little sister, for not we are stuck way exists."

Dedhóo ónket'i gáhín ts'eghenidhe éhsán. "Edíaa,
Young men two   with they woke up   then. "Little sister,

kónti óon edulian, edulian adundi,"
like that then nothing, nothing you will say,"

łéghededi.
they said to each other.

   I dedhóo ndaghededzed úh xeda ghedhéhxe
   Those young men they went hunting and moose they killed

édé; tl'unh sóon, tl'unh ghetthé.   **Edhéh**
then; rope then, rope they cut in strips. Hide

agheleh **tl'unh** **ghehtthé.** **Dándét'i** **sóon**
they were making rope they cut in strips. How many then

xedadhéh **tl'unh** **aghinli** **sóon?** **Ehsóon** **edu** **i**
moose hide rope they made then? Then not those

dedhóo **ye'inh** **i** **éhsán** **xónht'e.** **Úh** **ddhenítah**
young men he sees them that then like that. And everyday

ét'e **sóon,** **yíyueh** **lígin** **sóon,** **dígeh**
the same then, below the other one then, land

dawónged **éhsán.** **Dígeh** **konge** **yidigíi** **k'oh** **éhsán,**
she dug a hole in must be. Land digging above cloud must be,

wonged **éhsín.** **Sóon,** **"dijin!** **dijin!"** **ddheníghádé.**
she dug maybe. Then, "pound! pound!" everyday.

Úh **eyi** **dedhóo** **sóon** **ehxéhle** **níaghet'ah.**
And those young men then evening they came back.

Aidihdah **sóon** **etsính** **adlíi** **eyi** **dahghedínhlá**
On purpose then pemmican made that they spread out

níoghe'ah. **"Duhden** **dzeníghádé** **tl'a** **ye** **dah'in,**
they put it there. "Here everyday then what you're doing,

'dijin! **dijin!'** **dahdi** **úhzonh,** **ye** **ah'in**
'pound! pound!' you two make sound always, what you two have

sóon?" **guyéhdi.**
then?" he said to them.

"Tl'a, **i** **díáa,** **'etsính** **saújon,'** **di,** **dzenítah**
"Well, that little sister, 'pemmican I like,' she says, everyday

két'e **etsính** **k'adek'ah** **úh** **i** **a'adi** **sóon,"**
the same pemmican she pounds and that sounding then,"

di. **Gáa** **lónts'edi** **kughedi,** **sóon** **ndaghededze**
she said. Really true they thought, then they went hunting

ddhenítah **két'e** **ínyá.** **K'oh,** **k'oh** **éhsán** **ghaghenigé.**
everyday the same then. Clouds, clouds must be they dug into.

Yíyueh **sóon,** **yíyueh** **sóon,** **di** **k'oh,** **k'oh** **éhsán**
Below then, below then, those clouds, clouds must be

ghaghenigé. **K'oh** **éhsán** **ghaghenigé** **éhsín.** **On**
they dug through. Clouds must be they dug through maybe. But

gáa **guzí** **odacho,** **níoghenigé** **éhsán.**
really their soul the size of, they dug as far as must have been.

Ghinxe **úh** **sóon** **ech'ún** **ndaghedet'ah** **éhsín** **sóon**
After sunset and then another way they went back to maybe then

kughedi. **Sóon** **líenghedénila** **sóon,** **ghets'endéhtin**
they thought. Then they closed it [hole] then, they went to sleep

ínyá.
then.

Xetl'íonh sóon ech'úin ndaghedéht'a, i dedhóo
Morning then another they went back to, those young men

ehsíin ech'úin ndaghedéht'a. "Edíáa, di tl'unh
which were another they went back to. "Little sister, this rope

se'e níonhthah úh. Nándeduhłéh, nándeduhłéh édé
really you put [around] and. I'll let you down, I'll let you down then

yuyúéh ndéh ninendilu, édé nandelin ndéh édé. Di
below earth you dangling, then you dangling earth then. This

tl'unh wonht'inh, édé ndek'éh i tl'unh kéndaduhsuh
rope you will pull, then after you that rope I'll slide down

éhsín," yéhdi. Ehsóon mbedéédzé sóon
maybe," she said. Then her younger sister then

ndadehlu, ndadehlu. Héé! i xedadhéh
she was dangling, she was dangling. Hey! that moose hide [rope]

netlon, netlon náint'in. Gáa se'e mbelonh
lots, lots hanging down. Already really its end

audadih úh éhsán tl'unh nínkin. Tl'unh nda'edah,
happening and then rope loosened. Rope moving,

tl'unh nda'edah éhsán. Edin ju sóon se'e
rope moving must have been. Her too then really

ndáwotsed úh déyendéhtl'un sóon, mbedéédzé
strong [securely] and she tied then, her younger sister

k'éh nda'edéhlu ínyá, dendúhts'áde.
after she swung down then, hanging on.

Se'e tékeh, sahgeh woti ninlin, se'e
Really on the water, river main one flowing, really

tékeh, úh gecho xónht'i se'e jon, ehdacho
on the water, and big spruce like that really here, bald eagle

ndahthekon. I t'oh ekeh sóon mbedéédzé
nesting. That nest on it then her younger sister

ghinlú. Yek'éh ndá'edéhlú éhsán, edin
was lowered to. After her she swung down must have been, her

ju sóon yek'éh, at'in kudi. Ínyá gáa se'e
too then after her, she was she thought. Then already really

dígeh gots'ín xónhén niwonhtth'e éhsán. Eyi ehttha
earth toward near about then must be. That eagle

t'ohcho, ehda t'ohcho ek'eh, łeghadlú.
big nest, eagle big nest on it, they swung into.

Edu aghedeháa k'ehéh gúnlin, gáa kaa
Not they going a little way exists, still

ndádínhtthah. Wonlin deddheh úhzonh,
quite a ways [down]. Something passing by usually,

wonlinghedi deddheh ehsíin, wonhteghedlinh,
animals passing by that were, they begged,

wonhteghedlinh, wonhteghedlinh éhsán. Gáa
they begged, they begged then. Really

edulin guk'ínhín niwon'ah, edulin guk'ínhín niwon'ah
nothing their way happened, nothing their way happened

éhsín.
maybe.

Nóghe sóon ghetl'eh, ghetl'eh
Wolverine then he was running along, running along

éhsán. "Ehtsíe, nondahxindah, nondahxindhah,
must have been. "Grandfather, take us down, take us down,

hén?" yéhdi.
okay?" she said to him.

"Ndahxendáwohyeh édé zonh. Nondahwohdhah sóon,"
"I'll play with you all then only. I'll take you down then,"

kéhdi.
he said to them.

"Úh tl'a, nondahxindhah, nondahxindhah,"
"And well, you take us down, you take us down,"

yéhdi. Úh sóon, Nóghe sóon nókinla.
she said to him. And then, Wolverine then he took them down.

"Se'e éddhé kónt'e ehsíin tl'adah ndahxendáwots'eyeh,"
"Really bluff like that which is edge we play,"

yéhdi. Úh sóon éddhé se'e xónht'i níghenit'a
she said to him. And then bluff really like that they went

sóon tl'ade'eh ndahtl'aghedendéhke sóon. Nóghe sóon
then the edge they sat down then. Wolverine then

guets'ín déhtl'a gi'ekedinhdi úh,
toward them he went they pushed him down and,

gi'ekedinhdi úh, sóon taghedéhtl'a.
they pushed him down and, then they ran off.

"Éé, ju ué dindi, éé, ju ué dindi, dechin
"Hey, also whistle you say, hey, also whistle you say, tree

ué dindi, ué dindi, éé, ju ué dindi,
whistle you say, whistle you say, hey, also whistle you say,

ué   dindi   úh."   Di   dechin   łínt'ónh   sóon,   "Uí,
whistle   you say   and."   Those   trees   all   then,   "Whistle,

uí,   uí,"   éhdi   úh.   Nóghe   dedzíin   ats'ejíi
whistle,   whistle,"   they said   and.   Wolverine   where   happened

mba'élính.   Éé!   łínt'ónh   mba'élính.   Di   dechin
he was confused.   Hey!   all   he was confused. Those   trees

xéṉdét'i sóon   łínt'ónh   "Ui,   ui,"   éhdi.   Edulin,
that many then   all   "Whistle,   whistle,"   said.   Nothing,

mba'élinh,   dedzíin   awoji   mba'élinh,   ts'edi.
he was confused,   where   it happened   he had no idea,   it is said.

Storyteller's Commentary

Góon   edahdíhi?   Góon   xónht'ia?   Xónht'e   azonh.
[Question] you all know? [Question]   it like that? Like that   only.

Yi'ónéh   ui   ndahxéts'edi   edon.   Edu
Somewhere whistle   someone says to you all so what.   Not

kinka   xáhdeh   éhsín.   I   wodehts'ín   újon.
for someone   you all do that maybe.   This   much more   better.

Eyóon   duh   dene   nde'áh,   dene   nde'áh.
Like that   now   people   he tricks, people   he tricks.

Kawoghedéhon   edawahdíhi   adehsi.
He's looking for that   you all know   I say.

　　Ndahtlon   ndahxéhwohdeh   édé, kénét'i   sadzee   wohdeh
　　You all many   I'll talk to you all then, ten   hours   I talk

eghon   gáa kaa   wohdeh   éhsín,   eyóon.   I   guhyeh
even   still   I talk   maybe,   like that. That   like that

xéwóht'in   óon   ats'edi,   eyóon   duh.
it does that   then   they say,   that is   now.

　　Duh ndáten   ehsíin,   ndáten   ehsíin   eyi,   eyóon   duh
　　Now prophets which are,   prophets which are that,   that is   now

ndahxe'iyuné gha yaghawoni'a   ats'edi.   Ndahxetá   ts'ín
our spirits   for opening to heaven it is said. God   to

yaghawoni'a   ats'edi.   Eyóon,   eyóon,   eyóon   eyi
opening to heaven   it is said. That is,   that is,   that is   those

dene   k'oh   woningéd   on   yaghawoni'a   ts'edi.
people clouds dug a hole in   but   opening to heaven it is said.

Eyi   awónht'e.   I   xónht'ia.
That   it is.   That   like that.

Éé, ndéét'i ts'ídoa ehsíin, ndahxéét'i ts'ídoa ehsíin,
Hey, like you children that are, like us children that are,

mbéhts'edi úh mbéhwots'edeh edawodíh édé,
one talks to them and one talks to them when it is known then,

edawodíh édé kéhwodeh. Gúhts'edi edahdi
it is known then he tells about it. That way it is said you all say

úh sedhage kehwahdeh, kehwahdeh.
and in my language you all talk about, you all talk about.

Ts'egu edewon degúh mendaych wodek'éh
Girls even what way in front of her [vision] happens

i k'ándetah. Yi'ónéh dzahdawónht'e ehsíin
that looking for it. Over there it's bad that may be

gots'ín edu wok'áts'endetah. Ts'egu edewon
to there not one looks for it. Girls even

mendayeh wodek'éh ehsíin. Mendayeh
in front of her [vision] happens that may be. In front of her [vision]

wodehk'éh wok'ándetah. Xónht'e'a ts'egu ts'inlin,
happens she looks for. Even like that girls they are,

ts'egu ts'inlin edewon, di ts'ído ewon, ts'ído
girls they are even so, these children even, children

ehdah ats'edidleh yídeeh ts'egheda ts'ín édé.
too make for themselves ahead live to then.

"Eyi sendayeh xéwoht'in gúhye xónht'e,"
"That in front of me [vision] it will happen that way like that,"

kuts'edi. Edu endádla úh dene ats'edidleh.
someone thinks. Not hard and person makes their own.

Gúhye óon ju xónht'e deeti ats'edeh. Xónht'e
That way then also like that elder one becomes. Like that

yídeeh ghahda úh, éé, got'ónh wowodihé
ahead you'll all be living and, hey, long ago stories

ndahxedasi gha. "Sets'ídoé nendayeh
I will tell you [future] "My children in front of you [vision]

godek'éh, ehsóon ekoin dechintahin kónt'e
happens, maybe over there in the bush like that

k'ánet'in," łéts'ededi. Wonlin
you look for," they say to each other. Something

káłets'ededi. Wonlin dahé gáa
try to do to each other [using powers]. Something some already

mendayeh edu wodek'éh ehsíin la, xónht'e, xé
in front of them not it happens whatever is, like that, just

mbedhedhe	**ka**	**gheda**	**xáat'in.**
his death	for	they live	like that.

2 Wolf and Wolverine's Revenge

Storyteller's Introduction

"Wonlinghedi ehsíin edahdíh wonlin edahdíh,"
"Animals that are I know something I know,"

kuts'edi, on héé, shinze onht'e. Di i
someone thinks, but hey, for nothing it is. This that

wonlin, wonlin łáts'ut'ah íin kuts'edi.
something, something they give each other before they want.

Ndahxin dene ídlin óon. Wonlin enłándít'ah
Us people we are then. Something we give each other

igha édé. Mbeyoan, eyóon dene ts'ínhze ahthít'e.
[future] then. Old/weak, that people side we are.

Wonlinghedi yet'áin ghedi ehsíin ju. Gáa
Animals they depend on they live that are also. Already

xónht'i a'onht'e. Wonlin yet'áin ehsíin yutón úh
like that it is. Animal depends on it that are it holds and

di yek'ewoghintheda ehsíin kek'íneshíh. Gúhyeh
that they used up that are on someone throw. That's the way

xónht'e dene ewón xónht'e. Ghedi ewón xónht'e edu
like that people even like that. Animals even like that not

íhk'eh kawots'edeh wonlinghedi edu mbéhchehts'edah.
brave speaking with animals not bothering them.

Gúhjúh xéwónht'e. Aunét'e dah óon, tee sedadi.
And again it's like that. Many ways then, father told me.

Eyóon aht'e. Endádla wohteh wodih edahdíh i
That way I am. Really very story I know that

á'aht'e.
I am.

Edu sin. Sin got'ónh wodene; aht'in ele. Ewón di
Not me. Me long ago people; I was not. Even this

Ekucho ets'edi, kólaa, eyi mbewodihé, Tee
Ekucho they called him, old man, these his stories, Dad

úh mbewodihé. Dets'ín ondadhi ehsíin, ech'ingúh
and his stories. Where elders that are, differently

111

xádawodinda la gua édé, wónjonh udhohtthon kuhdi
presenting ideas   a little then,   trying hard I listen to   I wanted to

eyóon. Sek'ánahteh   éhsín. Kólaa   ehłin-e déhsi.
like that. You all look at me   maybe. Old man   I am   I say.

Dáht'it'áh ju   edu edehkoh ju   asíleh   ele
Why am I   also not cold   also I came down with   nothing

úh. Yandí'a i la   kólaa   ehsíin. Monhts'ú'iya úh
and. I sit   those old men that are. I respect   and

satinthene   wonlin   adídleh   édé   mbets'áhndi. Eyóon
pitiful for me something we do   then I help him.   That

wot'áh   ghehda   aht'e. Gúhyeh   óon
by those means I live/survive I am.   That's the way   then

xéts'int'e.   Úh deneti   ndahts'ín   wodeh   édé,
you should be. And people/leaders to you all   he speaks   then,

kíi, kíi xónht'e elin,   xónhjide elin gúhyeh.
just, just like that he is,   bad like that he is that's the way.

Eyi la   edu xónht'e dene   ts'inlin   élé.
That   not like that person someone should be   not.

Wotloan   kehe   wodih edahdíh, dúyé.
Many ways ways   stories I know,   lots.

Wolf And Wolverine's Revenge

Wot'ónh ehsíin ju,   dene éhdi.
Long ago   about   also, people said.

  Ts'íyoan   éhsán, mbets'ídoa ónket'ía wónlin
  Old woman   then,   her children two small existed

gheludh   úh   kek'éh   táyah,   xónht'e.
she was pulling and after them moving camp,   like that.

Níts'indeh   éhsín ke'oín.   Edu, edu etene
Where they are camped maybe off to the side. Not,   not on the trail

úh tíndeyah   ts'ín dets'ídoa   k'éndíh.
and going off to the side   to   her children she took care of.

  Xónht'e   ínyá xoniá,   t'oji   ayeh'in.
  Like that then suddenly, breast [premonition]   she had.

T'oji   ak'ehín   ts'edi   enłii
Breast [premonition]   usually happens it is said   the same

xát'in   úh. Dene, dedhóo júh łínt'ónh yídeeh
that was happening and. People, men   also all   up ahead

ndadzed ts'ín nidé'in   úh   kek'éh   ts'adeel
hunting   to   they went and   after them they were moving camp

á'awónht'e úh.   Eyi   tah   éhsán, etahezun
it was   and.   Those among   then,   young women

kúannínidel ehsíin i   yéhda ghedel   éhsán
married   each   those too   they were going then

a'onht'e.   "Sechée   t'oji
it was.   "My daughters-in-law   breast [premonition]

ahse'ien   edu shínze   éhsín. Tégeh
when this happens not   for nothing maybe.   Carefully/slowly

xá'udendah'ính   kek'éh   ahthít'in, édé   újon," éhdi.
look out for yourselves after them we will be,   then   good,"   she said.

Ts'íyoan éhsán etahezun   gutah   ts'ín éhdi
Old woman then   young women amongst them to   she said

ínyá.   "Ehtsún,   ndetsóan   k'ázé éhsán
then.   "Grandmother, your little shit   lumpy then

andch'in,"   giyéhdi.   I   t'áh
it was doing [this] to you," they said to her. That because of

mbadzahdáts'edi   sóon.
what they said to her made her sad   then.

Níts'indeh   kek'éh   ts'endet'ezi   éhsán, dahyahdhé
Making camp   after them bedding down   then,   snow on branches

edekéghelú   úh. Tíndéhya   ts'ín,
she knocked down after herself and. She went off to the side there,

sóon mbets'ídoa ghameh   udhéhtth'on,   xetl'in ghádéh.
then   her children   for them she was listening, night   throughout.

Gáa   k'elc   ndawodágah, k'íodéhthahá ts'adéhle
Already almost sun coming out, about that time   people coming

édhin éé,   "Tá! Tá!" ts'edi;   ts'ídoa   kedídinh
sounds like, "Dad! Dad!" they said; children   to meet

niwónhthed   ínyá. Éé!   xoniá   "waa! waa!" wodéja.
you could hear then.   Hey! suddenly [cries of pain]   were heard.

Ketah   ets'ewónh edhin   éhsán.
Among them killing   sounding like   then.

Dets'ídoa   dek'ehnínila sóon ek'énda'inludh úh   sóon.
Her children she put on   then   pulled onto trail   and then.

Kek'éh   sóon tadéhtl'a,   edin zonh.
After them then   she ran after, her   only.

Eyián etsinwonlonh,   dedhóo zonh déhtth'i
There   people had killed game, men   only   were sitting

lóon   éhsán.   Ts'íyoan   ketontl'a.   "Éé,   jon
must have been   then.   Old woman   ran amongst them.   "Hey,   here

yídín   edulin   ndahxets'ído   ghede   éhsín."
back there   none   all your children   alive   maybe."

    Ts'íyoan   éhsán   kéhdi   úh,   ehkeguh   ónket'ene
    Old woman   then   she told them   and,   young men   two people

kúan nínit'a   éhsán   yídééh   inhshíhxoghehthe.
living together   then   back there   they were both anxious to go.

Gots'ín   kedídih   ghedetl'eh,   ónket'i   inhłétlazé.
Over there   to meet   they ran,   two   each-other's-in-laws.

"Éé,   edu   kaa,   edulini   ghedi   ehsíin   edu   kaa
"Hey,   not   yet,   nothing   living   that is   not   yet

kets'eṇdáhłeh,"   kólaa   kéhdi   úh.   Gáa,   guk'ínhín
just leave them be,"   old man   said to them   and.   Yes,   their way

níoni'on.   Téeh   éhsán.   Kíi,   kíi   ats'et'in.
was being taken.   Carefully   then.   Then,   then   they stayed.

   Gáa,   yahk'i   kíoghindhed úh   ndatsidetle   úh
   Yes,   winter   ended   and   snow drifting   and

awodadi   úh éhsán.   Gáa,   ónk'etene   ehkegu
it was coming to   and then.   Really,   two people   young men

inhłetlazé   onht'e   úh.   Eyi   éhsán   łígé,   éhsán
each-other's-in-laws   they were and.   That   then   one,   then

se'e   yéhdi,   "Seyéh   dáunendí   éhsín?   Kaa,
really   he said to him,   "My brother-in-law   how are you   maybe?   Yes,

ke'edúdleh.   Gok'éh   aúdeh   gok'áṇdútse,"   éhdi
we'll do likewise.   After them   let's go   let's look for them,"   he said

óon.
then.

   "Dáneht'e   éhsín   seyéh,   ni   tl'a,   dáneht'e
   "How are you   maybe   my brother-in-law,   you   well,   how are you

éhsín?"   yéhdi.
maybe?"   he said.

   "Kaa,   eyóon   aht'e,"   sóon   éhdi,   mbeyéh.
   "Yes,   like that [able]   I am,"   then   he said,   his   brother-in-law.

Łíé   ju,   "Dáneht'e   éhsín,"   łéghededi.   "Kaa,
One   also,   "How are you   maybe,"   they said to each other.   "Yes,

eyóon aht'e,"   éhdi.   Éhsán   eyi   ónk'et'ene
like that I am,"   he said.   Then   those   two people

inhłétlazé.
each-other's-in-laws.

Éhsán gáa kek'éh ghedéht'a. Nóghe łígé elin,
Then already after them they went. Wolverine one was,

łígé Dígahi elin, aghejá éhsán kek'éh aghet'in. Éé,
one Wolf was, they became then after them they were. Hey,

kíi élính két'eh óon. Ts'iuné, keeh edah'inh.
just he's confused like that then. Wolf, tracks he knew to see.

Edu takédedeh'ính. Gáa, kek'éh łaheindi.
Not he misses seeing. Yes, after them always.

Éé xoniá ndáts'edéh. Eyi éhsán kets'ído
Then suddenly people camping. That then someone's children

edulin úh aghinleh éhsín i wonh ndághintl'a úh.
nothing and they made then that purpose they ran into and.

Ndághendeta kedhonah. Nóghe ju edin
They were looking for something around. Wolverine also him

onht'e úh kedádeh, nándetá úh, ah
it was and he was searching around, searching and, snowshoes

dáhtheleh éhsíin ju ehxáh úh. Xoje ju
hanging up that were also he chewed up and. Snares also

łint'ónh ghedéhch'ul úh. Kón, mbéhdats'edik'on
all they tore up and. Fire, with-it-fire-is-made [flint]

éhsíin ju nighedíleh úh. Gáa, xéghededéht'in.
that are also taking them and. Yes, they were always doing that.

Xoniá, se'e łahdinh zonh wots'ín kóán
Suddenly, really one place only from small fire

andat'ín, wots'inh łint'ónh kón andat'in. Éé!
was making itself, from there all fire was appearing. Hey!

gáa, endádla. Gáa, łint'ónh dene tinghenihthe úh
yes, it was hard. Yes, all people started to suffer and

gáa. Xoni donk'e dahani edulin deyah, ewon
already. Finally hunger some people nothing go, but

łét'e gáa dene echeghedéh. Łáhdinh zonh kón
the same still people they were bothering. One only fire

andat'ín.
was appearing.

Ts'íyoan ndádéh líin kúan wots'inh zonh; łint'ónh
Old woman living before house from only; all

kónandat'in úh edawoghedíh. Eyi sóon xetl'itah kéteh
fire was appearing and they knew. There then nighttime every

kéhcheghet'áh. Úh Nóghe xoni i ts'íyoan
they were bothering. And Wolverine finally that old woman

tah   ná'iníntón,   xetl'ee ts'ín,   thetin   gha
on her body   he looked for, night   time,   she sleeps   for

ayínlá.   Yets'ín   wonlin   onlá   úh
he made her.   To her   something he made [medicine power] and

yéhdinya   óon.
he started working on her   then.

   Xoniá   dúhde   se'e   detl'eh   ts'ín.   (Góon
   Suddenly   right here really her crotch   toward.   (Question

xéwondeh   éhsín?   Nóghe   nelin.)   Jon   se'e   detl'eh
you do like that maybe?   Wolverine you are.) Here   really her crotch

ts'ín   éhsán.   Kón,   mbéhts'ehtthenlih,   kón
toward   then.   Fire,   with-it's-struck,   fire

ndáts'edihk'on   ehłii   xáichogáa   deéntl'un   éhsán.   Nóghe
fire is started   that one this small tied on   then.   Wolverine

gots'ín   yinkandéhk'a   yetl'unhén   k'eyinihxá
toward   putting his head [mouth]   her string   he bit off

úh   tandadéhtl'a.   Ée!   gáa, kón   nendúé.
and he ran away.   Too bad! yes, fire nothing.

   Kólaa   łígé   éhdi,   "Goka   súdahdi,   duh
   Old man   one   he said, "For some reason you all look for, now

wolée   xúle   éhsán   agúnhteh   úh.   Kaa,   edulini
something gone   then   that is happening now and.   Yes,   nobody

gondíh   igha   éhsín,"   'éhdi   úh.   Edzach'idé,
living   [future] maybe,"   he said   and.   Leg muscle,

xedadzach'idé   thegoni,   tthindéhgoni   xáidedhi   k'éndíh
moose leg muscle dried,   stiff-dried   this long   keeping

líin   xáinton   úh.   Yéh   éhsán,   xónht'e   ts'ín
before he took out and.   Over there   then,   like that   out

éhsán   eyi   endéhtthe   yeghonh.   Dechin   ehdzoicho
then   that   he propped under   for him.   Log   big trap

onlíi,   eyi'endéhtthe   úh   sóon.   Éé!   gáa,
that he made,   he propped up [the log] and then.   Hey!   yes,

łínt'ónh   ndághendetah   úh.
all   they were looking for   and.

   Eyi   dechin ehdzoi ts'ín   Nóghe   gáa   mbadúyé
   That   log   trap   toward   Wolverine   really   hard for him

awójá.   Éé!   gáa,   yéh   kíi   uhwoyín   yets'ín
it happened.   Hey!   yes,   there   just   anywhere   toward it

yambeh   andajá   úh
for his benefit [Wolverine's] he went that way [new directions]   and

gots'ín mbeyi'endéh'á. Gáa, endádla. Yéh andaghet'ín
toward it was propped up. Yes, it was hard. There they were again

gots'ín mbeyi'endéh'á.
toward it was propped up.

Xoniá ye'oneh yedéh'in gua, gáa, Nóghe yeyueh
Suddenly to the side he glanced a little, yes, Wolverine under it

ghehtl'a. Dijin! wodéjá.
he ran. Crash! [sound of falling log] happened.

"Éé! ehdzo ndádenikin edhin," ghedi.
"Hey! trap it fell sounding," they said.

Kets'ín tauwedéhtthe, edhin éhsán.
Toward someone they started running, sounding then.

"Seyéh, sa k'éhsín udedinghelá,"
"My brother-in-law, sun direction [way] roll yourself over,"

éhdi úh sa k'ésín edit'e úh xondéhtl'a.
he [Wolf] said and sun direction he flexed and suddenly ran off.

Taghedéhtl'a úh yelíín woda.
They ran off and whatever will live.

Gáa, eyi se'e kéghedídla. Edulin dene ghede
Yes, that really they did the same. Nothing people living

ehteh ju.
that were also.

Storyteller's Commentary

Dáhse'e xewódeh? Wohteha wodih edahdíha, i
Would we do like that? Strongly/lots stories I know, that

a'onht'e. Ehxele dah, Ehtsée dadi éhsín
it is. In the evening each, Grandfather what he says maybe

kudahdi. I yohani— Jackáa—
you all might wonder. That what's his name— Jack Danais—

mbets'ídoa on ehxeli dah óon segáh ghedéhtth'i.
his children even in the evening each then with me they visit.

Gúhyeh óon dehsi. Ye ghon tínt'ónh edulin edayedíh,
That way then I speak. What for all nothing they know,

ewon edulin onht'e kudahdi.
but nothing it is you think.

Ts'égu edcwon wonlindah wodat'in édé, eyi
Girls even of some event she sees for herself then, that

wot'áhwodéh'a a'wónht'e. Dechintah wonh. Edéhtl'éhkúan
important   it is.   In the bush cause.   School

edu at'in dah, yéh shíh ts'ín ndádeghaht'a.   Gulóon
not be   each, there hill to   look for yourselves. Wish

kudahdi,   édé eyi la wot'áh wodéh'á. Edu deneti
you all want, then that important.   Not adults

ts'ilin wots'ín tindah   xéts'int'in awónht'e ele. Ewon
be   until   on your own be like that it is   not. But

sin mbetah dene ghinlé, ndetsée   ju   yetah dene
me   among   person I was, your grandfather also among people

ghinlé ehsíin la, mbetá   dechintah ts'ín yeh'á.
he was that were, his father in the bush to   he was directed.

Azon wonejídé, edon,   dechintah ts'ín dene
Even frightening, so what, in the bush to   person

ets'eh'a.   Xetl'int'onh, xetl'ets'in úh, xetl'egeh
he will be directed. Morning,   nighttime   and, nighttime

xoje ats'eh'in úh xédé wonlindah níowots'enihthid
snares doing   and just something expect the unexpected

úh xóje ats'ehin úh xónht'e. Gua   ka
and snares doing   and like that. A little of something for

k'éts'ededah. Se'e wolin nandeteh   ehłii
walk for yourself. Really animal looking for something like

ets'e'in, zonh óon, di setthíghá ets'eht'e,
act like, only then, this my hair   to be the same,

mbek'ánita.
look at it.

Úh kíi lon wonlin   utsintl'a ts'ídoa ahłíin,   don
And just place something jump up children you all are, maybe

gáa éyona kudahdi   édé dzahdé xá'edingaédé. I   zonh
yet able   you all think then badly   thinking.   That all

ndahdahndatse edewon edawahdíh. Eyi la mbet'ain
overpowers you but then you all know. That upon it

ghets'edi onht'e élé. Azon jon the'on   edewon
they say   it is not. Only there positioned but still

mbek'ánahte edon edu mbet'áhwodéh'in onht'e élé.
you all see it even so not important   it is   not.

Onk'edinh óon, xónht'e,   edawahdíh. Edu wot'ainh
Two ways   then, it's like that, you all know. Not upon it

wots'edi onk'edinh wonlin   wónlin.
living   two ways   something it is.

Mbetsie   ju   onhndadhi onht'e dándahxéhdi
Alexis Seniantha   also elder   he is   what he says to you

éhsín.   Edu setá   wónlin wodah   wonlindah   lon
maybe.   Not my father being because for something wish

kudahdi   gha wóh'on ónkehdaht'éle,   ni
you all think for it is   two of you [two children listening], you

ju úh, ni ju úh. Ůh dene netlon. Azon
also and, you too and. And people lots.   Even

kets'enelin   edon,   gáa, wonlindah lon kuts'edi.
treat with respect even though, yes, somehow   wish want.

Gúhzonh óon újon.
That way then it would be good.

Yidét'ónh, ndahthet'ónh dene   ehsíin   línt'ónh óon,
Long ago,   before you   people that were all   then,

wonlin   edawohdíh kudi,   línt'ónh zonh dene
something to know   they wanted, all   only people

yawoghinle   eyóon   onht'e.
they have been that is it is.

Sin la ededehgheli t'áh, di segón   úh ndét'e. Di
Me   just fool around cause, this my knee and like you. This

segon   jon úh, jon úh, wok'ánita   éhsín la ededéhghel
my knee here and, here and, you look at it maybe   fool around

úh sin a'adéhdleh eyóon onht'e. Xónht'e óon edu, edu
and me I did to myself that it is. Like that then not, not

ts'ído jon aseuntl'unh   úh, edu ts'eu kedeya
child here when I was in diapers and, not woman attack/wrestle

dahwónlin. Saújon edon xédé menéhílned eghon
never been. I like her but just respect her but still

mbéhnda'edlo úh. Gáa, dlo t'áh i   zonh. Edu
I laugh with her and. Yes, joke with that is all. Not

inhk'ehi ka dene ghinlé. Gúhyeh óon xéts'int'e
daring   for person being. That way then that is how

óon ts'egheda.
then one lives.

Jon ndaídehi la, andéhthít'e Gadéhtl'un ts'inh óon
Here we are living, all of us Gadéhtl'un from   then

ahthít'e. Dene lígé ts'inh zonh óon ahthít'e. K'inhts'ín
we are.   Man one   from only then we are. Way from

awónht'e. Eyóon   awónht'e úh.
it is.   Like that it is   and.

On ndahxéhwohdehí tah ju dene gheda k'ehéh
But telling you all a story with also people living way

ndaxéhwohdeh. Edu łahdin keh zonh dene ehwohdehi
I tell you about. Not one side with only people tell story to

wóh'on. Di ewon jon wonlin adéhdlehi a'úht'eh
should be. This even here something I do for myself as it is

óon. Di sekahtheya yuhin déya. Jon kíi yeh dene
then. This he got me here I went. Here just there people

sét'ia ehsíin. Wonlinah dedhóo ahłin wonlin ka
like me that are. Somehow small boys you all are something for

sudahdi. "Ehtsée, di dint'eeh," kedahdi. Gah
pray for. "Grandfather, this cook yourself," say to someone. Rabbit

tenáa sets'ín dashí edon, mehniduhtl'e éhsín. "Héé!
small/frozen to me threw but even, I'll grab it maybe. "Hey!

setsée, su'asenelá," dúhsi éhsín. Eyi la kíi
my grandson, you did well for me," I will say maybe. That just

edu óon edawahdíh. Uuhghen xondahten xáhchi úh
not then you all know. Goose take it out pluck it and

ndáehtthi. Edu sin ndaht'ain wowohdíi gha
I eat repeatedly. Not me upon you I will live for

andahxesi ndahxin, ndahxin edeghahdi gha ahsi.
I'm telling you you all, you all live for yourself to I say.

Wonlin ts'ín kólaa ehsíin wodehi, mbedhá
Something to old men that are what they say, his words

kaúyats'inlin igha édé, yídeeh ts'egheda ts'ín wogha,
ashamed of [future] then, in the future living to for,

kíi ka'élính. Dats'et'inh wonlin kasuts'ededi ehsíin ju
just confused. How you do animal pray for that is also

ka'élính i la mohúyawonlin-a.
don't know that to be ashamed of.

Di edéhtl'éhkúan aht'in dendahxets'edihin. Eyi la
This school you all are at you are being taught. That

anét'e újon aghaht'in gha'on edéhtl'éhkúan
this many good to be for school

dendahxets'edihin. Wotah ju dene, kólaa ehsíin,
you are being taught. In addition also people, old man that is,

ndaxehwodeh édé, mbeghá máhsi kudahdi. Úh
talk to you all then, for him thankful you should think. And

se'e jon mbedaghah ahchud úh duhden
really here words coming out of his mouth grab onto and here

nina'on.   Jon xa'aht'e   mbek'eh édé.
put it here. Here you all be like that on it   then.

Edet'áhwodadhi   éhsín. Łígé elin
Benefit yourself with your own efforts maybe. One   who is

edet'áhwodudhi éhsín.
will benefit himself maybe.

Eyi   xónht'i   wodih   óon,   mbekehwohdeh
That   like that   story   then,   with it I tell story/advise/lecture

igha.   Edu sa'inhtthi se'e   seuyon   két'e.
[future]. Not   right for me really suitable for me   seems like.

Ye ghonh onht'i?
Why   it is?

Got'ónh   ndahxethet'ónh   k'íodakehí,   eyi   mbek'eh
Before   before you all   things that happen,   that   on it

wohdeh ighá . . .   dahsee   łonduhsi?   Eyi eghon
I talk   [future] . . .   how could   I tell the truth? That   even

wots'i edek'eh nineht'ah i   k'enhen awónht'e
a lie   on myself I place   that   way   seems like

egohi   núdlin   úh. I   t'áh   edu se'e
that might be   expected and. That because of not   really

me'enéhłin et'e.
I don't like   like that.

3 Wolverine Steals a Child

Nóghe **dene** **ndéh'in** **ts'edi** **tl'a.** **Gáa** **k'ozonh**
Wolverine person he stole it is said well. Already recently

kuán **níniya** **úh,** **mbedené** **úh,** **mbetsuan** **úh,**
he was married and, his wife and, his mother-in-law and,

mo **úh.** **Taghedet'ea** **úh** **zonh,** **úh** **éhsán,**
mother and. Three living together and only, and then,

aghet'in **éhsán.** **I** **méhndádzíin,** **mbedené,** **ts'ídoa**
they were then. That her son-in-law, his wife, child

ah'in **éhsán,** **cho** **wóhda'echo** **éhsán.**
she has [pregnant] then, big big with baby then.

Mbedené **ndádzé** **úh** **ndádzéd** **éhsán.**
Her husband he hunts and he hunts then.

"**Ebé,** **embé** **ndéhtthen;** **embé** **duhts'elin**
"Stomach, stomach fat; stomach I'll broil

ndéhtthen. **Edu** **nánedzé** **úh** **élé** **úh.**
fat. Not you go hunting and not and.

Edhinhxin **édé** **embé** **sets'ín** **adungé.** **Embé**
If you kill something then stomach to me you pack back. Stomach

wohbeedzin **wohkádhin** **endehtthe** **óon.** **Edulin** **kasúdindi,**
broiled I want to eat I want/need then. Nothing you hunt for,

edhinhxin **óon** **kónt'i** **edu** **sets'ín** **níani'áh**
even though you kill then like not to me you bring

élé," **yéhdi** **úh** **éhsán.**
not," she said to him and then.

Ínyá **mbatedlinh** **t'áh** **éhsán.** **Duh** **ndádéhdzédi**
Then she begs him for that with it then. Now he went hunting

Ionh **éhsán.** **Wozen** **i** **t'áh** **sóon.**
[past] then. Darkness that with/because of then.

Ye'on **ghinté** **úh,** **xeda** **at'in** **on**
Where it [moose] was last known to be he slept and, moose was by

ndéhtin **úh** **éhsán,** **at'in** **Ionh** **éhsán.**
he went to sleep and then, he was [past] then.

Mbetsuan   sóon   gu'on   ndadeh. Gu'on
His little mother-in-law   then   beside them she lived. Beside them

mbetsuan   ndadeh   lonh éhsán.   Mbets'ín
his little mother-in-law she lived [past] it must have been. To her

tón-ets'edah,   áán, mbets'ín tón-ets'edah.
crawling up to her, yes, to her   he was crawling up to her.

Nandeteh *   dah,   sóon mbets'ín
She was repeatedly going to sleep   every time, then   to her

dedhóo   ndadedah   úh   sóon.
man   he was repeatedly going there   and   then.

"Sehndadzíin at'in," kudi,   "sehndadzíin at'in,"
"My son-in-law   it was," she thought, "my son-in-law   it was,"

kudi   úh   éhsán. K'aa, k'aa, xetl'iónh ni'íyah
she thought and   then.   Well, well, morning   she got up

éhsán. K'aa, yets'ín tón-endadah   úhzonh
then.   Well,   to her   he was repeatedly going up to   always

i   t'áh   éhsán. "Sehndadzíin at'in," kudi
that   because of   then.   "My son-in-law   it is,"   she thought

éhsán. Tl'a mbetúé   gáh   theda   úh. "I
then.   So   her daughter with   she was sitting and. "That

setúé   di   xónht'i éhsán. Sehndadzíin   at'in,"
my daughter this like that then.   My son-in-law   it was,"

kudi   éhsán; mbetsóné éhsán at'in. Yc   gha dene
she thought then;   her feces   then   it was. What for   person

andat'ính   úh   sóon? Yets'ínndadedah la   éhsán. Yets'ín
appear to be and   then? To her he went repeatedly then.   To her

tón-edah   lonh éhsán. I   t'áh   éhsán, gáa,
he crawled up to her [past] then.   That   because of   then,   yes,

xónht'e éhsán, gáa, mbedené gáa, ts'ídoa
like that then,   yes,   his wife   yes,   child

wohteh   ah'in. Gáa, k'elonh ts'ídoa
really [advanced pregnancy] she had. Yes,   almost   child

wónlin nínéni'on éhsán. Kaa   mehndadzíin   ndádéhdzéd
born   formed   then.   Already her son-in-law   he went hunting

úh   éhsán. Sa   dadéhk'ali   úh   awójá   éhsán,
and   then.   Sun shining brightly and it happened   then,

---

* This means that the same thing is happening each night.

mehndadzíin k'awu ndádéhdzéd   úh   éhsán.
her son-in-law again   he went hunting and then.

Ddhenéhtah mbetúé   thetin.   I   t'áh
In the daytime her daughter she was sleeping. That because of

éhsán i   gáa   mehndadzíin ndádéhdzéd   úh   sóon.
then   that already her son-in-law he went hunting and   then.

"Sehndadzíin at'in," kudi   tsían   t'áh   éhsán.
"My son-in-law he is,"   she thought useless because of then.

Mo,   mbetúé   ts'ín sóon déhtl'a. Úh gáa   ehsóon
Mother, her daughter to   then   she went. And already then

ddhenéh tadíenh sa   dahdéhk'ali   úh   éhsán,
day   middle   sun it was bright and white and then,

mbetúé   ts'ín déhtl'a. Úh   mbetúé   gáh   kúinya
her daughter to   she went. And her daughter with she went in

éhsán, mo.   Edu yéhdi   a'onht'e ínyá.
then,   mother. Not speaking to her it was then.

"Ené, ené, seyá   k'áninta,"   éhdi   éhsán.
"Mom, mom, my lice you look for," she said then.

Mo   k'eh nítthíet'on   éhsán. Jon   yetthíghá
Mother on   she placed her head then.   Here her hair

utón   ketthí   yehk'ath   úh,   edu
she holds someone's head she moved it around and then, not

ndáidah. Łehen   ndéhtin úh sóon.
moving.   Continuous she slept and then.

"I   xóhłeh,"   kudi   éhsán, mbetúé,   ts'ídoa
"That I do like that," she thought then,   her daughter, child

dzahdonht'e t'áh.   "Setúá,   sehndazíin   at'in,"
bad   because of. "My daughter, my son-in-law he is,"

kudi   t'áh   éhsán ayeh'in.
she thinks because of then   she had [she felt like].

Jon   mbetúé   yek'eh tthíh'on,   thetin
Here her daughter on her   she placed her head, she was sleeping

úh   éhsán, yetthíghá t'áh xéyeh'in   éhsán. Jon
and then,   her hair   with she was doing like then.   Here

echitth, eyi tuhtsindzatth'ené echi elin,   eyi jon
awl,   that loon leg bone   awl   it was, that here

ahkáhé   edet'á   ehton   éhsán, xáye'on
pouch/pocket inside here it was place then,   she took it out

éhsán. Jon   ekehgód,   ekehgódé,
then.   Here side of the ball of the foot, side of the ball of the foot,

tthinh   tsían   ju   ayeh'in   úh   éhsán.   Jon   mbetúé
axe   useless also she had   and then.   Here her daughter

i   tl'a,   k'íi   edu   ats'ut'in,   on   duh   k'íondeji
that well, just   not   worth doing, but now   dangerous

xéts'edeh   igha.
to do that [future].

Úh   eyi   mbetúé   yek'eh   nitthíeton   éhsán.
And that her daughter on her she placed her head then.

Yedzieh,   eyi   edzachí   tsían   íin,   yedzieh   yintthe
Her ear,   that leg bone awl useless before, in her ear she placed

úh   éhsán.   Eyi   yelainhshí   ínyá   mbetúé
and then.   That she pounded on then   her daughter

tthídáudéh'éé.   Úh   gáa,   detúé   dhéhxin.
she stiffens.   And yes,   her daughter she killed.

Mbetúé   dhéhxin   éhsán.   Yehndazíin   gáa   kaa
Her daughter she killed then.   Her son-in-law still

dude'inh   sóon.   Eyi   tlian   gha   kúan   awóndlá,
gone away then.   That dog   for   shelter she built,

det'úzáa   deintl'un   sóon.   Tse   cho   yegáh
her little bitch she tied up then.   Firewood   lots beside her

níndénila   úh.   Xáuwinhkin   úh   duhdíin   ts'inh,
she piled up and. She cleared a place and right there from,

guts'ínhín,   me   cho   onlá   úh   éhsán.   I
on their side, wall [shade] big   she made and then.   That

t'úhze   tsían   kón   gáh   dendéhtl'un   úh   éhsán.
bitch   useless fire beside she tied it up and then.

T'úhzáa   kón   gáh   yn'cníh'á   úh   éhsán,   kón
Little bitch fire beside she was sitting up and then,   fire

ts'ín   theda,   mbodat'in   úh   éhsán.
toward she was sitting, it appeared and then.

Déyendéhtl'un   úh   éhsán . . .   i   mbetúé   sóon.   Duh
She tied it up   and then . . .   that her daughter then.   Like

yehák'ehé   (Tl'a   i   éhsán   duh   ketthíthéh   cho   t'áh
this way   (Now   that then   now   wig   horrible with

ats'et'in).   Jon   wots'inh   dúhyeh   di   mbetthíthéh,   línt'ónh
going on).   Here from   to here   this   her scalp,   all

detúé   tthíthéh,   ejinhinch'í   úh.   I   éhsán   mbetúé
her daughter scalp,   she tore off and. That then   her daughter

tthíthéhcho   t'áh,   yet'áinla   sóon   yéhgon   úh   sóon.
horrible scalp with,   she stuffed   then   she dried it and then.

Yetthíthéh t'áh tthíh'on   éhsán. Mbetúé
Her scalp   with   she put on her head   then.   Her daughter

déhludhi   sóon   yéh, ondéhthahin   niyénilu   úh
she dragged   then   there,   a certain distance   she dragged her   and

sóon.   Edhéh   egoni   yegha   niténihká   úh   sóon.
then.   Hide   dried   for her   she spread   and   then.

Yéodinkín,   et'adhicho   ehdah   yéodin,   daetthie
She covered her up,   big smoked hide   also   she covered,   branches

ehdah   i   netlon   yédinlá.   Duh   xónht'e. Ts'ído,
also   those   lots   she piled on.   Now   like that.   Child,

sóon eyi,   mbetúé   nínitsa   úh   éhsán.
then   that one,   her daughter   she buried   and   then.

"Eyi   duh   dáyínlá   onht'e?"   kudi   éhsán.
"That   now   what did she do   it is?"   he thought   then.

"'Embé   kuhdi,'   dindi   úh   óon   embé   ndegha
"'Stomach   I want ,'   you say   and   then   stomach   for you

nίanehgin.   Dáninlá,   úh   edu   sindi   edu
I packed back.   What did you do,   and   not   you say to me   not

ká'anet'in,   dondih   úh   edu   sindi   deneh'á
you're like that,   why is that   and   not   saying to me   ignoring me

sóon?"   mbetúé   ts'ín   éhdi   úh   éhsán.
then?"   her daughter   to   he said   and   then.

Yetthíghá inhchu   igha   úh   éhsán.   Jon   yetthíghá
Her hair   he grabbed   [future]   and   then.   Here   her hair

t'áh xáinlá   sóon.   "Sets'ín   ndahładeniyah,"   yéhdi
with   he pulled   then.   "Toward me   you turn around,"   he said to her

úh   éhsán.
and   then.

Yetthíghá inhchu   xáinlá   ínyá,   mbedené tthíghá
Her hair   he grabbed   he pulled   then,   his wife's   hair

gahdin'on. Mbetúé   tthíghá t'atthih'on,   tsían
he took off.   Her daughter's   hair   she's wearing,   worthless

lonh   óon mbetthí tsían   dahdéhk'ale. Kóncho   t'áh
[past]   then   her head   worthless   white.   Big fire   with

yetthí   enihdí.   Kóncho   t'áh yekadéhghe;
her head   he struck her into.   Big fire   with   he struck her into;

yedhéhxin,   yedzíninhxe   úh   sóon.   Hée,   yeóné
he killed her,   he struck her to death   and   then.   Hey,   on the side

yayínhtin   úh   sóon.
he tosses her   and   then.

Deghelé t'onghintsín újon níawonitsin úh sóon,
His pack packed it well he arranged and then,

edhéhxe íin ts'ín deyah igha éhsán. Úh
where he killed [moose] before toward he goes [future] then. And

jon eyi mbetsun tsían, dzíinxeli,
here that his mother-in-law worthless, the one he clubbed to death,

sóon yéh ya'ínhtthu. I dedené tthí, tthí
then there he threw her. That his wife scalp, scalp

dihts'inch'ili, ju éhsán. Yehxal úh éhsán cyi
that was torn off, also then. He rolled it up and then that

edet'áyat'ón éhsán.
he stuffed it in his clothing then.

"Déé sóon ajá?" éhsín kudi. Yeninlú
"Where then happened?" maybe he wondered. She dragged her

líin k'ínhín sóon, yek'éh déhya
she was [before] way then, after her he went

xáajá. Ínyá mbedené mbódekin cho
it happened like that. Then his wife she covered horrible

theda úh yek'ewodéhkin éhsán.
laying there and he uncovered then.

Yebé k'eh níadedih úh yebé k'eh déhdi.
Her stomach on he felt and her stomach on he felt.

Ts'ídoa gáa kaa ndáidah éhsán. Mbedené chon eninht'a
Child still moving then. His wife's womb he cut open

úh i ts'ído xáinhtin úh. Gahdhéh t'áh se'e újon
and that child he pulled out and. Rabbit skin with really well

ayínlá úh gahdhéh t'áh yinhtin úh éhsán.
he did it and rabbit skin with he put and then.

K'éyehteh. Dih úh, gah úh, xeda úh,
He carried [the baby] around. Grouse and, rabbit and, moose and,

xónht'i úh, xónht'i dhéhxe édé yetthíghon yaleh.
like that and, like that he killed then its brain he makes with it.

Mbetthíghon aleh t'áh, godahi ek'a ewon ayeh'in
Its brain he used that with, something fat even he has

édé. (Tl'a, díin wots'inh idahátsinhin wónle? Yidét'ónh
then. (Well, where located store it was? Long ago

idahátsinhin guxúle úh.) I t'áh éhsán gáa, i
store nonexistent and.) That because of then yes, this

ts'ídoa xónht'ia k'éndíha; k'éyehteh łaheindi
child like that he's caring for; he carried it around always

k'éyehteh.
he carried it around.

Xattheeh	la	yegha	tth'a		ayeh'in,	netsédláa
First		what for	sphagnum moss		he had,	small

úh	éhsán,	la k'éyegeh,		k'éyegeh		úh,
and	then,	he packed him around,		he's packing him around		and,

ndádzéd	óon	k'éyegeh,		k'éyegeh
he's hunting	even then	he's packing him around,		he's packing him

éhsán.	Nechá	gua	ajá	éhsán,	gáa,	nechá	gua
then.	Big	a little	he became	then,	yes,	bigger	a little

ajá	éhsán,	újon	gua	ndáidah		éhsán.
he became	then,	well	a little	he's going around		then.

I	mbetá	k'éyegeh		úh	endádla	éhsán,
That	his father	he's packing him around		and	tired	then,

"Debé	éhsín,"	kudi	éhsán.	"Sechuen,	yeh	dih
"He's hungry	maybe,"	he thinks	then.	"My son,	there	grouse

inde	k'éh	ndohtlah.	Edu	wontse	ele,	ts'aya.
flew off	after	I'm going.	Not	you cry	not,	somebody's coming.

Nógha	tl'a,	edu	dene	eteh	ehteh.	Gáa,	dáhseé
Wolverine	well,	not	person	he was	all the time.	Yes,	unexpected

k'aondeh	éhsín.	Edu,	edu	'Ta'áh'	dundi	úh	mbets'ín
it will happen	maybe.	Not,	not	'Dad'	you say	and	to him

gundeh	ele.	Eghatthelé	edon	edu	'Ta'áh'
you speak	not.	Sound coming	even	not	'Dad'

dundi,"		yéhdi		éhsán.
you [future] say,"		he said to him		then.

Xa		t'edzecho,	tíé	xónht'i	tah	éhsán.
Driftwood stump		big flat,	one	like that	within	then.

Dechin	dedhecho	eyéhtl'un		éhsán.	Xayéh
Tree	long/big	he hung him [on]		then.	Moss on stump

yeníeninhtthí		eyi.	"Seda	dahtheneda,"	yéhdi
he put him in with stick		there.	"For me	you sit there,"	he said

éhsán.	Gacho,	gacho	dáitthi	cho	tah
then.	Big spruce,	big spruce	branches	lots	among

ye'eninhtthi	éhsán.
he put him in	then.

Eyi	dek'ehyidle	t'áh	eht'o,		ayíhthen	úh
That	pacifier	with	he [baby] sucked on,		he left	and

éhsán.	"Di	neht'o,"	yéhdi		sóon	yedhá
then.	"This	you suck,"	he said to him		then	his mouth

yi'on.   Ek'á xá'at'aii   cho   dahe'ał   úh   ayínlá.
he put it in. Fat   cut out that   much   he's holding   and   he did.

"Edu   ta'áh dundi   ele."
"Not   father you say not."

"Nógha   tl'a, edu dene   eleh   ehłeh   egúh   yí
"Wolverine well, not person he was usually in the past   what

kaa sóon sechuen ch'a ahjá,"   kudi   úh.
for   then   my son   left   I did,"   he thought   and.

Mbetá   dih   ónk'etía   zonh, k'ahu   ech'uín
His father   grousc two small ones only,   again   another

dahndadéhde,   yinghon   éhsán. K'awu t'áhin
they landed together, he killed them then.   Again   back

yets'ín   —ínyá kaa, duhyi,   joan, k'a   xáh,   yéh
toward him —then well, there it was, here,   again   stick,   there

yechuan eyanínhtthe   k'a.   Ínyá indayedéxel óon,   ínyá
his son   he stuffed him   again. Then   there it fell   then,   then

k'a   k'éch'in'intth'áhdhe   lonhán.
again   he wore out one spot moving around then.

Ínyá ts'ídoa k'a   nídedínhchú.   Ínyá ts'ídoa
Then   child   again   he [Wolverine] took. Then   child

ndéh'in úh sóon.   Ée,   kaa,   mbetá   yek'éh   tl'a,
he stole   and then.   Hey,   of course,   his father   after him   well,

k'íadah.   Yech'ahín   at'in,   sóon gáa, yek'éh déhtl'a.
he followed. Avoiding him   he was,   then   yes,   after him he went.

Xattheeh la gáa, níniya   úh,   níniya   úh,   xattheeh la.
First   yes,   he came   and, he came   and,   first.

Ghinté, Nóghe   ghinté la, tth'a tseláa thehła.   K'ahju
He slept, Wolverinc he slept,   moss   wet   he placed. Again

wodééh ndaetéi, k'ahju yetth'a   tsclé thehła úh. I
ahead   he slept,   again   his moss   wet   he left   and. There

wots'inhá, gáa, ah   xácho t'áh déhya
from,   yes,   snowshoes this big with   he [the son] went

ayínlá. Gáa, ah   t'áh niyah   úh ayínlá.
he made. Yes,   snowshoes with   he was going and   he made.

Gáa, tl'a, yek'éh, kaa yek'éh, k'íadah   úh,
Yes,   well,   after him,   still   after him, wandering around and,

gáa, łíónh yeyíhxáyah   úh. Jon   ju dónk'é
yes,   all   ahead of him he went like   and. Here   also hunger

ehdah onht'e   éhsán. Gah   úh   dih   xónht'ia.
also   he [the man] was   then. Rabbit and   grouse like that.

Xóndínk'on úh,   xóndínk'on   úh,   atthe   édé   k'awu
He camped   and,   he camped   and,   he ate   then   again

seníandetl'un   i   k'ahju   yek'éhda.
he got dressed again   that   again   he went after him.

Gaá,   yek'éh   k'íadah   úh.   Dehxéli   tah   két'e   óon
Yes,   after him   he went   and.   Nightfall   during   the same   then

ah   ech'un   aleh.   Inhde   aicho,
snowshoes   another   he [Wolverine] made.   Next [size]   that big,

inhde   aicho.   Xoniá   ahcho   t'áh   yek'agáh,
next [size]   that big.   Suddenly   big snowshoes   with   beside,

detah   dih   ka   k'égezeh   úh.
in the woods   grouse   for   back and forth between [zigzagging]   and.

K'édondadáh   Nóghe   tsian   eninlú,   wohdludhi
He wandered around   Wolverine   worthless   he dragged,   toboggan

t'áh   k'é'idluh,   eninludh   éhsán.
with   he was pulling around,   he dragged   then.

Kaa,   dih   ka   ehda,   k'édondadáh.   K'egahín
Yes,   grouse   for   also,   he wandered about again.   Alongside

dih,   mbetá   yek'éh   k'íadah.   "Káa,   sechuen   at'in,"
grouse,   his father   after him   he went.   "Yes,   my son   he is,"

éhsín   kudi.   Mbetá   yek'éh   k'íadah,   ahcho
maybe   he thinks.   His father   after him   he went,   big snowshoes

t'áh   k'íadah.   Dih   xadáheh'ih   k'é   wónlin.
with   he went.   Grouse   he plucked   place   was.

"Éé,   gulóon   sechuen   woh'in,"   ee   kudi   úh.
"Hey,   hopefully   my son   I will see,"   just   he thought   and.

Gáa,   duh   mbek'é   wodetlege,   jon   dih   xáinhch'il   úh
Yes,   now   its place   soft [fresh],   here   grouse   he plucked   and

edelé   ndáda'ehk'ahe   detleh   úh   sóon.   "Héé,   yéh la
blood   drips   fresh   and   then.   "Hey,   there

xódeh'ín,"   úh   kudi;   yeh   yedai   sóon
he might go,"   and   he thought;   there   for him   then

yendadah'ín   úh   éhsán.   Mbetá   déhtl'a   ehdin-á
ahead of him he went   and   then.   His father   went   thoughtfully

yeghon   náinya.
for him   he came [they met].

"Éé,   sechuen,   se'e   kanejá.   I   t'áh,
"Hey,   my son,   really   like that it happened to you.   That   because,

no,   ndetsun,   kayínlá.   I   t'áh   se'e
your mother,   your grandmother,   she did.   That   because of   really

tegúhtheni neɳdéehshon úh.   Se'e   tegúhtheni
hard times   I raised you   and.   Really   in hard times

néɳdéehshon úh.   Ůh   k'éɳdehgeh,   úh   nenehk'inł,
I raised you   and.   And   packing you around,   and   you were heavy,

i   ka   neya'enihged   íin.   Kaa,   Nógha   wodén
that   for   I hoisted you up   before.   Well,   Wolverine   where

déhtl'a.   'Dúh   óon   edu   kadundí,'   dehsi   'Ta'áh,
he came.   'Now   then   not   for you say,'   I say   'Father,

Ta'áh,'   dindi   igha   édé.   Ayínlá.   Anínlá,"
Father,'   you say   [future]   then.   He did it.   It happened to you,"

yéhdi   éhsán.
he said to him [his son]   then.

  "Ínle,   Nógha   tsían,   'Ni'a,   ni'a,   sechuen   enet'e.
  "No,   Wolverine   useless,   'You,   you,   my son   you are.

Sian   ndetá   aht'e,'   séhdi.   Nógha   kaa,   séhdi
Me   your father   I am,'   he said to me.   Wolverine   well,   he told me

i   t'áh."   Dih   ka   k'étl'eh   úh,
that   because of."   Grouse   for   he ran around following   and,

mbetá   dih   ka   k'íadah   úh   sóon,   mbetá
his father   grouse   for   he went around after   and   then,   his father

yeghon   noeja   úh   sóon.
for him   he came back   and   then.

  "Héé,   sechuen   sian   ndetá   aht'e.   Duh   dáɳdét'i
  "Hey,   my son   me   your father   I am.   Now   how many

dzenéh   óon?   Shíh   teh,   onk'eh   shíh   teh   óon,
days   then?   Hill   over,   two   hills   over   then,

nink'áɳdehtn,   ndck'éh   k'étl'eh,   k'étl'eh.   Naɳdahtéh   k'é
I looked for you,   after you   I walked,   I walked.   You slept   place

ech'unh,   ech'unh,   ech'unh   ah   t'áh   anileh   úh.
another,   another,   another   snowshoes   with   he makes you   and.

Ónk'edeh   zonh   óon   neɳdatselé   inhła.   Ůh   i
Two places   only   then   wet ones   were left.   And   there

gots'inh   łínt'ónh   kíi   sech'ahín   aɳdeh'in   a'onht'e.
from there   all   just   away from me   you were taken   it was.

Sian   ndetá   aht'e.   Gáa,   donk'e   ju   ndek'éh   ddheníi
Me   your father   I am.   Yes,   hunger   also   after you   day

ghádéh   k'ehtl'eh   úh   sóon,   i   t'áh   dehbé
all during   I walked   and   then,   that   because of   I was hungry

eɳdádla,"   yéhdi   éhsán.
really,"   he said to him   then.

Dih   dahé yanilá,   mbetá,   dahé dih
Grouse some he gave him, his father, some grouse

ghanila   úh sóon. Yetáh   theya ts'ín
he gave him and then. With him he went to

éhsán.
then [he returned to Wolverine].

    "Tee, gáa, dih kandet'ian   zonhan dhéhxin.
    "Father, yes, grouse that small amount is all only   I killed.

Kíi gotene   ehwondih,   edu újon dhéhxe," éhsán
Just all frozen I think maybe, not   well I killed," then

yéhdi.
he said to him [to Wolverine].

    Diháa,   di inghon, dahé éhsán yegáh
    Little grouse, this he killed, some then   beside him

ninila   úh. Dih   yehóon ts'ín dedhal   úh
he placed and. Grouse there   to   he threw and

yek'ádánehta   éhsán. Yek'ádánehta,   eyi
he [Wolverine] inspected them then.   He inspected them, there

wots'ín yedadhał   úh éhsán. "Dih,   dih dezeni,
to   he threw them and then.   "Grouse, spruce grouse,

mbetl'elé nechá   éhsín, dih dezeni   mbetl'elé nechá,"
its gizzard big   maybe, spruce grouse its gizzard big,"

ts'enidheni.
he [Wolverine] thought.

    "Gotá   gháts'inleh," yéhdi
    "Someone's father give it to,"   he [Wolverine] said to [the boy]

úh édé.
and then.

    Uh, "Níon setá   anet'e séhdindi.   Dónht'e íin,
    And, "You my father you are you said to me. Whatever before,

'Tee' gha auhłeh adindi? Kíi edu dene   inh'ín. Yelíi
'Father' for I'll do you say? Just not person seeable. Whatever

setá   wolé adindi. Nion, 'Ndetá   aht'e,'
my father be   you say. You,   'Your father I am,'

séhdindi   úh. Édé káa, dzahdándehłeh igha,   edu
you said to me and. Then yes, I'll ruin you   [future], not

gundeh   ele, edu 'Tee' séhgondeh   ele. 'Edu
you talk [future] not, not 'Father' you talk to me not. 'Not

sechuan   anet'e,' séhdindi.   Dádindi   úh
my little son you are,' you say to me. What are you saying and

adindi?" yéhdi.
what are you saying?" he [boy] said [to Wolverine].

Mbadzahdádi. Nóghe yadzahdádi
He didn't like what he said. Wolverine he didn't like what he said

éhsán. "Tl'a, dih dinzi," úh. "Káa, kónt'i zonh
then. "Well, grouse you cook," and. "Yes, like that only

eh'in úh a'onht'e," yéhdi éhsán. "Gulóon
I saw and it is," he said to him then. "Hopefully

mbedihé tthidutth'i," kudi éhsán.
his grouse it would fall into the fire," he [the son] thought then.

Dih ena'intthi ínyá, dih
Grouse he [the son] skewered and put to cook then, grouse

ena'intthi ínyá. Dih jon yeyádhé yanitthe úh
he skewered then. Grouse here its breast he skewered and

yenáintthe ínyá. Jon dééh déhtl'a tthidatth'é
he skewered it then. Here back it moved it fell in the fire

mbedihé éhsán.
his grouse then.

"Ni'edínchu'a. Dándúhłi anet'in?"
"You pick it up. What do you think I'll do with you you are?"

yéhdi. Ye'ín'eh detl'eh éhsán. "Ni'edínhteh!"
he said. Short of it he reached then. "You pick it up!"

yéhdi éhsán.
he said to him then.

Yets'ín xá'ajá úh la dúhyeh xónht'e kóncho
To him it happened like that and right there like that big fire

t'áh, yetthí ndadéhxe. Kón t'áh
with, his head [Wolverine's head] he struck. Fire with

ndáiyedéhxe, diéhtthiedatth'e. Tthidatth'é úh
he struck him, he fell head first into the fire. He fell into the fire and

éhsán yek'in é'edinlá. Eyi k'ehduecho ju
then on him he kindled the fire. That big coat also

tthidinshí, eyi ju. Héé, tleh t'ehze cho, dene
he threw in the fire, that too. Hey, grease black horrible, person's

tlezé t'ehzecho éhsán. Łe xáingóde úh ayínlá.
grease black horrible then. Smoke billowing out and he did.

Eyi yeghohdludhécho ju k'eyedéhłe úh ye'ahé
That his big toboggan also he burned and his snowshoes

ehdah. Łínt'ónh yek'ehdéhłe úh. Edulin úh ayínlá úh
also. All he burned and. Nothing and he made and

éhsán.
then.

Úh	gáa,	dzeelonh	gua,	xetl'iónh	goin'a,	wots'ín
And	yes,	high	a little,	morning	being,	until

éhsán,	mbetá	da	i	theda.		Mbetá	da,	ka	i
then,	his father	for	that	he sat waiting.		His father	for,	for	that

theda.	Ínyá	mbetá	edhatthinle	edhin,		úh	goin
he sat.	Then	his father	sounding in,	sounding like,		and	there

óon	k'ánehta.		Ínyá	mbetá	dih	xaninlá,
then	looking in that direction.		Then	his father	grouse	he gave,

ínyá	yets'ín	nda'edah.
then	to him	he came back to him.

"Sechuen,	sian	ndetá		aht'e	úh	sian	ndetá
"My son,	me	your father		I am	and	me	your father

aht'e,"	mbetá	yéhdi	úh	sóon.
I am,"	his father	said to him	and	then.

Eghatthée	tl'onh	éhsán,	eghatthée	tl'onh	éhsán.	Kaa,
They ate	after	then,	they ate	after	then.	Well,

i	mbetá	yeghonh	ndáiya	úh	xoghedéhk'ón	úh.
that	his father	upon him	he came	and	they camped	and.

Eghatthée	tl'onh	újonh	níaghenetl'un		úh	éhsán
They ate	after	well	they dressed again		and	then

ghedéht'a		sóon.	Gáa,	ghedéht'a		úh	sóon
they both went		then.	Yes,	they both went		and	then

ghat'ah.		Łáhúh	gheghinté	úh	k'ahju
they both were going.		Once	they slept	and	again

ndághedéht'a		i	t'áh	éhsán.
they both went on again		that	with	then.

"Kaa,	yuúh		dedíeh	ehsíin	ka	ahthít'in,"
"Yes,	over in that direction		his land	that was for		we will be at,"

kudi		éhsán,	ndaghedéht'a		lonh	úh.
he thought		then,	they both moved on again		[past]	and.

Ínyá	mbechuan	yídeeháa		gheyał		úh
Then	his son	a little ways ahead		they were going		and

yídeeh	dih	ka.	"Tee,	ndeda	yundahéh	dih
ahead	grouse	for.	"Father,	ahead of you	ahead	grouse

ka	duhtl'a,"	éhdi	éhsán.
for	I'll go,"	he said	then.

"Áán,"	yéhdi.
"Yes,"	he said.

"**Yídeeh dih   ka   dehtl'a,**"   **kudi**   **ínyá.**
"Ahead   grouse   for I'm going,"   he [son] thought   then.

Kaa, yek'éh   at'in,   gáa, yek'éh se'e.   "**I   Nógha la**
Yes,   after him   he was,   yes,   after him   really.   "That   Wolverine

edu   dene   et'e,"   **kudi   t'áh   sóon.   Se'e**
not   person   he was,"   he thinks   because of   then.   Really

łíndi   t'áh yek'éh   at'in.   I   ts'ído onht'e
with all his strength   with   after him   he was.   That   child   he was

úh   yeyihxádéhtl'a   úh   gáa, yek'éh   gheyah
and   he outdistanced him   and,   yes,   after him   he was going

úhzonh.
always.

"**Téé!**"   **éhdi   edhin.**
"Father!"   he said   calling out.

Úh   mbetá,   "Éé!"   yéhdi   ínyá.
And   his father,   "Yes!"   he said to him   then.

"**Duhdei   ehtsée   egenihsudi**   **guk'éh**
"Here   grandfather   they have dragged [toboggan]   after them

duhtl'a,"   **k'ahju'a ndadedi.**
I'll go,"   again   he repeated.

K'ahju'a i   denecho, xónht'e dene,   denecho xónht'e:
Again   that   giants,   like that   person,   giants   like that:

inhch'ónh   da'áhí,   keníhshon   íin   cho
opposite each other   facing away,   grown together   before   big

dene   i   éhsán. Wohdludhicho t'áh   tl'a,   i   ts'ído
persons   that   then.   Big toboggan   with   well,   that   children's

wohdludháa   k'íadluhi   ét'in, t'áh k'éghedluh.
small toboggan   pulling along   like,   with   they pulled along.

"**Duhde   ehtsée   egiyenihsudi,**   **guk'éh**
"This way   grandfathers   they have pulled through [here],   after them

duhtl'a'a,"   **éhdi.**
I'm going [okay?],"   he said.

"**Ínle, sechuen, i   dene   k'é'ezoe   tl'a,**
"No,   my son,   those   persons   that travel around pulling   well,

łéts'áhgohincho   **úh mondeji   ats'edi.   Denecho**
they are split/grown/horrible   and   dangerous   said to be.   Giants

ets'edi,   mondejide.   Héé, sechuen,   edu
they are called,   dangerous.   Hey,   my son,   not

kawonedeh,"   **mbetá   dóon   ka   wotthílé k'ih**
you talk about that,"   his father   in vain   for   clearing   place

xadahtle **éhdi,** **éhsán** **yek'éh.**
running on and off   he said,   then   after him.

Gáa, **eya** **úhtla.** **Gáa,** **łínt'ónh** **yeyíhxadéhya.**
Yes,   there   his tracks ran off.   Yes,   all   he outdistanced him.

Gáa, **wozenáa** **ajá** **éhsán.** **Ndetée** **igha**
Yes,   it was getting dark   became   then.   For him to sleep   [future]

sóon, **dih** **ka** **k'íadah** **úh** **dih** **dedéhghin'a.**
then,   grouse   for   he went around for   and   grouse   kill for himself.

Ndéhtin **kéte.** **Kíi** **wohk'ón** **awódlá** **éhsán, mbetá**
He went to sleep   like.   Just   small camp   he made   then,   his father

dejiháa **k'eh** **nitthíton** **úh** **sóon.** **Ndéhtin**
his little gloves   on   he placed his head   and   then.   He fell asleep

úh **sóon** **ndéhtin** **ínyá.**
and   then   he went to sleep   then.

Xetl'inh **xetl'iónh** **la** **ni'íyeh,** **yek'éh** **déhya.** **K'a**
Tomorrow   morning   he got up,   after him   he went.   Just

yek'éh **niya,** **ddheneh** **tadienh,** **etthénáa**
after him   he followed,   day   middle,   a little bit of meat

ts'inda, **xónts'edík'ónhín** **ninwontthed** **úh.**
that's been eaten,   camp   he arrived   and.

Debé **úh** **éhsán** **xónduk'on** **kudi.** **"Gukóné**
He's hungry   and   then   he will camp out   he wants.   "Their fire

k'é **auht'e,"** **éhsín** **kudi,** **ínyá** **guk'éh** **gheyah.**
place   I will be,"   maybe   he thought,   then   after them   he went.

Gáa, **guk'éh** **gheyah** **ínyá.**
Yes,   after them   he went   then.

Ínyá **mbechúan** **goin** **kek'éh,** **detsée** **guk'éh**
Then   his son   there   after them,   his grandfathers   after them

déhya **ínyá,** **káts'edhéhxin.** **Giyedéht'e.** **Gitth'ené**
he went   then,   but he was killed.   They cooked him.   His bones

zonh **dahdinhłai** **éhsán.**
only   they scattered   then.

Yetth'ené **ehdah** **i** **etthítth'enáa** **ehdahi,** **yetth'ené**
His bones   also   that   his small skull   also that,   his bones

łínt'ónh **náhthehtsin** **úh** **sóon.** **Ndetéh** **igha,**
all   he gathered   and   then.   He goes to sleep   [future],

ehtienh **awodídlá** **sóon,** **se'e** **dets'ído** **eghasulin.**
sleeping place   he made   then,   really   his child   he prayed for.

Yasulin **dúyé** **at'in** **sóon.**
He prayed for him   really hard   he was   then.

"Héé, sechuen xetl'eet'ónh lon.
"Hey, my son morning he wished.

Kíi kaṇdádéhtsed úh sóon, sechuen lon.
Just as strong as he was and then, my son hopefully.

Xetl'eet'ónh lon sets'ín gundeh úh.
Morning wish to me you will be talking and.

Lon ndute.
Hoping he would sleep.

Gulon ndawoda,"
Hopefully he will be living again,"

kudi éhsán.
he thought then.

Yegáh ndéhtin úh yetth'ené edet'aeya éhsán.
With him he slept and his bones he put in with him then.

Ndéhtin yechonhda'áh, sóon ndéhtin ínyá.
He went to sleep facing the other way, then he slept then.

Xetl'onh'a kón ndats'edíhk'on edhin ínyá. Ínyá
In the morning fire was being lit sounding like then. Then

mbechuen at'in. Dene andajá, k'ahju. Úh kón
his son it was. Person he became again, again. And fire

ndadéhk'on úh éhsán. Mbetá da kón dadéhk'on—
he kindled again and then. His father for fire he made—

yelíín ju ts'endúhthi úh.
whatever also one should heat and.

"Sechuen, eyi diháa detah theda íin
"My son, there small grouse inside left before

nehsi'á. Eyóon dih detah theda, sexehthéhé
I say to you. There grouse in it it's sitting, my bag

t'á. K'ahju edulin sedhéh ndádonjá élé.
inside. Again nothing before me you take off again not.

Sedhéh ndadínja édé, k'ahju éhsán eyi ehtsée
Before me you go ahead then, again then those grandfathers

aṇdeguleh éhsín. Ndetsée k'ahju
they'll do it to you again maybe. Your grandfathers again

aṇdegínlá édé dáuhndeh? Gáa, k'ahju
they did it to you again then what will you do? Yes, again

ele ndek'éh ndaduhtl'a," yéhdi éhsán. "Káa, kíi
not after you I'll run again," he said to him then. "Yes, just

káa, xoniedi yeníhts'énenehthe."
yes, all in all you tired me out."

  Kaa, eyi   detsuan   dhéhxin,
  Yes, like that his little grandmother/mother-in-law he killed,

da   éhsán at'in.
because of then   he is.

  Úh eyi, i t'áh,   xetl'iónh nighit'a úh k'awu
  And that, that because of, morning   he got up and again

ndághedéht'a úh éhsán. Xóghedéhk'ón lonh   úh
they both went off and then. They camped out must be and

éhsán, mbetá gáh k'ahju ndatthée   úh.
then, his father beside again he ate with again and.

  K'ahju'á, "Tee, ehtsée   degenihsudi
  Again,   "Father, grandfathers they have passed through pulling

guk'éh duhtl'a," k'ahju'á ndadedi.
after them I'll go,"   again   he repeated.

  Anah! I   dene ka kíi detá   tíndahninhthén.
  Oh dear! That person for just his father he kept wearing him out.

Héé, mbetá dúyé ayéhdi. Kaa, k'ahju la detá,
Hey, his father really he told him. Yes, again   his father,

mbetá, yek'éh déhya úh la gáa, xénude'in
his father, after him he went and yes, going on endlessly.

Kaa, eyi ju, k'ahju nanéhtin lon.
Yes, that also, again slept again wishing.

  K'awu ndágiyedéht'e   lonh úh i gitth'ené,
  Again they cooked him again [past] and that his bones,

tínt'ónh na'inlá;   gitth'ené, tínt'ónh tadinshid. Úh
all   he found again; his bones, all   crushed.   And

ongiyedéla   úh. Gitth'ené k'eh edintl'eh i
they threw them away and. His skull on he drew on there

éhsán. Giyanihthe;   mbetthítth'ené giyatthée
then. They put it up on a pole; his skull   they ate

éhsán; gitthítth'ené k'é edintl'éh éhsan.
then; his skull   place he wrote on then.

Giyaníhtthi   úh éhsán guwonhnoya.
They put it on a pole and then he stumbled onto them again.

  Gáa, eyi taguh   yetth'ené gáh ghinté úh. Gáa,
  Yes, then three times his bones by he slept and. Yes,

tíónh edu dene andajá.   Gáa, ónk'eh zonh
all   not person he became again. Yes, twice only

ayínlá, úh i t'áh ju ayínlá. Gáa, mbetá thún
he did, and that because of also he did. Yes, his father in vain

ayínlá. Sóon mbetá thún ayínlá, kíi mbetá —gáa,
he did. Then his father in vain he did, just his father —yes,

i denecho k'éh at'in.
that giant after he was.

"Sechuen, gúgúhłe íin," kudi éhsán.
"My son, I'll do them in as they did before," he thought then.

Wozen úh éhsán i níniya. Wozen úh sóon
Darkness and then there he arrived. Dark and then

guk'éh gheyah. Kón déhdeli mbódat'in úh
after them he was going. Fire glowing red appear and

éhsán. "Xaguéhła édé," sóon kudi éhsán
then. "What if I did this to them then," then he thought then

guk'éh. Jon ní'egheniludhi cho líi.
after them. Here they've dragged up to horrible must have.

Guméné ta'ánh ní'egheniludhi cho líi,
Their wall behind pulled up to horrible must have been,

gughohdludhé. Ínyá dene xónht'e ninénihshon
their toboggan. Then person like that grown

cho, inhch'onh yuhdéhtl'a úh guk'ándutah
horribly big, opposite each other he moved up on and to look at them

kudi. "Dáahła édé?" sóon ondé éhsín
he wanted. "What might I do then?" [suspense] maybe

kudi'á éhsán. Eyi ghohdlui íinh éhsán,
he thought then. That toboggan behind in cover of then,

guts'ín déhge úh gáa, edu se'e tonht'in níniya
to them he crawled and yes, not really far he arrived

éhsán.
then.

Guts'édécho, mbóh'ín! Yéht'a úh
Their big blanket, bang! He shot them [with arrow] and

éhsán. Jon sunteh sóon yetthíghá tah nits'é
then. Here conveniently then his hair among he grabbed

úh sóon. Inhk'eghedéht'a.
and then. They fought each other.

"Edin asínlá," kudi i t'áh; jon
"He did it to me," he thought that because of; here

inhk'éghedéht'a i t'áh inhk'oh k'eghenizí,
they fought each other that because of each other's necks they broke,

úh   **łéghedhéhxin.**
and   they killed each other.

    Łéghedhéhxin   **éhsán. Ka,**   **i**   **Nógha**
    They killed each other   then.   Well,   that   Wolverine

ats'inlá   **íin**   **k'ínhín, ka, di**   **ju**   **i**   **denecho**
as was done to him   before   way,   yes, this   also   that   big person

tthidintin.   **I**   **t'áh,**   **yekóné k'é**
he put in the fire.   That because of,   his fire   place

et'eh   **tthigiyedintin**   **úh**   **yewohdludhécho**
using what's available   he put in the fire   and   his huge toboggan

ju   **onlá**   **i**   **ju.**   **Łínt'ónh**   **i**   **ju**   **yewohdludhécho ju**
also   he did   that   also.   All   that   also   his big toboggan   also

tthidinlá   **úh,** **łínt'ónh**   **eyi** **ju**   **yek'e'edéhłe.**
he put in the fire   and,   all   that   also   he burned them.

Edulin úh ayínlá.
Nothing and he did.

    Héé,   **mbechuen**   **wonh**   **na'edindheł.**
    Hey,   his son   for   he thinks about all the time.

K'íadaha   **dah**   **ndatseh**   **úh**   **sóon,**
He went wandering   all the time   he cries now and again   and   then,

héé,   **mbadzáhagúnt'e.**   **Ehłéh**   **ets'edi.**
hey,   he was sad.   Always   it is said.

    I   **se'e**   **tegúhthene**   **dene.**   **T'oye**   **t'áh**   **yenéhshon,**
    That   really   pitiful   person.   Milk   with   he raised him,

Nógha   **ets'edi. Dzahdonht'in**   **ínyá, Nógha,**   **dene**
Wolverine   it is said. He was bad   then, Wolverine,   person

ghinlé t'ónh. Keké ju   **wónlin**   **ts'edehde**   **édé,**
he was   before. Feet   also   somewhere   when they went   then,

wónlin   **ts'edehde**   **édé**   **gáa.**
somewhere   when they went   if   yes [the end].

4 The Children Raised on Fat

Storyteller's Introduction

Etundaht'ine.   **Yundét'ónh**   **dene**   **di**   **ndéh gok'eh**
You all are pitiful.   Long time ago   people   this   land   on it

wonlin   **aint'in**   **wolinyendaé.**   **Dechintah**
something   he was [they were]   animal.   In the bush

woyendaé duh   **yainlin.**   **Gúhyi**   **andet'e,**   **gúhyi**
animal   now   they were.   Even though   how many,   even though

dene   **inle**   **ehłeh**   **ts'edi.**   **Kónti**   **ghadéhi**
people   they were   all the time   it was said.   Like that   even them

i   **ghendaé**   **gúhyi**   **edandahxodíh.**
those   animals   even though   they knew us.

  Etundaht'ine.   **Nógha,**   **Nógha**   **ets'edi,**   **tl'a, di**
  You all are pitiful.   Wolverine,   Wolverine   they call him,   well,   this

ndéh gok'eh ende'ính úh   **ju**   **úh. Wonlin**   **ehsíin**
land   on it   steals   and   also   and. Something   every

dzaohłeh   **i**   **nidheni**   **úh**   **nidheni**   **yendaé**
he destroys   that   that he wants   and   that he wants   animal

ehłehi.   **Dene**   **elin**   **t'ónh gáa kaa**   **int'e**   **ts'edi.**
all the time.   People   they were   before   already   he was   it is said.

Eyi   **daúhłin agiyéhdi.**   **Eyi Nógha**   **dene**   **elin**
That   what kind   they said to him.   That Wolverine   person   he was

t'ónh;   **kagigiyegú'ah**   **ehłéh**   **ts'edi.**
before;   he used to do that   all the time   it is said.

The Children Raised on Fat

Tai,   **tai**   **ts'ído**   **ndéhshon. Gonh**   **yendéh'in**
Three,   three   children   he raised.   Someone's   he stole them

ts'ído   **yendéhshon. Eyi**   **ghádé**   **éhsán.**
children   he raised.   That   way   it must have been.

  Nógha   **gondié edats'edíh**   **duhden**   **ts'ín agúnht'e.**
  Wolverine   story   was known   now   to   they are now.

141

Se'e godéhtthed úh ónk'e dene, ónk'e dene
Really first beginning and two people, two people

ndéhshon.
he raised.

Dene nde'in ndehsheh. Óon yidahúh guyek'éndíh
People he stole he was raising. Then above he kept them

úh guyu'éh úh guyu'éh ts'ín mbetthéné kúen
and under them and under them to his meat house

gúnlin. Ekoin wonlin łínt'ónh andet'ehi. Di
it was. Down there something all assorted. This

ndéh gonk'éh łígé ghedé gha yehła, eguh
land on it one year for he put them, there then

yidahúh dene k'éndíh úh ek'á zonh. Ek'áé'
above people he was keeping and fat only. Fat

et'in zonh. Úh etthén kin la i dene, ek'a
just like only. And meat by means of those people, fat

zonh kin gondih. I t'ah xoni
only by means of they lived on. That because like that

gonlonhan ndéhtthene, ajá ínyánítsene.
at the end he got fat, it happened then he got fat.

Guadzahdonht'e. I ek'a zonh guadzonht'e.
They [children] didn't like that. That fat only they didn't like.

I gukaa giyendedih woden ndadetl'eh éhsín.
That for them they were trying where he is going to maybe.

Ech'uin ndadéhtl'a úh, éhsán ekonh
Another he went back to and, it must have been path

ndádetl'a íin ts'ín sóon, dedhóoa ekoin nandeta
he went on before toward then, the little boy there he looked

ínyá. Kúendatl'ek'é kegúh'on déhłíe sóon ekon
then. His entranceway he found out his companion then there

lonh. I dene at'in ekoin mbetene yueh
must be. That person he was there his path below

guin'a. "Ek'on gok'anata," yéhdi úh
it existed [Wolverine]. "There let's look," he said and

yetsonhtla.
he informed him.

Ek'on t'ónh giek'éhguełégetthé. Héé, héé, anet'e
There after they went following after him. Hey, hey, all sorts

dene yek'áh ehsíin łínt'ónh ts'ek'ah eyont'in. Ek'a
people eat each one all edible like. Fat

zonh gúadetsé.   (**Eyóon   duh   mbek'ehín   dene   ene'ín.**
only   he fed them.   (There   now   his way   people   steal.

Netloni   dene   ene'ín   édhi,   ts'ído.   Ezhi,   i
Lots   people   steal   currently,   children.   That,   that

Nógha   k'éhín   óon   at'in.)   Úh   ekon   kuehin
Wolverine   way   then   it is.)   And   there   inside

ndagiyeht'a   úh,   gindahtthon.   Etthén
they went there   and,   he didn't know about them.   Meat

agiyadídlá   edu   nechái   etthén
they made for themselves   not   big   meat

agiyadídla.   Gokat'a   úh   dekeagíta
they made for themselves.   They got out again   and   they went back up

úh, exeleh sóon goin   nontl'a.
and,   evening   then   toward   he returned.

"Ye gha sekúen   ts'inh,   sekúen   ts'inh   ndahtthí
"Why   my house   from,   my house   from   your heads

ndáhchedhekóh?"
wander?"

"Úh ye gha ek'a   zonh,   ek'a   zonh   ndahxenánendíi?   Úh
"And   why   fat   only,   fat   only   you gave us?   And

yueh   wonlin   netlon   ekenendih?   Dondih   i   t'ah
below   something   lots   you keep?   How's that   that   because

edu   ndahxaedintsi?"   giyéhdi.
not   share with us?"   they [children] said to him [Wolverine].

I   kaa   sóon   guedhéhxe   akehe.   Gukaa
That   because   then   he killed them   he tried.   Because of them

gueyendehdíh   úh,   eyi   dene   yanéhshon
he was thinking about them   and,   those   people   he raised

onht'e   úh   giyendáhguyon,   it'áhan   giyet'ahan at'in
they were   and   they were smart,   because of   they oppose   he was

giyet'ahan   at'in.   "Guanhdíh   edhin   edé
they oppose [outsmart]   he was.   "If you live   like that   then

yundahéh   edhin   édé   mbet'ain   ekúhyeh aaht'in
in the future   like that   then   depend on it   that way   you all will be

igha   igha.   Óon   andahxoh'in   eghon,
[future]   [future].   Then   I tried for you   but,

dzáhehsáhłae.   Guanhdíh   edhin   edé   ene'ín
you all did something bad   to me.   If you live   like that   then   stealing

dene   aaht'e.   Gots'i   dene   ju   aaht'e."
people   you all are.   Lying   people   also   you all are."

I   **Nógha**   **dene**   **eli**   **t'ónh**   **kádi,**   **ehłeh**
That   Wolverine   person   he was   before   he said,   in the past

ts'edi.   **Eyóon**   **kegúnhté**   **óon**   **jon**   **aaht'in**   **ndahndagúle**
it's said.   That   that way   then   here   you all are   your parents

ndahk'éndíh.
keep you.

Storyteller's Commentary

Nógha   **ets'edi**   **úh,**   **Ts'ahle**   **ju**   **úh,**   **onk'ion**   **di**   **ndéh**
Wolverine   it is said   and,   Frog   also   and,   those two   this   land

gok'eh.   **Se'e**   **xatthee**   **wondít'ónh**   **dene**   **újon**
on it.   Really   in the beginning   a long time ago   people   good

onlá   **ehłeh**   **ts'edi.**   **Ts'ahle**   **ju**   **ehtthi**   **edehtthíh**
they made   usually   it is said.   Frog   too   straight   he shoots

igha   **k'éts'egeh.**   **Yahk'eh**   **édé**   **mbek'éts'endih.**
[future]   he was carried on.   In winter   then   he was kept.

5 Wolverine, Giant Skunk, and Mountain Lion

Storyteller's Introduction

I   daháni tl'a, netlon dene kehyawodeh úh i
That some   well, many   people tell stories   and that

dene netlon kehyawodeh úh. Eyi, i,   i   t'áh
people many   tell stories   and. That, that, that because

edu łéét'e   daháne ju   ech'uh, ech'uh xónht'e
not   the same some   also different, different like that

łondi.   Edu łíónh   dahé zonh edahdíh.
they tell the truth. Not everything some only   I know.

Wolverine, Giant Skunk, and Mountain Lion: Part 1

Edu łínt'ónh,   úh eyi Nóghe,   Nóghe,   eyi la i
Not   all,   and that Wolverine, Wolverine, that   that

Ehtsée   séhwodeh úh yídeéht'ónh úh, edu duh,
Grandfather talked to me and long ago   and, not now,

tonht'et'ónh. Eyi dene,   Nóghe   ju dene elin úh
a long time ago. That people, Wolverine also person was   and

Nóda nechi, Nódacho cyi úh. Eyi mbekeeh wots'a'in.
Cat   big,   Cougar   that and. That his tracks they saw.

Édé yáts'ítse,   yáts'ítse   úh éé,   tonht'in
Then everyone cried about it, everyone cried and hey, long ways

ats'edeh   úh. Mbeda ats'int'e édé mbekeeh wots'a'in
they moved and. For him   to be   then his tracks they saw

xónht'e édé edawodíh úh t'ahín andadeh,   úh
like that then he knew   and back   he went again, and

kek'éh,   úh kek'éh   at'in úh, dene t'áhge.
after them, and after them he is and, people he catches up with.

Édé łíónh dene eghon.   Dene eghon   Nóda   ju
Then all   people he killed. People he killed Cougar also

úh.
and.

145

I   xá'at'in   úh, Nózíen nechi, Nózíen nechi, ju.
That   he does that and, Skunk   big,   Skunk   big,   also.

Mbekeeh wots'a'in édé, dene   yá'ítse   úh héé, gáa
His tracks they saw   then, people they cried and hey, already

edu ts'eghedi'a igha   kughedi   t'áh.   Dene tonht'in
not   they live   [future] they thought therefore. People far

ts'ín   ats'et'in úh   goin níts'indeh xónht'e   éhsán   gáa,
towards they lived and there moving   that way   then   yes,

xéts'ejá   éhsán   yáts'ítse úh.
they did that then   they cried and.

Dene sóon netlon i   at'in éhsán. Tsá   ndadeh,
People then many   there were   then.   Beaver living,

tsá   ndadeh éhsán. I,   wóhdli éhsán tsá   kín
beaver lived   then.   That, cold   then   beaver cache

éhsán, tthinh t'áh yagiyínhshú   úh,   tsá   mbedage
then,   axe   with they cut it open and, beaver its den

ehsíin   tsá   k'ághendetah   éhsán. Nóghe   keeh
whatever is   beaver they looked for   then.   Wolverine   tracks

wots'a'in. Sóon ats'ejá   ínyá, "yuhaán,"   gáa
they saw.   Then it happened then, "come here,"   already

tonht'e ón   éé,   nechicho úh   kek'éh.
far   but hey, big one   and following.

Nóghe   gáa   kets'ín gheyah.   Úh   éhsán eyiá
Wolverine already toward   he was coming. And then   that

xónhén, xónhén ajá   éhsán. Éé!   ghedi   éhsán.
close,   close   it happened then.   Hey! they said then.

I   Nóghe   éhsán, "Éé! tlahzé   gheyał,"
That Wolverine then,   "Hey! brother-in-law is coming,"

yéhdi   ínyá. "Éé!   tlahzé,   tsá   k'ándetah."
he said to him then. "Hey! brother-in-law, beaver you look for."

Sóon Nozian ju   yéhdi   éhsán, gáa   yets'ín
Then Skunk   also   he said to him then,   already there

at'in   ínyá xónhén ningéd   úh   éhsán.
he was then   close   he came crawling and then.

Ndadendéhgé   úh   éhsán ketahín eledzi ts'edi.   I
He turned around and then   toward   spray   it is said. That

éhsán xáaje   sóon mbeyinhdleé łíónh Dene   déhtsin.
then   if he did that then his spray   all   people stinky.

I   t'áh   Dene t'andek'éh úh éhsán. I   éhsán
That because of people die   and then. That then

ndadendéhge úh sóon mbeché xóonlá,   se'e
he turned around and then his tail he raised [he did that], really

ya'ínli   igha   úh éhsán.
he sprayed [future] and then.

Nóghe   éhsán "t'ong"   wodi   i
Wolverine then   [spraying sound] he makes sound [Skunk] that

elé   éhsán,   yetsónék'é éhsán, xónht'e
where he urinates it must have been, his anus   then,   like that

éhsán yígé. Yígé   sóon se'e edegha   yuge   úh sóon,
then   he bit. He bit it then really real hard he bit it and then,

"Úú úú úú," éhdi   éhsán.
"Oo oo oo," he said then

Dene línt'ónh sóon mbets'ín déhya,   i   yohani
People all   then   toward him he went, that something

(tthunh ets'edi) satsóné nedééh, i   beeh ét'i t'áh,
(spear   called)   metal   long,   that knife like with,

i   úh éht'o t'áh ju úh, téht'o xúle. I   sóon
that and arrow with also and, gun   gone. That then

eyía xáat'in éhsán gáa   yedhéhxin, Noziencho. Úh
that like that that   already he killed him, Big Skunk. And

éhsán i Nóghe   éhsán yúgé   úh, "Úú, úú, úú,"
then that Wolverine then he bit him and, "Oo, oo, oo,"

éhdi   éhsán.   Diín   ndáts'in ts'ín   goin ts'ín
he said it must have been. Where wind   toward there toward

i   sóon. Jon xónht'i éhsán yedaege sóon,
that then. Here like that then he bit him and then,

xáajá   jon dahé.   Nozien ledzé mbek'eh
it happened like that here something. Skunk spray   on him

dahé ajá,   i   óon duh dendítl'édze ts'edi.   Úh
some it happened, that why now yellow   some say. And

k'uen   tsian   íin   sóon   tadéhtl'a éhsán.
groundhog worthless before and then he ran off then.

I   dene   úh éhsán, i   dene ehsíin, sóon,
That person and then,   that person that was, then,

línt'ónh nechá úh gáa, lahéindi xáatin, xáatin. I
all   big   and yes, all the time like that, like that. That

t'áh   dene   netlon   dhéhxe,   xódleh   ghedi   éhsán.
because   people   many   he killed,   let's do that   they said   then.

Dene   łínt'ónh   beeh,   beeh   t'áh   éhsán,   łínt'ónh   Nózien
People   all   knife,   knife   with   then,   all   Skunk

nechi   sóon   tagiyendint'á úh,   netsédle   úh   sóon,
big   then   they cut it up   and,   small   and   then,

yágiyeleh,   łínt'ónh.   Nózien   netsédláa   gha   di   éhsán
they threw it,   all.   Skunk   small   for   this   then

yágiyeleh,   łíónh,   łíónh   xéginlá   éhsán.   I,   i
they threw it,   all,   all   they did like that   then.   That,   that

gáa   úh   éhsán   dene   eyi   gáa   i   wots'inh
already   and   then   person   that   already   that   from there on

Nózien   nechi   xúle   igha.
Skunk   huge   gone   [future].

Wolverine, Giant Skunk, and Mountain Lion: Part Two

Úh   i   łíé   i   gáa   i   ét'é   ju.   Nóda   nechi   sóon
And   that   one   that   already   that   like   also.   Cat   big   then

mbekeeh   wots'a'in   k'awu   ju   sóon.   I   éhsán   dene
his tracks   they saw   again   also   then.   That   then   person

sóon   yekeeh   wa'in   sóon,   yekeeh   wa'in   sóon.   Eyi
then   its tracks   he saw it   then,   its tracks   he saw it   then.   That

óndedah   édé,   "Sek'éh   audeh   éhsín,"   kudi
he went home   then,   "Following me   it might   maybe, "   he thinks

éhsán   mbekeeh   ét'e   goin'á   niyá.   Ah   tl'a
then   his tracks   like   there   they went.   Snowshoe   back

xedadé   elin.   Mbedzihdé   xónht'i   ehłíi   eyi
moose antler   it was.   Caribou antler   like that   one that is   that

ah   di   ét'i,   di   ét'i,   ah   adłíi   sóon.
snowshoe   this   like,   this   like,   snowshoe   made like   then.

Eyiá   tsá   ndadeh,   i   ju   tsá   ndadeh.   Tsá
That one   beaver   living,   that   also   beaver   living.   Beaver

ekín   nechi   la   éhsán   ekín   ttheeh   ehteni,   ghanishí
cache   big   then   cache   in front of   ice,   they cut it open

eyiá   ínyá.   I   éhsán   k'elezonh   sa   ndá'áh   úh,   éhsán
that   then.   That   then   almost   sun   setting   and,   then

i   dene   níniya   éhsán.   Ínyá   tl'unh,   mbexehthéh   i
that   person   arrived   then.   Then   rope,   his pack   that

the'on   mbe'ahé   ju.   Mbe'éht'o ju   i
sitting there   his snowshoes also.   His arrows   also there

thela   éhsán i   xehthéh, mbexethéhé, t'áh éhsán
they were sitting then   that pack,   his pack,   with then

tl'a, éhsán.
well, then.

Eyi tsá   ndadeh i   éhsán tutah   teniya,
That beaver living   that then   in the water he went into,

tutah   teniya   lonh.   Xúle eduliné úh éhsán
in the water he went into [past].   Gone nothing   and then

i   xehthéh t'á nándeta ínyá eyi i   ts'ídoa, i
that pack   inside he looked then   that that child,   this

ét'ia   minlá,   minlá jon ts'ín, jon ts'ín
just like [small] his hand, his hand here up to, here up to

enúdlin   k'eingé thegon. I   éhsán, i   xónht'e édé,
undoubtedly bitten off dried.   That then,   that like that then,

tatlidi úh xónht'i éhsán, ege   elin mbetáhtheton. Úh
soup   and like that then,   spoon it was placed in there.   And

dene tl'a, jon ts'égu, ts'ídoa t'óyé, ts'ídoa
people well, here woman, child   breast, child

t'óyé   eyi xónht'i thegon i   ehdah
breast [from a nursing mother] that like that dried   that also

éhsán detahthehła sóon. Éé,   sóon dene   sóon
then   was put in there. then.   Hey, then person and then

oníya   ínyá   edu edayedíh ínyá.
he was frightened and then not he knows   and then.

Xoniá,   xoniá i   téeh,   téeh   ts'ín ínyá,
Suddenly, suddenly that in the water, in the water to   then,

"Non, non," éhdi   éhsán ll'unh xónlá.
"Here, here," he [Mountain Lion] said then   rope   he did that.

"Non!"   éhdi   xáaja.
"Here!"   he said it happened like that.

Téeh ts'ín xáaja   i   yinhchu úh   sóon,
Water into it happened that he caught it and then,

xéyínlá   i   tsá   nechi, tsá   łínt'ónh
he did like that that beaver big,   beaver all

edeindéhtl'un, tsá   sóon   łíónh xáinla éhsán.
wrapped,   beaver like that all   pulled out then.

Ts'e'in xadéhya   éhsán edege   i   yah
Outside   he [Mountain Lion] went then he shook that snow

tah, tu   yah   tah   ké'edeghel   úh   ju
on,   water   snow   on   he [Mountain Lion] rolled himself   and   also

at'in   éhsán.   Xáat'in,   edega   úh   éhsán.
he was   then.   It was like that,   he shook himself   and   then.

Di   jon   tl'a,   di   jon   di   ónket'i   di   xónht'i   la,
This   here   well,   these   here   these   two   this   like that,

kewonyenhén   ets'edi,   kewoyenhén   ets'edi,   xónht'i
someone's shadow   it's called,   someone's shadow   it's called,   like that

éhsán.   Tsá   netlon   éhsán   yahdíeh.
then.   Beaver   many   then   on top of the bank.

"Tsá   únda   ndóté,"   éhdi.
"Beaver   let's eat   let's sleep/camp,"   he [Mountain Lion] said.

Éhsán,   "Dúhden   ajá   édé   sets'ín   audeh,"
Then,   "This way   it happened   then   toward me   it might happen,"

kudi.
he [Wolverine] thought.

Éhsán,   "Sendatthéeh   tsá   łíé   dinghéh,"
Then,   "In front of me   beaver   one   you pack,"

éhdi,   tsá   ndéhtin   úh
he [Mountain Lion] said,   beaver   he [Wolverine] took   and

éhsán.
then.

I   deghelé   t'á   sóon   tsá   dahé   ninla
That   his [Wolverine's] pack   in   like that   beaver   some   he put

úh   éhsán   di   yendattheeh   sóon.   I   dechin   wónlin
and   then   that   in front of him   then.   That   tree   existed

ndetéh   igha   éhsán   yendattheeh   niya   éhsán,
you go to sleep   [future]   then   in front of him   he got up   then,

"Di   sóon   di   k'ándehta,"   úh
"This   then   this   I'm watching for,"   [Wolverine thought]   and

sóon.   Mbewonyenhén   wónlin   yets'ín,
like that.   His [Mountain Lion's] shadow   it was   toward him,

inhshi'etl'eh   úh   sóon   yandaítl'eh.
he made a false start   toward   and   then   he [Mountain Lion] jumped.

"Tl'a, dánet'in?"   yéhdi.
"Well,   what's with you?"   he [Wolverine] said to him.

"Se'ahé   la'edáa,   se'ahé   di   kónt'i
"My snowshoes   got caught,   my snowshoes   this   like

mbela'edáaka   i   t'áh   aht'in,"   éhdi.
it got caught   that   what happened   I am,"   [Mountain Lion] said.

Kets'ín   inhshi'etl'eh   ínyá.
Toward someone he made a false start towards then.

Gáa   k'elazonh detah   xáaja   éhsán. Éé!
Already almost   in the bush like that then.   Hey!

ndákedihthon   wónjonh se'e   deghade k'etah,   i
he chased around good   really   hard   in the willows, that

éhsán   i   xehthéh ehdah   ondéhla.   Éhsán
then   that pack   that too he [Wolverine] threw away. Then

dechin, dechin, dechin dzelonh (ah)   xónht'i sóon,
tree,   tree,   tree   up high (snowshoes) like that then,

i   dene   di xónht'i ah   t'áh at'in
that person [Wolverine] that like that snowshoes with he was

éhsán.
then.

Di   ah   xónht'i yátl'eh. Úh   goin   sóon
Those snowshoes like that he jumps. And that way then

se'e   ke'in,   se'e   ke'in,   sóon edin ju
exactly mimicked, exactly mimicked, then   him   also

ah,   mbedzihdé ah,   adlíi sóon. Nódacho
snowshoes, caribou antlers snowshoes, made then.   Mountain Lion

úh   dechin dzelonh xónht'i, xónht'i sóon. I   dene
and   tree   top   like that, like that and then. That person

sé'edeghae ya'ítl'eh sóon.   Ah,   mbe'ahé,
really hard   jumps   and then. Snowshoes, his snowshoes,

xónht'i xéyínlá   éhsán yinkah déhtl'a.
like that he [Mountain Lion] did like that then   through it he ran.

Úh sóon i Nódacho   ju gúhyeh ajá   ínyá,
And then that Mountain Lion also that way it happened then,

mbe'ahé   telah   ajá,   dendítthé   yuéhdétthie
his snowshoes on the side it happened, he got hung up upside down

éhsán.   Éé,   sóon,   éé,   tsá   undá íin.
it must have been. Hey, like that, hey, beaver he ate before.

"Nohsinhte, nohsinhte," éhdi   sóon
"Get me down, get me down," he [Mountain Lion] said and then

i   dene   sóon Nódacho   dendítthé   úh sóon.
that person then Mountain Lion hanging down and then.

Eyi kón onlá   got'ónh mbéhkódikonhin
That fire he [Wolverine] made at that time matches

ju   xúle   úh. Éé tl'o   úh xónht'i adlíi. Eyi
also nothing and. Just grass and like that he made. Those

egháddhé,   egháddhé   ets'edi,   di   ét'i   egháddhé.
shavings,   shavings   they're called, this same as shavings.

Eyi kón,   kón, kón ts'ek'ali ets'edi,   tthe   sóon
That fire,   fire, fire flint   it's called, stone then

xéyeh'in   [gesturing] ínyá. Kón   adeh   sóon, kón
he does that [gesturing] then. Fire happened then, fire

dedéhk'ón   éhsán.
light up   then.

Eyi Nódacho   sóon dénida.   Mbe'ahé   ónket'i
That Mountain Lion then hanging. His snowshoes two

onht'e úh   yuehdéhtthé úh . . . . "Hee! segóhdli, uu!
two   and upside down and. . . . "Hey! I'm cold, oo!

uu! uu!" ndadedí   úh   sóon.
oo! oo!" was saying and then.

I   dene   sóon mbechina   se'e   xónht'e
That person [Wolverine] then at the base really like that

éhsán kón déhk'ón   úh eyi éhsán at'in   éhsán. Úh
then   fire he started fire and that then   he was then.   And

eyi tsá łíé nidínhtín éhsán, tsá   ya'it'a   úh
that beaver one he took   then,   beaver he butchered and

éhsán, tsátthén   det'ééh.
then,   beaver meat   he cooked for himself.   **Tsátthén**
                                                 Beaver meat

det'ééh   úh   sóon etthi   úh   sóon.
he cooked for himself and then   he was eating and then.

"Hee! uu! uu!" ndadedí   xoniá.   Edu
"Hey! oo! oo! " he [Mountain Lion] was saying suddenly. Not

ndaidah dúhden   wots'inh, elé,   elédz,   úh
moving   from here   from,   he urinated, he urinated, and

dúhden,   dúhden   yuhín   xónht'i. Mbetthítáhín tu
from here, from here   upside down like that. Top of his head water

ndát'eh. Ínyá   xoniá   edu naidah úh   sóon
dripping. And then   suddenly not moving and then

yueh   xónht'e sóon. Mbedzíaten úh   sóon.
upside down like that then. He froze   and then.

I   dene   ehsíin   sóon gáa, yek'án̲detah
That person [Wolverine] that was then yes, he was watching

úh   sóon,   gáa, yek'án̲detah. Xoni   dahani
and then,   yes, he was watching. Maybe others

mbechidle   egóhó   gik'éh   ajá édé, xoni
his [Mountain Lion's] brothers possibly they follow came then, maybe

sóon ndats'edeh ehsóon   kudi   t'áh éhsán.
then   meet up   must have been he was thinking with then.

Eyi i   sóon gáa, se'e ehten, ehten úh sóon. I
That that then yes, really frozen, frozen and then. That

ju éhsán dechin, dechin t'áh éhsán, eyi ye'ahé
too then   stick,   stick   with then,   that his snowshoes

xéyeh'in   éhsán. Eyi Nódacho   ndádéhtth'e.
he was doing like that then.   That Mountain Lion he fell.

Ehten úh sóon,
Froze and then.

Eyi táyedehshi,   táyedehshi   eyi ju netsédláa
That he was cutting it up, he was cutting it up that too small

úh ayínlá. Úh łínt'ónh sóon, Nozien k'ehín łíónh
and he did. And all   then,   Skunk   way   all

ónyedéhla   sóon. I   úh sóon. I
he threw them away then. That and then.   That

dene   ehsíin sóon tadéhtl'a.
person [Wolverine] that is then ran away.

Tadéhtl'a úh éhsán di   mbek'ehdue xónht'i éhsán.
He ran away and then   this his jacket like that then.

"Uuwii!" éhdi   éhsán. Yahk'eh   xéyeh'in. Yahk'eh
"Oo wee!" he said then.   On the snow   he did that. On the snow

xéyeh'in   ínyá, ee, wónjon edeghah. Ndáts'e. Yah
he did that then, hey, well   really hard. Windy.   Snow

netlon sóon yah xádéhton wots'ín. Wohteh yah
lots   then snow that deep up to.   Really snow

ajá   ndáts'in t'áh Nódacho   ah   t'áh
happened   wind   with Mountain Lion snowshoes with

úhya   iin   mbekeeh xúle. Úh eyi dene   ju
he passed before his tracks gone. And that person also

tadéhtl'a   úh tadéhtl'a   Dene, Nódacho,   gáa,
he ran away and he ran away. Person, Mountain Lion, yes,

tandéhtth'e. Úh Nódacho   mbekeeh eddha,
he died.   And Mountain Lion his tracks snowed in,

mbekeeh eddha   úh, ndátsihtlah úh, mbekeeh edu
his tracks snowed in and, blizzard   and, his tracks not

kíodat'in.
visible.

Mendajíné sóon yek'éh   déhyeh, édón   edu
His relatives then following him he went, no matter not

edayedíh. **Úh** **eyi** **ju** **netsédle** **łínt'ónh** **ayínlá** **eyi**
he knows. And that also small   all   he made then

wots'ín **óon** **edu** **móndeji.** **Úh** **xattheeh** **la** **i** **Nóda**
from   then   not dangerous. And originally   that Cat

nechíi **la** **dene** **k'ésín** **ndake'edeh'eni,**
big   people way   tracker [follows tracks, curious]

ndake'edeh'eni **uye.** **Ts'edi** **gáa,** **xónht'e.**
tracker   he was called. It is said yes, like that.

6 The Man Who Sought a Song

Dene mbetá éhsán, tl'a, ndéét'c, shin kandeda
Person his father it must have been, well, like you, song going for

ayínhthén, mbetá "shin kaneyah." Tl'a, kawodi
he was made to, his father "song you go for." Well, sounding

Dene Dháa kawodi. Godahi i t'áh, ghedi
Dene Dháa sounding. Something that because of, living

kałéts'et'íi. Eyi t'áh éhsán mbetá yéhdi úh
for helping each other. That with then his father he said and

sóon.
then.

Di xáicho t'ónh wots'inh éhsán, godah
This this big before from it must have been, somewhere

ts'ín k'íadah úh ayínhthén, mbetá éhsán. Héé,
toward he went and he made him, his father then. Hey,

mbedonhxá dendéht'ehzi cho, (i ndét'i cho), úh
his beard it became black big, (that like you big), and

ajá ts'ín éhsán, gáa xódé.
it happened until then, already happening.

Mbetá gugáh nonja, mbetá gugáh
His father with them he came back, his father with them

nonja.
he came back.

"Sechuen, ni elin anet'in?" yéhdi.
"My son, you it is you are?" he said to him.

"Áán," éhdi.
"Yes," he [the son] said.

"Úh júh?" mbetá yéhdi éhsán.
"And what else?" his father said to him it must have been.

"Élính, edu edahdíh edulin. Sin gua
"I'm not sure, not I know nothing. Me a little

godeh'in," mbetá yéhdi.
I saw something," his father he said to him [he said to his father].

"Edulin   wónlin   łínt'ónh,"   éhdi.
"Nothing   exists   all,"   he said.

"Úh dóndih   úh sóon aht'e éhsín?"
"And what's the matter with and then I am   maybe?"

mbetá   yéhdi.
his father said to him.

"Yéh   xónht'i   mo   tuhtl'ah   yeh ts'égu ghinlé
"There like that mother by the door with woman was

ehsíin.   Yeh   níniya   ghinlé ehsíin éhsán. Mo
she was.   There he was born before she was then.   Mother's

ké   ch'ilé,   di   xónht'i ke   dháa   k'eh
moccasins ragged,   this like that moccasins ordinary on

éhsán.   I   nítthínit'áh,"   mbetá   yéhdi   úh   sóon.
then.   That sleep on them," his father he said and then.

Detá   gugáh   nandéhtin   éhsán. Mo   ké
His parents   with them   he slept again then.   Mother's moccasins

k'eh   jon níthíeton   agiyínlá.   Mbetá   yéhdi
on   here he laid his head on they made him. His father said to him

éhsán. Mbetá   ju,   mo   ké   ch'iláa   mbek'eh
then.   His father also, mother's moccasins ragged   on it

níatthinit'ah,   yéhdi   úh. Mo
he slept on again, he said and. Mother

ghindá k'é   éhsán, yi'ónéh   di
where she sat/where she gave birth then,   off to the side these

dechin yi'ónéh   ndadéhlá   úh   éhsán
sticks   off to the side they were laid out and then.

"Nintéh,"   mbetá   yéhdi.   Mo
"Go to sleep," his father said to him. Mother

ghinda k'é   éhsán. Mbeké   ch'iláa
where she sat/where she gave birth then.   Her moccasins ragged/small

k'eh   nítthínt'on   ayínlá   sóon
on   he laid his head he [his father] made him then

nandéhtin.
he went to sleep again.

"Sechuen, na'iht'óyí   tl'onh k'ahu   dechintáhín
"My son,   breastfeed again after   again   in the bush

ndadindah. Kíi kánet'e   anet'e édé   kíi, wonlin
go again.   Just you are like that you are then just, something

dhé kats'e'áhi ehłíi unht'e   édé
liver taken out   it is   you would be like [future] then

dágot'e?   **Ye**   **t'áh**   **kededundi,"**   **mbetá**
what would happen?   What   with   look after himself,"   his father

yéhdi   **úh**   **éhsán.**
said to him   and   then.

    "Áán,"   **éhdi**   **éhsán.**
"Yes,"   he [the son] said   then.

    (Mbetá),   **mo**   **mbet'óyé**   **yon'áa,**   **mbedonhghácho**
(His father),   mother   her breasts   old/small,   his big beard

díjadhi   **éhsán**   **(ndéét'e)**   **ehkegucho**   **ehłíi**
blond [light]   then   (like you)   big young man   being like

mbedonhghácho ajái   **wots'ín,**   **éhsán**   **dechintah**
his big beard   came to be   until,   then   in the bush

at'in. . . .
he was. . . .

    Edulin   **wónlin**   **éhsán.**   **"Xénedeh,"**   **mo**   **yéhdi**
Nothing   was   then.   "Do this,"   mother   she said to him

i   **t'áh.**   **Mbetá**   **yéhdi**   **i**   **t'áh**   **éhsán.**
that   because of.   His father   he said to him   that   because   then.

Mo   **ehdah**   **nda'eté.**   **Mo**   **ké**   **k'eh**
Mother   where she sat   he slept again.   Mother   moccasins   on

ndatthíe'ón.   **I**   **t'áh**   **i**   **i**   **sóon**   **na'inhlúnh**
he slept again.   That   because of   that   that   then   he sucked again

úh   **ayínlá,**   **tl'a,**   **k'ahju.**   **I**   **t'áh**   **éhsán,**   **i**
and   he was,   well,   again.   That   because of   then,   that

naint'ó   **úh**   **ayínlá**   **i**   **tl'onh**   **úh**   **éhsán.**
sucking again   and   he did   that   after   and   then.

    "Sechuen, kónt'e úh   **wonlin**   **ndadintl'a.**   **K'ahju**
"My son,   like that   and   something   you go again.   Again

ndasont'in   **dánet'in?"**   **ka**   **mbetá**   **éhdi**   **úh**   **sóon.**
you see me   how are you?"   for   his father   said   and   then.

    K'awu   **dechintahín ndadéhja**   **t'onh**   **níadét'in.**
Again   in the bush   he went back to   after   he was gone back.

Edu se'e   **tonht'e**   **nda'úhda;**   **k'awu**   **níanonja.**
Not   really   far/long   he is gone again;   again   he came back.

    "Úh   **júh?"**   **mbetá**   **yéhdi.**
"And   what?"   his father   said to him.

    Ndutíin   **wok'ándeta**   **úh**   **sóon**   **gáa,**   **edunkaa**
Sleeping [future]   he was looking for   and   then   yes,   hardly

endotéen.   **Kin**   **wonlin,**   **kin**   **ninkuhlin**   **úh**
he'll sleep there.   Just   something,   someone   he was expecting   and

sóon. Gáa   kíi   ndetéh   gha   edu   adeh
then.   Already just   before sleeping [future] not   try

eyónht'e,   gáa,   k'íadeh.   Gáa,   se'e
it seems like, yes,   he was walking around. Yes,   really

tenihxe,   gáa,   xetl'eeh tadienh éhsán, gheyal   ínyá.
getting late, yes,   night   middle   then,   he was going   then.

Jon   uhshiné ónk'et'i cho   náin'a   tl'a,   inhgagáh
Here   stumps   two   big   were standing well,   together

náicho   ehłíé,   xónht'i éhsán
where it was grown out   that kind, like that   then

náin'a.   Mbegeze   nítthíonht'áh   nutéh
were standing. Between them he lay down between   he wanted to sleep

sóon kudi.   Yegeze   nítthít'on   éhsán.
then   he wanted. Between them he lay down   then.

Ndéhtin,   gáa,   atthée   tl'onh éhsán. Ndéhtin.
He went to sleep,   yes,   he ate   after   then.   He was sleeping.

Gáa, dejiháa   nínihtthu k'eh éhsán, elian
Yes,   his little mitts   he placed   on   then,   spruce branches

ndadezíhí   k'eh ndéhtin   ínyá. I   éhsán, eyi
that he broke on   he slept   then.   That   then,   those

uhshinécho china ndéhtin. Úh   gáa,   se'e   sa   xádadeh
big stumps   base   he slept.   And yes,   really sun   setting

úh.
and.

"Jon, yudi!"   yéhdi,   uhshiné yéhdi.
"Here,   up here!" it said to him, stump   it said.

Ndáidlo   mbeyí   ededéhdhe, kón ts'ín   ni'íyah
He fainted away   his breath   stopped,   fire   toward   he got up

ínyá mbeyí   ededéhdhe. Yéh   ndáitth'ed úh   sóon.
then   his breath stopped.   There he fell   and   then.

Dáṇdéhthah eyi   ghinda lon   éhsán.   Nía'íjá.
How long   there he was   [past] it must have been. He got up.

I   t'áh   éhsán i,   yéh ndáitth'e úh   sóon
That   because of   then   that,   there he fell   and   then

ndahtsodadi   úh   éhsán.
he came to [woke] and   then.

Gáa, xódé   nia'íja   sóon, "Héé, kagot'in
Yes,   already he got up then,   "Hey,   vision

ónt'enya,"   teé   adi,   "máhsi.   Setá
things happen like that,"   father said,   "thank you. My father

éhtsonhtl'adinh, edu   nindhain dehtl'ade eguh," úh
I'll visit,   not   far   I went   since,"   and

kudi   éhsán. Mbetá   sóon   yéhdi. "Teé   kaséhdi
he thought then.   His father then   he said. "Father he said to me

úh   teeh   k'ont'uh ot'uh   a'adi
and carefully   like this that's how it is that's what he meant

mbets'onhtl'ah," sóon kudi   éhsán. Atthéedi tl'onh
I'll visit him,"   then he thought then.   He ate   after

éhsán dctá   ts'ín andéhja.   Mbctá   dadi   éhsán.
then   his father to   came back to. His father he told then.

"Teé,   uhshiné ndéehjidi i   t'áh   kíi
"Father, stump   I'm scared that because of just

dukandoteh   i   t'áh   eyi dechin chinah
how would he sleep that because of that tree   base

nítthíndeht'on.   Ndodúgal   úh   uhshiné
I laid my head down. When the sun is coming up and stump

sets'ín wodeh. I   t'áh   seyi   ededéhdhe lon
to me   it spoke. That because of my breath   stopped   [past]

úh   se'e   edu ka   ts'enanehdhe. Kónt'i ele   adindi,"
and really   not yet   I woke up again. Like that was it you said,"

sóon detá   ts'ín éhdi.
then   his father to   he said.

"Éé, sechuen, edu kádindi.   Kaa   kut'a. Gots'inh
"Hey, my son,   not you say that. Already quit.   About that

edu   sendaédondí   ele.   Kíi gots'ín   zonh   aut'e
don't say anything to me   not.   Just about that only   it will be

édé,"   mbetá   yéhdi   ínyá. "Áán, tl'a, se'e
then,"   his father he said to him   then.   "Yes, well, really

guk'ánita   edu inhłáhdinh zonh," sóon mbetá
look for purpose not one place   only," then   his father

yéhdi   úh   éhsán.
he said to him   and then.

Yéh   k'ahju ndadéhja, k'ahju ndadéhja   úh   sóon.
There again he went,   again he went back and   then.

Gáa, gheyah   gheyal   ínyá. Éé, ts'enida
Yes,   he was going he was going then.   Hey, where people passed

cho   líin   sóon kek'éh gheyah.   Joan denáa
big/many   that was then after it he was going. Here small people

wolíi cho.   Héé, dene   wolíi ndadeh.   I   éhsán
lots   many. Hey, people lots   living.   That then

konhnái'á   éhsán.   Kegáh   kóntahniyah   éhsán, kegáh
he came upon then.   With them   he was visiting   then,   with them

theda úh.
he sat and.

"I   dene   dat'in   líin   at'in   etundét'ine,
"That person what doing was before he is   he is pitiful,

mba'edahtsi   sóon,"   kólaa   líi   kéhdi
give him something to eat then,"   old man same   he said to them

éhsán.
then.

Gigha   etthén   théht'ee.   I   ts'éu   líé   sóon   yets'ín
For him meat   they cooked. That woman one   then   to him

újon   éhsán, yegha   etthén   théht'ee   úh sóon
good   then,   for him meat   she cooked and then

yatáhthe'on. Tleh   ehdah, xónht'i   xeda   tlehé   xónht'i
put out.   Grease   too,   like that moose grease like that

tené,   ehdah sóon yenihchu   úh éhsán.
hardened/frozen, too   then   she gave him some and then.

Atthéed úh. "Edu dahé xáhnidunt'ah ele. Línt'ónh
He ate   and. "Not some store away   not. All

aneleh," giyéhdi   úh sóon. I   etthén
you do,"   they said to him and then. That meat

mbets'enihchu   i   cho   línt'ónh ghedéhtthe éhsán.
that they gave to him that big/much all   he ate   then.

"Edu kóntahínduntl'a ele. Kíi jon   anet'in," giyéhdi
"Not you go visiting   not. Just here you are,"   they said to him

éhsán.
then.

I   gugáh   ghinte éhsán. Xetl'inh   xetl'íonh k'achu
There with them he slept then.   Tomorrow morning   again

giyénihchu   úh éhsán. Dene   líé i   gohndáithahdi
they gave him some and then.   Person one there came upon them

sóon.
then.

Giyéhdi,   "Dónt'e   líin   aunet'e   etundet'ine?
He said to them, "Whatever it is before how was he   pitiful?

Kíi t'inthen igha   theda líin.   Dát'in   líin   at'in?
Just poor   [future] he sits before. What is this before he is?

Táuts'edóshul édé.   Mbet'á   nóts'edéhli wolé.
Cut him open   then. Inside him urinating   it will be.

Ts'índáts'eya   édé   mbet'áin zonh,
Where you are going outside [to urinate] then inside him only,

mbets'ín zonh ats'ut'ín," ghedi   éhsán.
to him   only   you go,"   they said then.

   Goín   tágiyedéhshídli cho   úh. Táudéh'í
   There they cut him open awful and. Path to village or river banks

i   éhsán, kíi mbet'á   łón   dazedl i   cho   mbet'á
that then,   just inside him all   icy   that awful inside

ndáts'edeh,   ndáts'edeh. Héé, mbegha k'íodeke igha
him they went, they went.   Hey,   for him   vision   [future]

éhsán. Ambewo'inh   éhsán at'in éhsán. I   mbet'áin
then.   That is why that was then   it was then.   That inside him

zonh ts'inh ndats'edel,   úh   sóon dódéhthah
only   out   they were going, and then   quite a while living

éhsán, gáa, łíé sa   ndáts'edeh   éhsán.
then,   yes, one month they were living then.

   Tínts'enidah   éhsán, kíi   dene   xónht'e éhsán.
   They started to move then,   just person like that then.

I   ts'éu łíé sóon yek'ehdiya   éhsán. "Xoni   se'e
That girl   one then   by him she went then.   "Suddenly   really

ndahjá   édé," kudi   éhsán. Kíi   ke
he heals again then," she thought then.   Just moccasins

yaonlá.   Héé, ech'oh t'áh ke   újon   yaonlá
she made for him.   Hey,   quills   with moccasins good   she made

éhsán! I   dechin yegáh   nái'ai   di   yelá
then!   That tree   beside him standing this its branch

k'eyinhshi úh   yedátthic,   i   ke   tl'unhén t'áh
she cut off and its branches, that moccasin lace   with

sóon yegáh   ke   dadínla,   dahthela.   Úh
then   with him moccasins she hung up, she hung them up. And

k'ihdue ju. K'ihdue ju   onlá,   tl'a, eyi et'adhi
jacket   too. Jacket   also she made, well, that tanned hide

éhsán, ts'et'ai adlíi ju   éhsán yegáh   dadínhtthú
then,   shirtlike made also then   beside him she hung it

éhsán. Yegáh dídahyéhla úh   sóon. Tonht'in
then.   By him   she hung it and then.   For a long time

yegáh   dahyindá úh   sóon. Gáa   ts'edéhde ehsíin
beside him she sat   and then.   Already leaving   they were

óon, gáa, tonht'i   íin   yegáh   ghinda   i   tl'onh
even, yes, for a long time before beside him she sat   that after

éhsán.
then.

Gáa,   tínts'enida   ehsíin.   "Seyéhkáts'ededeh
Yes,   starting to move camp   after then.   "They're outdistancing me

ehsóon   wondejid   on,   aht'e,"   kudi   éhsán.
in case   frightening   even though,   I am,"   she thought   then.

Gáa,   gulaa   éhsín   guk'eh   déhya   úh   sóon   héé,
Yes,   finished   maybe   after them   she went   and   then   hey,

mbadzáhdáawónht'e.   "Etundet'iné   óon   ats'inlá,"
she was sad.   "Pitiful   even though   they've done,"

kudi,   yeghon   ndáidindhé.   Gáa,   yeghon
she thought,   about him   she was thinking.   Yes,   about him

náidindhe   óon   sóon, gáa, kek'éh   déhya.
she was thinking   even though   then,   yes,   after them   she went.

Yegáh   yéhadeh,   yegáh   dahyéhla   úh   sóon,   gáa,
Beside him   go with,   beside him   she hung   and   then,   yes,

déhya.
she went.

Xoniá,   gáa, tonht'e   gua   déhxedl   úh,
Suddenly,   yes,   far   a little   getting late   and,

"du du du du,"   gaa,   edítth'e   i   ghonh   éhsán.
[pitter patter sound]   yes,   he heard   that   because of   then.

I   dot   wodi.   Ndáudhetth'eni   edhin   ehsán.
That   pattering   sounded.   Something's sounding   even like   then.

"Séht'in, ni   tl'a,   wonlin   ts'eláa   ehsíin,
"Like me,   you   well,yes,   something   filth/contamination   that is,

łínt'ónh   ndets'ín   nídé'inhín   anet'e.   Wonlin   ts'eláa
all   to you   that goes to you   you are.   Something   strange

ehsíin   ndebé   t'á   ndets'ín   nídé'inh   i   anet'e.
that is   your stomach   in it   to you   toward you   that   you are.

Séht'e ni   tl'a,   wonlin   ts'eláa   éhsán   anelehí
Like me   you   well,   something   filth/contamination   then   that you

anet'e,"   úh   Nógha   ts'ín   éhdi.   Nóghe   ts'ín
do   you are,"   and   Wolverine   to   he said.   Wolverine   to

éhdi.   Nóghe,   dene   elin   t'ónh   éhsán.
he said.   Wolverine,   person   he was   before   then.

Éé,   yedhondetl'eh   edhin.   Áán,   yedhondetl'eh
Hey,   he ran around him   sounds like.   Yes,   he ran around him

edhin   úh   ejin   úh   yedhondetl'eh   úh   éhsán.
sounds like   and   while singing   and   he ran around him   and   then.

Xoniá   **"ghans, ghans,"**   **éhdi**   **i**   **tu**   **cho**   **úh.**
Suddenly   [chewing sound],   he said   that   water   awful   and.

Łínt'ónh   **yet'á**   **xáinghaz**   **úh,**   **mbet'á**
All   inside him   he gnawed it out   and,   inside him

ts'inhdahts'eyi   **i**   **cho**   **ehsíin,**   **łínt'ónh**   **xáingheh**
urinated   that   awful   that was,   all   he gnawed out

úh. Yebét'á   **yet'á**   **yedzéet'á**   **ehdah**
and. Inside his stomach   inside him   inside his heart   also

łínt'ónh   **yinhtthe,**   **edulin mbet'á**   **úh**   **ayínlá**   **úh.**
all   he licked,   nothing   inside him   and   he made   and.

  "Kont'úh   **ni**   **dáunleh?"**   **sóon**   **yéhdi**
  "Like that   you   what are you going to do?"   then   he said to him

éhsán. I   **Ts'iuné,**   **Nóghe**   **úh**   **Ts'iuné,**   **Ts'iuné**
then.   That   Wolf,   Wolverine   and   Wolf,   Wolf

éhsán.
then.

  Yegha   **yechontth'ené**   **inhts'ín**   **xénondla**   **éhsán. Yedazé**
  For him   his ribs   together   seated then   then.   His spit

t'áh éhsán yek'éh úh   **xéyínlá.**   **Yek'ínhín**   **ndadeyoł**
with   then   on him   and   he did like that.   In his way   he blew on

úh   **gáa,**   **i**   **ju**   **ayínlá**   **úh**   **sóon.**
and   yes,   that   also   he did   and   then.

  Gitthídíé   **nínihdí.**   **Níaíjá**   **sóon.**   **"I**
  He was sitting up   they pushed him up.   He stood up   then.   "That

ke   **duhthela éhsán, i**   **tádin'é,"**   **giyéhdi.**
moccasins   hanging   then,   that   you put on,"   they said to him.

Gigáh   **ke**   **ninila.**   **Ke**   **tagiycdin'é,**
By the   moccasins   he put.   Moccasins   they made him put on,

k'ehdue ju   **l'ón-ejah. Agiyínlá**   **újon, níagiyedénitl'un**
coat   also   he put on.   They made him   well,   they dressed him up

éhsán. "Kíi   **jon anet'in. Jon**   **theneda**   **gua**   **úh**   **jon**
then.   "Just   here you stay.   Here   you sit   a while   and   here

gheneda   **édé. Łahdéh**   **jon gheneda édé ndahk'éh**
you sit here   then. For a while   here   you sit   then   after us

donya. Úh   **ts'ído**   **ndeda**   **etthén**   **aguleh**   **éhsín.**
you go.   And   children   for you   food   they will make   maybe.

Ndahk'éh   **duntl'a,"**   **giyéhdi**   **éhsán.**
After us   you go,"   they said to him   then.

  Gáa, gidadéht'a   **t'ónh Nóghe**   **ju**   **úh. Gáa,**
  Yes,   they went ahead of him   before   Wolverine   too   and.   Yes,

Ts'iuné juh ét'e   ghedéht'a   éhsán. Gáa   eyi   łíé
Wolf   also the same they both left then.   Already that   one

xetl'ee ait'in   tl'onh éhsán. Gáa, xódé   guk'éh
night   he was there after   then.   Yes, already after them

déhya   úh. Éé, yídeeha yída   ke   edin
he went and. Hey, ahead   yonder moccasins him

mbaxónht'e   éhsán. Yída   kíi   wohk'ón   i   cho
for him like that   then.   Yonder just camping place that big

inhtadáanh.   Nóghe   ju   yetadáanh ndághinte
across from each other. Wolverine also across from he slept again

lóon, eghedin ju. I   tadáanh,   kúan wocho wóh'on
then, them   too. It across from, tipi   big   was located

éhsán   kíi etth'ené wodle   cho dahdínlá.
then   just bone   broken   big scattered.

"Ndeda etthén ní'ets'edintse, i   tl'a, ts'ído, tl'a,
"For you meat   they left,   and well, children, well,

edu dene eghinht'e úh. Yundahéh gua   dahthe'on édé
not people they were   and. Above   a little put up   then

náo'áh   ededunzí   úh wonk'áh," giyéhdi
take it down cook for yourself and you will eat," they said to him

éhsán.
then.

Gida   etth'ené k'é'eghenihxótli ju   éhsán. Gida
For him   bone   they broke it   also then.   For him

yídahúh dahthe'on. Gida   ni'eghenihchú.   Gida
up above they put up. For him they gave him some. For him

dechin k'eh dahgiyéh'on. Éé, ekín
tree   on   they put up.   Hey, cache [depending on]

ewoh   ndats'edeh   cho líin.   Mbeghá
for that reason they were living big before. For that purpose

xónht'e   sóon, i   níghenida lonh.
it was like that then,   there they camped then.

Ts'iuné wonlin xeda wónihthedi
Wolf   some   moose passed by where they had camped

k'íadheh,   k'é   wónlin úh. Tat'i cho dzí'eghenih'ál
he was chasing, place were   and. Three big   they killed

íin   éhsán thela   éhsán. Gitth'ené kíi mbetth'ené
before then   they were there then.   Their bones just its bones

zonh dahdínlá. Inhtahdáanh kúan wocho wóh'on   úh
only   he put up. Across from   tipi   big   was located and

éhsán. Di   etthénáa   mbeda   dahts'u'áh   éhsín
then.   That small amount of meat for him put up for him maybe

ts'edi   kaa éhsán. Woni'íi   k'én̠detah   ínyá
they said for then.   Where the trail is he looked around then

etthén dahthe'on   éhsán.
meat   was hanging then.

Kón déhk'on   éhsán. I   etthén en̠dáedatthé
Fire he started fire then.   That meat he skewered and cooked

úh   sóon. Gáa, eyi etthén ghetthédi i   tl'oanh. Gáa,
and then. Yes, that meat that he ate that after a little. Yes,

eyi etthén ghetthédi tl'onh éhsán k'ahju, k'ahju éhsán.
that meat he ate after then again, again then.

Nóghe   k'ahju yeghonh noetl'a   éhsán. "Konht'úh
Wolverine again upon him he came back then.   "Like that

yéh   dentl'a   gáa, yéh ts'enidáa   kek'éh
there you go over there yes, there someone is camping after them

niyah úh. Dúhden k'ék'edheh   ts'inh, sa
you go and. This way on the side [along the trees] along, sun

xá'áh ts'inh. Gáa, gacho   tíoden̠dáwół éhsíin.
rising from side. Yes, big spruce bent down whichever is.

I   nódehgáhi goin ts'ín úhtl'a. I   t'áh   i
That fisher there toward it ran. That because of that

ekoín ts'ín uht'íen úhtl'a, nódehgáhi úhtl'a édé, i
that way to marten ran, fisher ran then, that

k'éh tíduntl'a,"   sóon giyéhdi   éhsán.
after you start going," then they said to him then.

Goin déhya íin,   tl'adah,   gacho   táuden̠dáwół
There he went before, edge [of cliff], big spruce bent over

úh éhsán. Uht'íen kuetl'a lonh úh xóndéhtl'a
and then. Marten went in must be and he went out

lonh   úh k'ahju oneh ndadéhtl'a.
must have and again away he [marten] ran back.

I   kuehín wok'án̠dehta   ínyá, wonlin
That inside he [man] was looking then, animal [bear]

yek'án̠dehta   két'e sóon, kuehín wok'án̠dehta.
[bear] looking at him as if then, inside he was looking.

K'etthít'ah   úh yek'án̠deta   úh sóon.
Moving his head around and it was looking at him and then.

Yéht'ah   kuehín, yuht'ah i   t'áh,   yéht'ah
He shot it with arrow inside, he shot it that because, he shot it

etah   t'áh   yuht'ah.   Úh   sóon   xáiyeh-   nekínhlin
arrow   with   he shot it.   And then   he tried to pull out   heavy

t'áh   xáiyehtéh   igha   endádla   úh   sóon,   xáyedinhdi
to   pulled out   [future]   tired   and then,   he pulled out [paw]

úh   sóon.   Yinlá   zonh   kéts'enit'a   úh   sóon.   Minlá
and then.   Its paw   only   someone cut it off   and then.   Its paw

zonh   k'enit'a   sóon.   Deghelé   t'á   i   sah,   deghelé   t'á
only   he cut off   then.   His pack   in   that   bear,   his pack   in

yin'on.
he put it in.

   Gáa,   kek'éh   gheyah   úh   edu   se'e   tonht'i   déhya
   Yes,   after them   he went   and   not   really   far   he went

inya.   Éé,   k'awu   ínyá   ndághedéh   íin
then.   Hey,   again   then   where they were living   before

ndághedéh   i   cho.   Tl'a,   yéha   kíi   dechin   me
they were living   that   big.   Well,   there   just   stick   lean-to

zonh   éhsán.   Kónhnáinyá.   Gáa,   ketáhtheyá   úh
only   then.   He ran into somebody.   Yes,   he came up to them   and

sóon,   i   kólaa   yets'ín   újon   úh   sóon,   xehtl'ah
then,   that   old man   to him   he was nice   and   then,   far end

ndadeh   lonh   éhsán.   "Kíi   jon   segáh,   kíi   jon   segáh
he lives   must be   then.   "Just   here   with me,   just   here   with me

nitéh.   Kíi   jon   sian   zonh   aht'e   úh   dzahagút'eh.
you sleep.   Just   here   little me   only   I am   and   it's no good.

Ndecha   tíots'énitthé   úh,   héé,   sadzahagút'eh   ínyá.
Because of you   they left camp   and,   hey,   I'm sad   then.

Héé,   ni   tl'a,   anet'in   ehxondih."   Kegáh   níniya
Hey,   you   well,   you are   maybe."   With someone   he arrived

éhsán,   i   sah   inlá   sóon   xáin'on.
then,   that   bear   paw   then   he took out.

   "Ehtsée,   di   sah   inlá   dinzí.   Óhchudékon
   "Grandfather,   this   bear   paw   you cook.   I want to take out [bear]

nekinhlin   t'ah   edu   ahłeh   éyonht'e."   Sah   inlá   sóon
heavy   that's why   not   I do   unable to."   Bear   paw   then

kanin'on   xónht'e   ts'et'eeh.
he gave it away   like that   it was cooked.

   Mendá'ets'elúh   úh   ts'eht'ee   édé.   "Edulin   mbets'ín
   Hanging on a string   and   cooking   then.   "Nothing   to him

ndedhá   wo'ín,"   giyéhdi.   "Edu
your mouth   see,"   they said to him [Wolverine/Wolf].   "Don't

wontthi," giyéhdi   óon.
eat,"   they said to him   then.

Sah ts'inhtin ets'edi úh sóon goin. Tl'a,
Bear was found was said and then there. Well yes,

yedhéhxin óon goin wots'edéhthe úh sóon mbedage
he killed it then there everybody ran and then his den

wocho táugiyedéhshí úh sóon. Sah xáts'edéhlu, sah
big they broke open and then. Bear they dragged out, bear

xáts'intin xets'edendéhłe, Xágiyedendéhłe úh
they pulled out they singed [burned hair off]. After being singed and

sóon, níagiyénitín úh tá'ets'edéhshí'i,
then, they brought it back and they cut it up,

ts'ehkalicho úh. Sahcho endáits'ingé, sah
it was all spread out to cook and. Big bear they put up to cook, bear

endáits'inge úh sóon. K'itth'á mohinhtl'ónts'edeleh
they put up to cook and then. Birch cup they took turns

éhsán, kíi tleh déddhe cho. Ínyá i cho tleh cho
then, just grease bright lots. Then that lots grease lots

ehdah eghehda kíi etthén cho eghehda.
also they ate just meat lots they ate.

Xetl'íonh dáudígá   i kólaa úh ehkegu úh
Morning when the sun came up that old man and young man and

yegáh thetedz ínyá. "Donht'i t'áh wohteh
with him they were sleeping then. "Why is it really

ndawodígá edulin ndi'íyah?" kudi éhsán. "Kón
sun up nobody got up?" he thought then. "Fire

ndadúhk'ón," kudi ni'íya ínyá. I kólaa ínyá
I'll rekindle," he thought he got up then. That old man then

duhdin ínyá tleh cho xándatén. I ehkegu
there then grease lots oozing and freezing. That young man

ye'oneh thetin íin ju k'ándehta ínyá ju xónht'e.
next to him he slept before also he looked at then also like that.

"Héé, inhłah t'anghendéhkin, lonh. Éé, edin ayínlá
"Hey, both they died, must be. Hey, he he did it

suts'edi," sóon kudi.
they will think," then he thought.

Dene i łíónh ghedel i cho kón
Person that all moving that lots fire

ndadéhk'ón tl'onh. Dene łíónh at'in
he started a fire again after. People all they were

k'enet'e ónkeht'i mbetah dene, kúan wónlin. Eyi
twelve people, tipis were. There

se'e yéh sóon mbedeek'étl'ah sóon
really there then at the edge of the eye/off to the side then

xalonh ts'ín éhsán, łé'a edehts'ih, dechin
first [in front] toward then, little smoke rising, woods

méh. "Che wotl'onh édé woh'ín," kudi éhsán.
border. "Wait later then I'll look," he thought then.

I łínt'ónh kewonhín déhya úh. I kúan wotah
Those all among he went and. Those houses around

łínt'ónh dene, i łínt'ónh dene t'andéhkin. Łínt'ónh
all people, those all people died. All

tleh mbedhá xedandéhten, łínt'ónh
grease their mouths frozen around their mouths, all

t'andéhkin. Edulin. Kaa, eyi ghedi ndayínhdá
died. Nobody. Well, that being/animal that healed him

idahxádéh ehsán at'in. Úh i łahdi i kónaa
because of him then he is. And that place that a little fire

łe'a edehtsihí éhsán. Edahxá'edinká yek'ándehta
smoke that was rising then. He opened the flap he looked at her

ínyá ts'éu yaní'a.
then girl sitting there.

Ts'eú yaní'a sóon. "I lonh
Girl she was sitting there then. "That must be

sonhts'uya íin onht'e," kudi éhsán. Kíi
who cared about me before she was," he thought then. Just

yek'ándéhtón úh zonh líi éhsán ondéhja úh. Edin
he looked after and only just then he went home and. Him

i, Ts'iuné, xedatthén giyenihchú gáa káa dahé
that, Wolf, moose meat they gave him still a little

ayeh'in. I éhsán ndadéht'ee úh sóon. "Dih
he had. That then he cooked again and then. "Grouse

dhuhxe éhsín, kíi godah ts'ín duhshíin. Sóon
I'll kill maybe, just somewhere to I'll go. Then

ts'ih'áh ehsóon," kudi sóon, héé, ndejid.
I'll be discovered then," he thought then, hey, he was afraid.

Ndejid óon sóon, kaa, xónht'e on sóon at'in
He was afraid but then, yes, like that but then he was

inyá. I xónht'e on sóon káa, káa, gúlaa i
then. That like that but then yes, yes, finished that

tl'onh seníandétl'ún éhsán, i ts'uu ke
after he got dressed then, those girl's moccasins

yanila éhsán.
she gave to him then.

Káa, yek'éh déhya. Diín sóon déhya? Sóon gáa,
Yes, after them he went. Where then he went? Then yes,

gheyah gheyah úh. Héé, tonht'i déhya gáa,
he was going he was going and. Hey, far he went yes,

sa ndá'on ts'ín níniya. Xa'etenáa yáwolin, tl'a di
sun setting to he arrived. Patches of ice there are, so that

ts'uek'eh elin, migeháa xéwónht'i ehteni yáwónlin. I
muskeg it is, small lake it is like that ice there is. That

xónht'i. Se'e tadíénh ndadaya ínyá "sek'éh
like that. Really middle he crossed then "after me

ts'iwotla," kudi éhsán. Łáhín sóon łóninlin
snow drift," he wanted then. One place then flowing together

i cho, wónlin tu tadíenh ts'ín. Łáhín
that big, it was water middle to. One place

niwóh'á k'íodat'in ga th'édlé
trail to somewhere he saw [there appeared] spruce bunched

cho i táh éhsán. "Jon tl'a,
many/big that among then. "Here well,

xáehdá eyóon awonht'e."
I survive [I might survive here] like that I might."

"Nduhtée kuhdi," éhsán. Kúan awodídláa úh
"I want to sleep I want," then. Shelter he made and

éhsán ndetéh úh xáhgáhín dih ka
then he planned to sleep and evening grouse for

k'é'edah éhsán. Dih łíé déht'e úh dahé det'áh
he went for then. Grouse one he cooked and some in

theh'on éhsán. Dahé újon ayínlá úh éhsán
he kept then. Some well he did and then

xahniedet'in úh sóon. Gáa, eyi theda úh. Se'e
he saved it and then. Yes, that sitting there and. Really

sa xádadéh sóon.
sun rising then.

Sa xádadéh úh sóon. Kón, ndadéhk'ón éhsán ni'íya.
Sun rising and then. Fire, he started fire then he got up.

"Héé, jon sechon ndáudígá lóon. Sek'éh
"Hey, here while I'm sleeping bright must be After me

níudlin   egohón   aht'e,"   kudi   éhsán.
he expects   behind   I am,"   he thought then.

Deeh   ndehtin   ínyá.
Forward [he moved camp ahead] he slept   then.

Yahdínhan,   yihthehi mbéhchedinhsohle
Short distance behind,   fox   she was all covered with frost

úh   sóon. Gúhyeh niyaa   íin   gúhyeh'a
and then.   Like that where he went before like that

aht'as.   Etene niyaa   k'ehé mba'élính   úh,
she ran along. Trail where he went way   confused her and,

se'e etene   yáwóhts'in úh sóon, yek'éh   ét'e
really trail   she smelled it and then, after him the same way

ahtah   úh   sóon. Yetadáanh   níntl'a   éhsán. Héé,
she ran and then.   Across from him he came up to then.   Hey,

eyi   ndehtin éhsán i   thetin   edu
there she lay   then   there she slept not

yíndidính'a   sóon.
he noticed her/he paid attention to her   then.

  "Anáh, i   ghenda á'onht'e. Dhuhxe,"   kudi
  "Oh my, that animal   it is.   I want to kill her," he thought

óon sóon edu kudi.   Łáhín   ju   edu kudi.
but   then   not he wants to. One way also not he wants that idea

i   t'áh   éhsán.
that because of   then.

  Kíi   xónht'e éhsán k'ahju. K'ahju se'e   ddheníigháadé
  Just like that then   again.   Again   really every day

niya   úh   éhsán. Goin éhsán k'ahju yeda   nandéhtin
he went and then.   There then   again   for her he slept again

ínyá. Ée,   ndatsiedéhtlah   endádla úh sóon k'ahju
then.   Hey, again snow drifted lots   and then   again

éhsán gáa kaa yek'éh   at'in. Úh sóon i   ka'etenáa
then   still   after him she was. And so   that icy spot

yáhtheli   migeh, tl'a, ts'uek'é migeh
here and there [scattered] lake,   well,   muskeg   lake

łí   xónht'e. Eyi   éhsán nínida.   Se'e   wotthinlé
it was like that. That then   he camped there. Really clearing

dhénék'é   éhsán nínida.
smooth spot then   he settled.

  Nínida   éhsán i   tl'a, "Ónkeh egóho nduhtehin.
  He settled   then   there so,   "Twice or   I'll sleep.

Dát'in   **at'in?**   **Tthidóh'ính,"**   **kudi**
What is she doing   she is?   I will understand/see clearly,"   he thought

éhsán. Kíi i   **níniya úh kíi wotsineh**   **kúan**
then.   Just that arrived   and just roughly made   shelter

awóndlá éhsán, ndéhtin éhsán.
he made   then,   he slept   then.

K'a   **yek'éh yahdienh'a ndaetl'eh.**   **Gáa,**
As expected   after him   behind a little   she ran again.   Yes,

kaa yek'éh ghetl'eh   **úh. Yétadáinh**   **k'a**
still   after him   she went along   and.   Across from him   as expected

níntl'a   **úh sóon. Dek'ehdué t'óndadah. "Tse**
she arrived   and   then.   His coat   he put on.   "Firewood

deeh deduhłeh,"   **kudi,**   **dedhóo k'ehdue t'óndadah.**
ahead I'll move,"   he wants,   man   coat   he put on.

"Éé, jon kaa kíi mbet'áunhndá í xúle   **úh, edulin**
"Hey, here still just something to wear   nothing and,   nothing

t'áinhdáuh'á, ndek'éh á'aht'e úh. Ye   **kaa sech'áhín**
I'm wearing,   after you I am   and. What   for   away from me

anet'in?"   **xoniá**   **yéhdi.**
you are?"   suddenly   she said.

Úh sóon, "Dene i   **lonh,**   **ke**   **sek'eh**
And then,   "Person that must be,   moccasins on me

dathehła íin,"   **kudi**   **éhsán, kudi**   **éhsán.**
she hung   before,"   he thought   then,   he thought   then.

Kudi   **t'áh**   **éhsán yek'éh eyi yéhdi**   **éhsán.**
He thought about   then   after him that   she said to him   then.

Úh ndéhtin,   **úh tl'a i**   **dene**   **ju nandéhtin**
And he fell asleep,   and so   that   person   also fell asleep again

úh. Kaa, łáhín   **ndéhtin. Gáa, thetin, thetin.**
and. Yes,   a long time   he slept.   Yes,   he slept,   he slept.

Héé, se'e dechin nénihsódi, edulin wots'ín. Se'e
Hey, really poles   bare/smooth,   nothing there.   Really

dechin náninzódé náintthi éhsán, ayínlá. Yegha kúan
poles   bare/smooth he put up   then,   he did.   For her   dwelling

awóndlá úh yek'eh edulin ju   **ts'iht'ené mbek'eh**
he made   and on it   nothing also   dust   on it

theton. Se'e újon yek'eh dechiné dezódé awóndlá
located on.   Really well   on it   pole   smooth   he made

lonh óon. Dándét'e,   **tagúh**   **enúdlin déhxe wots'ín**
maybe.   How many times, three times must be   nights   until

éhsán. Ddheníighádé ju thetin úh xetl'inghádé ju
then.   Every day   also he slept and every night   also

thetin. I   sóon dát'in   sóon. Ts'enidhed úh
he slept. That then   what's he doing then.   He woke up and

sóon ts'enidhed éhsán. Ts'enidhe gaá xódé   tu
then   he woke up   then.   He woke up then   already   water

kudi   éhsán. Ts'enidhe, dahtthídít'on.
he wants   then.   He woke up,   he lifted his head.

Anáh!   i   dedhóo sóon łue ts'edáht'adhi ehsíin,
Goodness! that man   then   fish he cut in two   that were,

łue dzahdádlái.   Łue ya'ígundh úh yidáanh
fish cut up for smoking. Fish scored   and across from

té'ela   elin   cho téthel. Héé, ługe éhdahi k'uen
blanketed spruce lots laid out. Hey, fish   also   groundhog

xádéhdadhi   ehdah wolíi eht'ée.   Héé,
all prepared [gutted/singed] also   lots   she cooked. Hey,

yídáanh la yaníhgode cho inhkah   eyá theda.
across   piled high lots on top of each other there she sat.

Łue łíé ená'in'áh   éhsán, yets'ín niíya   éhsán. Áán,
Fish one put on a stick then,   to him   he got up then.   Yes,

wode'én gots'inh ayeh'in ju edu yéhdi   ele,   kíi
where   from   he has also not she asked not,   just

edu yets'ín wodeh   éhsán.
not to her   he spoke then.

"Síin   diáa   ghunk'ah   éhsín sóon. Éé, jon
"[Question] this little you want to eat maybe then.   Hey, here

kaa, mbet'aunhda'i   xúle   úh á'aht'e   úh. Dája
well, something to wear gone/nothing and I'm like that and. Why

i   ju sech'a   k'íodinlehí."
that also from me ignoring/avoiding/moving."

Úh   éhsán kíi edu yets'ín wodeh   úh.
And then   just not to her   he spoke and.

"Di síin   wunk'adh éhsín?" yéhdi úh.
"This [question] will you eat maybe?" she said and.

Diín wots'inh sóon k'i   tth'á ehdahi se'é
Where from   then birch cup   also   really

yadikazicho yaxáinton.   I   t'áh xegáh łue
decorated/big she took out for him. That with for him fish

nínikon éhsán, i   łue cho łíónh ghedéhtthé. Kaa,
she served then, that fish big all   he ate.   Yes,

kúla   i   tl'onh   éhsán.
finished that   after   then.

"Ka'ah,   sin   sets'inh   unk'adhin,"   éhdi.   Xetl'inh
"Wait,   me   from me   you are going to eat," he said. Tomorrow

xetl'iónh   sa   xadadel,   edu   k'a sa   xa'aht'ónh   éhsán,
morning   sun   coming up, not   yet sun   risen   then,

yechonht'onh   déhdzé.   T'onh   nide'in,   kaa,
before she wakes up he went hunting. Long ago gone,   yes,

inghon,   gáa, xeda   ghinghon, deyázé   ghinghon
he killed, yes, moose he killed, moose family he killed

éhsán.   "Suasínlá   etundet'ine at'in," kudi
then.   "She did good things to me she is pitiful she is," he thought

éhsán.   Ek'a ehdah, xedatthí   áunht'ehé ju,   yets'ín
then.   Fat   too,   moose head   whole   too, to her

níani'on   úh   éhsán.
he brought back and   then.

Úh   xetl'inh xetl'iónh   tl'a, kaa, "Ekon   onhk'e
And   tomorrow morning   yes,   "Over there butchering place

dit'áh   igha.   Etthén ahthídleh igha.   Héé, di,
we both go [future]. Meat   we will do [future]. Hey, this,

dete'e dáudleh   i   t'áh dáidóoge   úh
this   what are we going to do   that with we will pack back and

níawóoge,"   sóon kudi.
we pack back," then he thinks.

Áán,   ets'agheli t'áh   úh   xehtl'unh t'áh,
Yes,   packing   with that and   packstrap with,

k'é'ets'ehgeh   i   níghenit'á éhsán.
they packed it back that they arrived then.

Etthén gah   nighenit'á éhsán, "Godahts'ín k'íohtl'eh
Meat   with they arrived then,   "Somewhere   I'll walk around

sedaa   aneleh,"   yéhdi éhsán.
while I'm gone you do it," he said then.

Etthén inhk'á'endéht'a, etthén xedati   ts'ín, dint'i
Meat   cut for dried meat, meat   big moose   from,   four

zonh etthén onlá.   Tsiyaa tthén ju   onlá.   Etthén
only meat   she did. Yearling meat   also she prepared. Meat

inhk'é'enit'i   inhts'índient'i zonh onlá.   I   edhéh
that is cut for drying eight   only she did. That   hide

tselé cho kíi   i   thela.   Kíi   eyi   inhk'eh
wet   big just there placed there. Just those on each other

niyénilah,   kíi eyi yéhła   edu ayíleh. Úh   kíi
she placed them,   just that left them   not   she did.   And   just

i   theda, eyi etthén łínt'ónh onlá.
there   she sat,   that meat   all   she did.

7 Wolverine Is Outsmarted

Storyteller's Introduction

Tcguhtheni,   dániya.   Setá   xúle   úh   eyóon
Poverty,   I survived.   My father   gone/dead   and   that

aht'e.   Úh   ndahxin   dase'e   kahndeh?   Duh   di
I am.   And   you all   could you really   you do?   Now   this

káht'e   t'ónh   setá   xúle.   Ewon   kaa,   ghehda
I was like [this big]   before   my father   gone.   But   yes,   I lived

k'ehé   gokago'á.   Héé,   teguhthene,   edhéh   ndái'á
way   try to find.   Hey,   poverty,   hide tipi   put up

ndats'edch   úh   ah   edeh   edu   ts'edetl'eh.   Úh
we lived   and   snowshoes   without   not   get around.   And

ah   ets'edídleh   úh,   eyi   kaa,   ats'inlá   édé   kaa,
snowshoes   made yourself   and,   that   yes,   made   then   yes,

mbéhts'eghenda   k'ehéh   gukats'endehta.   Ehdzodzi   edulin
with living   way   look for.   Traps   nothing

ah'in   úh   dechin   ehdzodzi   eyi   kunde   agiyeh'in   ghádé
I had   and   log   trap   that   uncle   they have   by

kaa.   Dechin   ehdzoi   níndehkáh   úh   eyi'á   nóhthehi
yes.   Log   trap   set [with axe]   and   then and there   marten

thihdzoh.   Hée,   teguhtheni   setá   xúle   dándiya.   Edu
I trapped.   Hey,   impoverished   my father   gone   I survived.   Not

kondéhdíh   úh   ndahtí   ndahts'ín   gondeh   éhsín.
that well   and   your parents   to you all   speak   maybe.

Gutloan   k'ehéh,   iyá   ts'eghendáa   k'ehéh   agúht'e.
Many   ways,   there   to live/to survive   ways   there are.

Wolverine Is Outsmarted

Di   Nógha   zonhán   dzóont'ch   chłch   ts'edi.   Héé,
This   Wolverine   only   bad   traditionally   they say.   Hey,

ghonlindah   dene   dzáondéh   henidhen   gok'ándetah.
somehow   person   bad luck/mischief   he wants   he's looking for.

175

Di kón ts'etthính t'ónh. Eyi kaa, níats'endeh'inh,
This fire striker [flint] before. That yes, they hid them,

ewon gochonh nandeta úh kaa, yí'on édé. Eyi
but in their sleep he searched and yes, he found then. That

zonh óon mbet'áin ats'et'in ndiyedi'áh úh, yií'i t'áh
only then depend on it they are he takes and, what with

kón ndats'edúhtla? Eyi Nógha la, yundééht'ónh hee,
fire they light up again? That Wolverine, long ago hey,

dzóonht'eh ets'edi.
he was bad they said.

 Kot'uh gonhndáitla ínyá dechintah ts'endeteh. Héé,
Now run into then in the bush camp out. Hey,

gots'ín   dechintah ts'endeteh. Héé, gots'ín
toward someone in the bush camp. Hey, toward someone

újon ts'endeteh úh níoni'ón, mbetanáh
well camp out and became, across from him/across the fire

ts'endeteh.
he camped.

 Goké   tl'a, dahts'ela, goké
Someone's moccasins well, hung up, someone's moccasins

ndahthehts'eli, kón gah dahts'ela ínyá. Edu ts'endeteh
wet ones, fire by hung up then. Not going to sleep

úh sóon mbehuts'endih ínyá. Eyi'aá niítl'a
and then he's being watched then. Then and there he got up

niedeníta   se'e gok'ánehta.
[Wolverine] roused himself really he's looking [at the other person].

Kíi aidihdah ts'etin-á aets'edídla.
Just on purpose sleeping [the man] made himself.

Niítl'a,   ínyá eyi dechin thehton
[Wolverine] got up, then that pole he had positioned there

líin t'áh goké   endaedéht'ah. Thidi
before with with someone's moccasins he poked off. Embers

donlá íin eyi goké   dinhdinla.
he did that before those someone's moccasins he threw them in.

Thidi yekín kanondlá. Nandéhtin. Ndéhtin
Embers into he did again. He went back to sleep. He was sleeping

úh tl'a mbeké   dahtheli eyi
and then his moccasins [Wolverine's] that were hanging those

nits'edíhtin. Eyi ayínlá'a kehé
were taken. Those he has done like way

dinhts'edinla.   **Thidi   mbek'eh   andats'edla,**
he [the man] threw in the fire.   Embers   on   was again,

ndats'endéhtin.
he [the man] went back to bed.

Eyi   dene   ayínlá   íin   tl'a,   ke   onki
That   person [man]   he did   before   well,   moccasins   two

aych'in.   Ehtl'ónh   ndíitlah   ínyá   deké
he has.   In the morning   he [Wolverine] got up   then   his moccasins

káye'ín.   Ínyá   mbeké   xúle.   Úh   eyi   dene
he looked for.   Then   his moccasins   gone.   And   that   person

ayínlá   íin,   ke   ónki   ayeh'ín   úh,   ke   edenh
he did it   before,   moccasin   two   he has   and,   moccasins   without

níedíntin.   Ke   edenh   éhsán
he put himself in that situation.   Moccasins   without   then

ejihadéhtl'a   úh   kaa,   mbeké   ehten   úh   éhsán
he [Wolverine] ran away   and   yes,   his feet   froze   and   then

eyi   mbedzíaten,   ehłeh   ts'edi.
that   he froze to death,   traditionally   it is said.

Nógha   zonhán   kónt'e.   Eyi   zonh   óon   dzahagunht'e
Wolverine   only   like that.   That   only   then   trouble/mischief

gokago'á   ehłéh   ts'edi.   Ehtth'i   zonh.   Dene   ts'inli
look for   traditionally   it is said.   Straight   only.   Person   to be

eyi   gokóné   mbéhats'etin,   eyi   ju   mbech'a
that   fire   the one you use,   that   also   from him

ndáts'endeh'ín.   Héé,   kaa,   dene   chdinya.
they hide.   Hey,   yes,   person   beginning to work on.

Go'ahé   ju   łínt'ónh   nda'ał   úh   di   gokóné   ju
Snowshoes   also   all   he chews up   and   this   fire   also

mbech'a   ndáts'endeh'in.   Kaa,   i   ju   niyedí'on
from him   they hide.   Yes,   that   also   he took

lonh.   Dene   łíónh   kedeh   yií'i   t'áh   kón
must have been.   People   all   move around   what   with   fire

auleh   úh.   Úh   eyi   zonhon   edu   újon   ehłéh   ts'edi.
make   and.   And   that   only   not   good   traditionally   it is said.

Nógha   dene,   łínt'ónh   dzahaguht'ehi   gukago'á
Wolverine   person,   all   bad ways   looks for

ehłéh   ts'edi.   Eyóon   duh   ts'ín   gondadah
traditionally   it is said.   Like that   now   to   in the path of someone

nitth'e   sakeguht'e.   Di   łínt'ónh   ets'unúh
came to be   it seems like to me.   These   all   mysteriously

mbéhts'edíndhe.   **Tl'omónh   ts'ín. Kaa, eyiá**
keep doing something persistently. High Level to.   Yes,   there

dene   ndadeh édé   on,   kaa,   Tl'omónh. Di   gots'ídoa
person living   then but, yes,   High Level. This children

edu kaa újon, edu   aghedídleh.   I   kíi   mbech'a
not   still well,   not   make for themselves. That just from him

ehda   dene   ndadeh   kónt'e,   Tl'omonh   ts'ín. Héé,
also   people live   it is like that, High Level . to.   Hey,

edu újon, endádla.
not   good,   really.

8   Wolverine Steals a Wife

Nóghe,   Ehtsun,   Yahtl'uhimo,   ndetsun
Wolverine,   Grandmother,   Yahtl'uhi's mother,   your grandmother

íin, sehwodeh ehłeh. Ts'ído ehłin úh sehyawodeh.
past, told me   usually. Child   I was   then   she talked with me.

"Ehtsun,   séhwonedeh," ehsi. Séhwodeh.
"Grandmother, tell me a story," I said. She spoke with me.

Nóghe   kets'íyuen   ndéh'in. Dene   elin   úh
Wolverine   someone's wife   he stole.   Person   he was   and

kets'íyuen   ndéh'in úh mbetlazé   wónlin. Úh
someone's wife   stole   then   his brothers-in-law   were.   And

sóon diín   sóon ghedéhde ehsíin. Mbetsuan
then   someplace   then   they went   whatever. His little grandmother

gu'ón   ndadeh.
next to them   she lived.

Nóghe   ts'ídoa sóon, mbetsun   donge t'andetth'í
Wolverine   child   then,   his grandmother   hunger   dying of

yéhdi   úh   tsá   eghon   úh   edu   gi'inhchu. Eyi
she said   and   beaver   killing   and   not   feeding her.   That

ts'íyoan   gáa   donge   dzahdadeh úh, eyi ts'ídoa
old woman   already   hungry   getting worse   and,   that   child

gáa   necha   gua.
already   getting big   a little.

I   sóon mbetsun   edu   ghe'ets'inhchu,   úh,
That   then   his grandmother   not   they giving food to her   and,

edawodíh i   t'áh   eghon   etse   endádla.
he knew   that   because of   he's killing   cry [for things]   very hard.

Úh mbegha ets'eht'éi sóon ek'ade'ál,   i   t'áh
And   for him   cooking   then   he is chewing,   that   with it

éhégúh edebé   t'á eleh. I   sóon mbebé   t'á
but   to his stomach   in   he put.   That   then   his stomach   in

ek'adéh'ál. I   netloni adeh   édé, "Ehtsun
he chewed.   That   many   he made   then,   "Grandmother

k'áuhshá," éhdi   úh. K'ahu tsegehdínye   úh gáa,
to visit,"   he said   and.   Again   he would start crying   and   yes,

179

mbetsun   **ts'ín**   **déhya**   **édé**   **ju.**   **Mbetsuan**   **gah**
his grandmother to   he went   then   also.   His grandmother   with

kúinya   **édé.**   **"Ehtsun,**   **ndetth'éé**   **jon**   **dahdínkáh,"**
entered house then.   "Grandmother,   your cup   here   lift it up,"

yéhdi.   **Úh**   **dek'ihduáa**   **xá'in**   **úh.**   **Mbetsun**   **tth'á**
he said.   And   his small coat   like this   and.   His grandmother   cup

ekeh   **yaníhgódí**   **etthi,**   **xéyeh'in,**
into   a pile of   she eats,   he was doing this for her,

xéy'eh'in   **úh.**
he was doing this for her   and.

    Tsá   **k'ándeta**   **úh.**   **Tsá**   **eyi**
    Beaver   he [Wolverine] was looking for   and.   Beavers   that

níonle   **édé,**   **tsá**   **łígé**   **yi'onhteh**   **úh**   **ju.**
he would bring back   then,   beaver   one   give it to her   and   also.

Yebé   **t'á**   **eledz**   **úh**   **xónht'e**
Its stomach   in   he [Wolverine] would urinate   and   and like that

yayínhtéh   **úh.**   **Ts'íyoan**   **tsá**   **det'éé**   **édé,**
he gives it to her   and.   Old woman   beaver   when she cooks   then,

yatthéé   **édé**   **ndáedekuh,**   **úh**
when she ate it   then   she threw up,   and

xéyeh'in.
this [Wolverine] did all the time.

    Ts'ín   **éhsán**   **mbechoan**   **níaghinde**   **éhsín.**   **Kíi**
    Finally   then   her sons   they came back   maybe.   Just

andawudeh   **sóon**   **gich'á**   **tínida.**
she was still living   then   from them   they moved camp.

Xetl'eeh   **sóon**   **gich'á**   **tínida.**
Nighttime   then   without them   they [Wolverine and his wife] moved.

Yídeeh   **níghinida**   **úh**   **sóon**   **dágiyeh'in,**
Ahead   they made camp   and   then   whatever they did to her,

dáyeh'in,   **sóon**   **mo**   **gudadi.**
what he did to her,   that   [their] mother   she told them.

    Níghenidae   **sóon**   **xeda**   **ghinghon**   **lonh**   **úh.**
    Where they camped   then   moose   they had killed   must be   and.

Xeda   **ndéhttheni**   **ghedhéhxin**   **sóon,**   **tthidi**   **k'eh**
Moose   that is fat   they killed   and then,   the embers   on

echonyú   **dahthela**   **úh**   **agiyínlá.**   **Eyi**   **ts'úu,**
big intestine   he hung up   and   that they did.   That   woman,

kets'íyuen   **ndéh'in**   **íin**   **sóon,**   **gáa,**   **i**   **mbetlazé**
someone's wife   he stole   before   that,   yes,   that   his in-law

xeda ghinghon sóon ndaghedéh sóon.
moose they killed then where they lived then.

Xetlint'ónh sóon guk'éh gheyah, echonyú
In the morning that after them he was going, big intestine fat

tthie dahthela úh. "Xódlehin!" kughedi
in the fire was hanging and. "We will do this to him!" they wanted

úh. Echonyú tthie dahtheli sóon gughon
and. Big intestine fat in the fire was hanging and then to them

náiya.
he arrived.

"Éé, tlahzé, xeda újoni ghedhéhxin, héé, donk'e
"Hey, in-law, moose good they killed, hey, hungry

aht'e. Ehtsún újon ghe'endehchud íin,"
I am. Grandmother good I was feeding her before,"

éhdi úh sóon.
he [Wolverine] said and then.

"Kón ndái'a tthon ats'eh'in ts'edi úh.
"Fire came upon breechcloth people had it is said and.

Taméh ts'ehda úh xéts'int'e
By the edge [of fire] someone was sitting and this way you have to be

úh, ketthoné xéts'eleh úh.
and, someone's breechcloth one must do this and.

Yátsinéhtsedl úh uhá kendíchú sóon,"
Must shut one's eyes and and then we finally feed then,"

giyéhdi úh. Detthoné
they said to him [Wolverine] and. His [Wolverine's] breechcloth

xóonla, úh sóon ihk'ení'éé.
like this he did [lifted] and then with his legs spread.

Echonyúcho tthie ekéghingei sóon, gitl'éh
Big intestine fat in the fire they poked it then, in his crotch

eghendihdi ínyá. Éé, ndadíghel úh sóon
they shoved it and then. Hey, he started jumping about and then

giyedhéhxin. Giyedhéhxin úh sóon yah yinhín
they killed him. They killed him and then snow under

gidéhtin úh.
they threw him and.

Wok'éh éhsán yehłinghin gheyah. Nóghe
After that and then his wife was coming. Wolverine

ts'íyoan gheya, aluh úh gheyah.
wife was coming, pulling something as and was coming.

Mbets'ídoa gáa k'ela wónlin úh, ketah theya
His baby already almost existed and, among them she was

úh ketah theya úh éhsán. Etthén gugha
and among them she was and then. Meat for them

agheleh úh etsính, tleh ehdah agheleh úh,
they were fixing and pemmican, lard also they were fixing and,

héé, újon óon. Kik'e'in ghádedél i t'áh i
hey, good then. On to it they were urinating that with that

sóon héé, újon sóon guye'enihchú éhsán
then hey, good and then they gave it to them and then

yóghínkuh úh. Nóghe yadzáa sóon ghedhéhxin
they were vomiting and. Wolverine offspring and then they killed

úh mo ju ghedhéhxin. Gáa k'aa mbebé
and mother also they killed. Still yet her stomach

ndáedah éhsán gíníenit'a, gíxedidíhtin. Nóghe
was moving and then they cut into, they took them out. Wolverine's

yadzáa sóon nighedínhtin.
offspring and then they took them out.

Ónket'e, guch'á táwodéhtthe. Gik'ededéhya
Two of them, from then they ran away. They followed them

sóon, gáa dekie<u>n</u>dagéeniyo úh.
and then, then they were chasing them up trees and.

Nógiyehteh úh gik'eh,
They would bring them down and after them,

dekindatthí'odíhk'ón, úh xégiyéh'in.
they would set fire after them, and this they were doing to them.

"Yídeeh díeh wónh'on édé, ndahxe'éhdzoi díe
"In the future this land if it's still here then, your traps bait

edu wótthi éhsín," éhdi. "Setsindáhłeh,"
not eat maybe, " he [small Wolverine] said. "Leave us alone,"

guyéhdi. Úh gichá ndadéhde.
they said to them [to the men]. And from them they went back.

Úh gáa mbódat'in éhsán nóeja
And still can see them and then once he [Wolverine] came down

ínyá, "Díeh wonh'on wots'ín ndahxe'ehdzoi dié gheh'in
then, "Land until its end until your traps bait if I see

édé, edu ju ndahduye úh óon, edulin ndahdawo'á
then, not also your caches and also, nothing will be left for you

éhsín."
maybe."

K'ahju giyedéhthon, gáa gik'éh
Again they chased, at that time after them

dekindatthío. Dekindaítl'eh édé ju
they were setting fire up trees. Wherever he went up a tree then also

guch'a édé, gik'éh. Dátth'ie wolíi dechin chinah
to avoid them then, after them. Branches lots tree base

agheleh úh gik'éh dekitthíodík'ón úh éhsán,
they put and after them they set fire up after them and then,

tthídeleh. Tthídeleh t'áh kón
into the fire he urinates. Into the fire he urinates with that fire

ndanétthih. Úh gáa thún agiyíleh.
fire goes out. And then are unable to they do it [kill them].

Wozenáa úh awójá úh sóon audadi úh sóon.
Darkness and came and then it was happening and then.

T'andawodéhthe k'ahu, t'andadéhtl'a k'ahu,
Started running home again, he started running home again,

guk'éh gáa thún agiyínlá.
after them then unable to they did.

"Xónhaán mbek'éh ahthíjá," kughedi ínyá, héé,
"Near after him we went," they thought then, hey,

tonht'e ts'ín gik'éh ajá łonh. Se'e
long ways there after them they had gone this had happened. Really

dunka gukúan kendaghí'on donk'e gugha
very hard their house they found again hunger for them

endádla.
are tired/exhausted.

Úh eyi óon duh nighontth'e ts'ín óon,
And that then now after all that happened to there then,

nóghe ke'éhdzoi die nidíleh úh, dúye ats'inlá,
wolverine someone's traps bait he takes and, cache that you make,

édé ju kedúyé ehda úh. Gúhyeh'á ehtsun
then also someone's cache he eats and. That way my grandmother

séhwodeh ehłeh. Guyeh xát'in ehłeh. Nóghe
she told me usually. That way he used to do all the time. Wolverine

dene elín ts'edi úh.
person he was it is said and.

Xát'in kanende'ính duh ts'ín on, "xónht'e
That way he does from people he steals now finally but, "like that

sín," éhdi íin. "Ndahts'ín dene újon
maybe," he [Wolverine] said before. "Toward you people good

auhłeh,"   éhdi.   Uh   mbets'endéleh   ínyá
I will be,"   he said. And if they had left him alone and then

tadéhtl'a   ts'ín,   "Ndahxonhendeh'ính ighá   éhsín.
he ran away   from there,   "I am stealing   [future] maybe.

Díeh   wó'oin   wots'ín ndahxe'etthéné gheh'ín   édé
This land   its end   until   your food   if I am seeing then

edu mbeyiendakád igha."
not   I respect   [future]."

  On   donk'e   gik'éh   nindéhde. Se'e   edunka
  But hunger   after them stranded.   Really hardship

níaghindé.   Eyóon   duh   ts'ín Nóghe   díeh   wok'ih
they came back.   There   now   up to   Wolverine world   on it

at'in édé   ene'ính úh. Ju   onht'e úh   woyon ju
he is   then   stealing and. Here   he is   and   smart also

onht'e. Sedhéhxin igha   thun   ats'eleh ets'edi.
he is.   To kill him   [future] hard/slow to do   it is said.

Gúyehá   ehtsun   sehwodeh ehłeh.
That way   grandmother   talked to me used to.

9 The Young Man Who Sought a Wife

Storyteller's Introduction

I Nógha tl'a, i debét édé, debé édé.
That Wolverine well, that he's hungry then, hungry then.

Xónht'i ghetl'eł úh, ghetl'el úh, xónht'e
Like that he's going along and, he's going along and, like that

gáa, ghetl'eh édé. Yéh minlá xáaleh.
yes, he's going along then. There his hand he does like that.

Tl'a, minlá mbeláodedhi ghetl'el úh xónht'e
Well, his hand its tips get shocked while going along and like that

ghetl'el úh. Yah tah xáleh minlá láodindhe
he's going along and. Snow in he does that his hand tip-shocked

édé gáa, wonlin wónlin. Gáa, gots'ín at'in édé.
then yes, animal exists. Yes, toward there he is then.

Gáa, i wonlin i'áh úh etthi. Xónht'e
Yes, that something he finds and he eats. Like that

ghetl'el úh xá'aja edulin minlá edu
he's going along and he does that nothing his hand not

láodindhe édé. K'ahju ech'uin i xáajidi.
shocked on the tips then. Again another way that it happened like.

Minlá láodindhe édé gáa, goin. Gáa, wolin
His hand shocked on the tips then yes, there. Yes, something

i'áh, etthi. Ts'edi tonht'et'ónh.
he finds, he eats. It was said long ago.

Úh eyi tl'a, i di xattheeh se'e xattheeh, di
And that well, that this first really first, this

dígéh awójá éhsín úh, beeh ju xúle úh, chi
world came into being maybe and, knife also gone and, duck

ju xúle. Úh xónht'i édé tthee kade'áh
also gone. And like that then stone he [Wolverine] chews on

xéyeh'in, xéyehin óon. Beeh aleh ets'edi.
he did like that, he did like that then. Knife he makes they say.

Beeh aleh úh éhsán. Edin zonh beeh aleh ehłéh
Knife he makes and then. Him only knife he makes used to

185

i   tonht'et'ónh ts'edi.   Di   tl'a,   ende'ínhín la   gáa, eyi
that long ago   they said. This well, he steals   yes, that

mbaújon wonlin   ende'ính. Duh   on   łéét'e.   Xónht'e
he likes   something he steals.   Now   still the same.   Like that

uhtl'e   édé   nóda, ewon nóda ts'elúnh, édé   łínt'ónh
if he ran   then   lynx,   just   lynx   snared,   then   all

tayedehch'a úh. Héé, ndátse.   Xalonh ndátse.
he tears it up   and. Hey, he's strong. Really   he's strong.

Xeda, xeda   mbetthén, mbedzuetthéné nechicho eyóon
Moose, moose   its meat,   its breast meat   big lots   there

xónht'i, eteneh yéh dehtl'eh édé. Yahk'eh   mbekeeh
like that,   trail   there he runs off then. Wintertime his tracks

wónlin łaheindi. Tadienh yugé   łaheindi
they are   all the time. Middle   he's carrying in his mouth all the time

ghetl'eh   netinh. Edu ju   niyi'ah   élé. Łaheindi
he is going   it's heavy. Not   also he put it down never. All the time

mbekeeh wónlin jon   wots'ín. Héé, tonht'e, gáa,
his tracks   they are   here from.   Hey, far,   yes,

yídééh   ndats'edeh íin   xodéhthah éhsín gots'ín
back there   people living   before   that distance maybe   to there

gaa kaa mbeke   wónlin. Héé, ende'ính. Ndátse.
still   its marks   are.   Hey, he steals.   He is strong.

The Young Man Who Sought a Wife

Eyi la edu Nóghe   ayínlá, edu Nóghe   ayínlá. Héé,
That   not Wolverine he did it, not Wolverine he did it. Hey,

ech'uni, eyi Nóghe   wú   eht'olonh ayínlá. I   éhsán
another,   that Wolverine tooth   arrowhead he made. That   then

ech'un, dene   goin ts'ín   dene   déhyedé. Tl'a, jon
another,   person there toward people walked.   Well, there

kewónht'e dene   wónlin. Tl'a, dene   wónlin   sóon
the same   people   there were. Well, people there were   then

gots'ín   mbetá sóon, "Mo   tinthene mbedeé ju   xúle
toward   his dad   then, "Mom pitiful   her eyes   also gone

úh   di   ke   ndegha alehi,   jihé   ehdahi
and these   moccasins for you   that she makes, mitts   too

ndegha aleh.   Dene   k'ánitah.   Dene   enet'in édé
for you   she does. People   you look for. Person   you find then

xoni   mbetúé   nanihtin   édé.   Ndegha   ju   ke
maybe   his daughter he gives you then.   For you   also moccasins

auleh   úh   jih   ju   auleh."   Goin
she will make and mitts also she will make." Toward

k'énedah.   Mbetá éhsán yéhdi, "aan," éhdi   úh
he walked around. His dad then   he said, "yes," he said and

sóon.
then.

  Gáa   edéghin   éhsán. Déhya, ínyá   dene,   kólaa
  Already he packed back   then.   He went. Then   person, old man

úh   i   ts'íyoan   úh   mbetúé   łíé,   i   éhsán guwonh
and that old woman   and her daughter one,   that   then   upon them

náinya. I   gutadáinh   mbetá   úh   mo   úh,
he came. There across from them her father and mother too,

gutadáinh   éhsán mbetúé   theda.
across from them then   his daughter was sitting.

  "Éé,   setúé   ndawohteh.   Héé, máhsi.   Héé,
  "Hey,   my daughter   I'll give you. Hey, thank you.   Hey,

ndahgha wonlin   kasudindi   xúle úh   eyi sechuen," eyi
for us   something hunting for gone and that my son,"   that

mbets'égu, mbetúé   gáa   kúan theda.
his girl,   his daughter already   married.

  "Dedhóo ayeh'in, dedhóo ayeh'in ewon   sóon,"
  "Man   she has,   man   she has   that's why then,"

éhdi,   "k'éndu'ah kudi   t'áh."
he [Yamonhdeyi] said,   "trick   he wants with [by means of]."

I   dene   ehsíin la éé,   woyon,   woyon onht'e
That person that is hey [really], smart,   smart   he is

éhsán. Eyi mbetá   gutadáinh   i   at'in   éhsán.
then.   That her father across from them there he was then.

Eyi eli   thela.   Eyi tah   éhsán its'egháddhi,
That spruce boughs lying there. It   among then   shavings,

ah   xónht'i   ats'eli,   egháddhé netsédláa   netlon
snowshoes   like that are done,   shavings   small/fine   lots

thela   úh.   "Kúan thedi   onht'e," kudi.   Úh
are there and. "House living [married] she is," he thought. And

éhsán, "Ndewonh ndáuhdze." Et'onlééh éhsán awónht'e,
then,   "For you   I'll hunt."   Summer   then   it was,

"ndáuhdze," éhdi.
"I'll hunt,"   he said.

Dewonlin, tl'a, héé mbets'édé úh xónht'in eyi
His things, well, just his blanket and it is like that

déhghin,   dahé hé   úh mbewonlin sóon déhya
he had packed, some just and his things then he went

úh. Sóon gáa   k'íadah,   k'íadah   úh sóon
and. Then already walking around, walking around and then

i   dene   goin déhye ehsíin xúle. Eyi éhsán
that person toward he went must have gone. That then

i   dene, i   egháddhí, i ts'égu éhsín mbedené,
that person, those shavings, that girl maybe her husband,

éhsán keghon. Łínt'ónh dene ehsíin ghedeghón
then   was killing. All   men   each   he was killing them

éhsán at'in. I   éhsán gáa   k'íadah   i
then   he was. That then already walking around that

wots'ín   éhsán.
length of time then.

Sah, sah dek'ewoghínhthe   i   éhsán sah ghinghon.
Bear, bear they climbed up [a tree] it then bear he killed them.

Łíé éhsán, yedhéh yedhéh t'á xayint'á, yedhéh t'á
One then,   its hide its hide inside he skinned, its hide inside

yetthén ghinlá úh. Duhtédhin kudi   igha.
its meat he put and. Put up to cook he thought/wanted to [future].

Sóon déhya úh gáa   se'e sa nda'a úh sóon tu
Then he went and already really sun set and then water

wonlin úh awodi   "ch'úun."   Tu
there was and sounds like "slurp" [walking in water sound]. Water

tl'a, nídhuh két'i tah dechin ju ndádatóni
well, moss like in trees/bushes too where they are broken

netlon, "wotl! wotl! wotl!" dechin tats'ede'é edhin
lots,   "snap! snap! snap!" branches were broken sounded

te'e ju tee ju "ch'úun!"   tu éhdi.
slowly also slowly also "slurp!" [walking in water] water said.

Tu   wonlin   úh, "wotl! ch'úun!" wodi
Water there was and, "snap! slurp!" was sounding

éhsán. I   mé   onlá   kóan,   kóan   onlá.
then. There lean-to he made small fire, small fire he made.

Kóan,   kóan   sóon eyi mbek'eh ndaídín éhsán i
Small fire, small fire then that on it shines then that

dechin eli lá k'é'enihshi éhsán. Mbets'édé yedeniká
tree   spruce tips chopped off then. His blanket covered it

úh   sahdhéh i   éhsán   di   yetthí da'udenihdi ts'etin
and   bearskin that then   this   its head he covered up sleeping

ét'in   ketthíghá   dendéht'ehze sóon   kóan
just like someone's hair black   then   small fire

ménda'it'in.   I   mé   onlíi
lighting up then dark [flickering light]. That   wall [lean-to] he made

in-eh   ehda   ínyá   "ch'úun"   wodih.
behind   he was ready then   [walking in water sound] sounded.

Eht'o t'áh éhsán, i   sahdhéh wónjonh éhdi. . .
Arrow   with then,   that bear skin well   he made sound. . .

dechin éhsán dátthie, eli   lá,   i   éhsán é'idínht'ah
stick   then   branches, spruce tips, that then   he shot [arrow]

úh   "gotl, tl'u, tl'u, tl'u," deja   úh   sóon.
and   "snap, slurp, slurp, slurp," sounded and   then.

Nóghe   wú   eyi kéintl'un eyi se'e   dígeh kededih,
Wolverine tooth that tied on   that really ground near,

wodendít'ehze on   goin   yedintse ínyá, "téhdhin,"
dark   but   toward he let it go then,   [arrow hitting sound]

wodéjá. "Éé, dahełehya   ahła adindi!   Tl'a,
happened. "Hey, he's holding something I did   it made sound! Well,

eht'o dahgheli   i   ats'inlá   adih.   Dehełelih
arrow   he's holding that ready-made sounded.   He's holding

dahełelih,   ahłá adindin.   Edu dahyuleh éhsín,"
he's holding, I did   it made sound. Not   he's holding maybe,"

kudi   éhsán, kón   łonedenila éhsán. . . . Gáa
he thought then,   fire   he stoked up then. . . .   Already

xódé   úh sóon ndéhtin.
happened and then   he went to sleep.

Ndéhtin   úh gáa   atthée tl'onh ndéhtin
He went to sleep and already eaten   after   he went to sleep

ínyá xetl'íonh sóon goin   déhya. Tsádhéh, tsádhéh
then   morning   then   toward he went. Beaver skin, beaver skin

k'ihdue eyi cho   mbek'eh déhzo, i   cho   ínyá.
jacket   that big thing on him   frosted, that big thing then.

Se'e jon   ónéh ts'ín ajá,   se'e jon
Right here [pointing] around there it happened, right here

yet'áin.   Yedzeékín kaa, eyi Nóghe
his back behind him. In his heart yes,   that Wolverine's

wú   i   mani'á.   Yéht'a,   yedhéhxin
tooth [arrowhead] that was stuck in him. He shot him, he killed him

úh, úh sóon.
and, and then.

Ndadéhja úh. Goin i dene i éhsán i
He went back and. Toward that man that then that

dedhóo, i ts'egu dedené, goin ats'et'in ghedi
man, that woman her husband, toward someone was they said

t'áh sóon. Ts'endeteh kekéh xáat'in, ts'etin úh
so then. Someone camped following he was like, sleeping and

éhsán. Kechonh kewon, kechonh kewon, kewon.
then. While sleeping killing, while sleeping killing, killing.

Éé, dene netlon dhéhxe!
Hey, people lots he killed!

I éhsán i dene yedhéhxin úh éhsán. Ndadéhja,
That then that person he killed and then. He returned,

sahtthén sóon ndadéhjin, níaninla. I ts'égu
bear meat then he brought it back, he brought it back. That woman

éhsín éhsán ts'inh, juh kúan awóndlá lonh, ínyá.
must be then outside, also house she made then, then.

Yání'a i éhsán, "Dene, dene déhdzé
She was sitting that then, "Person, person he went hunting

íin níanontla," éhdi sóon. Mbetá guts'ín éhsán
[past] he came back," she said then. Her father to them then

déhya. Sahtthén ju goin déh'on úh éhsán.
she went. Bear meat also toward she took and then.

"I dene mbet'ádhin ghída íin dhéhxin ehxondíh,
"That person depending on living before he killed maybe,

dhéhxin ehxondíh," éhdi éhsán.
he killed maybe," he [her father] said then.

I úh sóon k'ahju éhsán eyi, i éhsán k'ahju
That and then again then that, that then again

yéh mbetá ehsíin eht'a, ehda t'a, eyi
there her father that was eagle feather, eagle wing feather, that

éhsán. "I eht'o gha diín wots'inh andaye'ính?"
then. "That arrows for where from he usually gets?"

sóon. I yéh inhtth'i éhsán goin déhya.
then. That there straight in one direction then toward he went.

Goin déhya.
Toward he went.

Ínyá di ét'i mbetúa úh mbechidláa eyi
Then this the same his daughter and her little brother that

éhsán. I et'ohcho ekéh éhsán ghekeh éhsán.
then. That big nest in it then they were sitting in then.

I et'oh nechi a'onht'e, yeyúhin éhsán dihyeleh.
That nest big it was, its bottom then tunneling up to.

Héé, k'elazonh mauni'á két'eh éhsán ayínlá
Hey, almost a hole [through] like that then he did

éhsán.
then.

"Non, tl'a, dá'etl'el úh édé, Ene, tl'a,
"Mother, well, she's coming back and then, Mom, well,

nda'etl'eh édé, ndáhchunh gua édé, Ene
she's coming back then, it rains a little then, Mom

nda'etl'eh," mbechóan éhsán éhdi.
she's coming back," her son then he said.

Úh eyi i ts'egu at'in sóon. "Ene
And that that young girl [eagle] was there then. "Mother

níantl'a nendádehsia." Eyi dene éhsán eghehdá
comes back I'll tell on you." Those people then they ate

eyi. Wonlin éhsán dene eghehdá. "Eyi gáa
those ones. Animals then people they ate. "That already

choan at'in édé, ene ndaetl'eh úh yaháa
a little rain it was then, mother [eagle] coming back and a little snow

ka'at'in édé setá ndaetl'eh," éhdi. "Choan edeyoh
if it is then my dad coming back," he said. "A little rain sprinkles

éhsán, gáa, Mo, Ene ndaetl'eh éhsán."
then, yes, Mother, Mom is coming back maybe."

I et'ohcho yíyueh éhsán dene at'in, at'in éhsán.
That big nest below then man he was, he was then.

Dene tadíenh wots'ín éhsán níanitin. "Jon
Person half up to then she brought. "Here

nedía i dajá?" yéhdi. "Yúyueh
your little sister that where is it?" she [mother eagle] said. "Below

setthí elie wohteh," éhdi.
my head hurts I'll sleep," she said.

Úh, "Héé, Ene, dédehdíe seghá újon ní'enichu,"
And, "Hey, Mom, I'm hungry for me well serve me well,"

yéhdi éhsán.
he [boy eagle] said then.

I dene éhsán, "Ye gha edintsé?" éhsán
That person then, "What for you cry?" then

etthi   gha níoni'on   úh   sóon.
he [boy eagle] eats   for getting ready and then.

Eyi   xát'in   ínyá ndadéhtth'e i   éhsán, i   dene
That   doing like that then he fell   that then,   that person

ehsíin   éhsán yedhéhxin. I   ehdacho   dhéhxin.
that was   then   he killed her. That big eagle he killed.

Godah   diín ts'ín níenitin k'ahju ínyá, "Diín
Somewhere   where to he put   again   then, "Where

wots'inh dene   ledíh," éhdi éhsán. Di   dene   óon
from   person aroma," he said then. This   person then

aneh'in, dene   óon aneh'in. "Yi'i'áh   dindi,"   sóon
he was,   person then he was.   "Whatever you say," then

yéhdi. Yéhtsén   dene   at'in edayedíh ínyá. K'aju'a
he said. He smelled him person he was he knew   then.   Again

ndahchunh éhsán, k'ahju éhsán   mbet'óhcho éhsán.
it rained   then,   again   then   his big nest   then.

Eyian mbetá   ju   kaa, "Sechuen, woden wots'ín
Then   his father also well, "My son,   where from

dene   ts'inh ledíh?" éhdi   éhsán.
person from   aroma?" he said then.

K'ahju   éhsán eyi   ndandadéhtth'e, eyi   ju   gáa
Again   then   that one he fell through,   that one also already

inhlah éhsán yet'á   onlá.
both   then   its wing feather he did.

"Úh di   dene la edu mbekín   ts'egheda
"And this person   not sustenance someone lives

mbets'odedene. Úh luge úh tl'a, eyi ehda ets'edi
he is no good.   And fish and well, that eagle called

gah   úh,   luge úh, eyi dih   úh, chi   úh, xónht'e
rabbit and, fish and, that grouse and, duck and, like that

mbekin ts'egheda. Dene la edu mbekin   ts'egheda,"
depend on one lives.   People   not sustenance one lives on,"

sóon yéhdi. "Édé i   ndegha luge auhleh
then he said. "Then that for you fish I'll do

mbek'ánontíin," yéhdi éhsán.
you'll be looking at," he said then.

Joan sóon tu   se'e dehdédhe éhsán luge at'in úh.
Here then water really clear   then   fish he was and.

Di   lééh ét'i t'áh dinlá   xonlá,   yenda yih
This ashes same with his hands he did like that, his eyes in front of

ajá. **"Góon** **újon** **mbek'ánitá?"** **éhdi,** **yenda**
happened. "[Question] well you see him?" he said, his eyes

yih **éhsán.**
in front of then.

"Áán, héé, újon mbodat'in."
"Yes, hey, well he appears" [the boy eagle said].

"Úh unitl'a," **yéhdi** **éhsán.**
"And you attack it," he said to him [Yamonhdeyi] then.

"Jidíhin," **éhdi** **ínyá. Ługe ínhchu.**
"Splash," he said then. Fish he [boy eagle] grabbed.

"Xónht'e nedih," **yéhdi** **éhsán.**
"Now eat it," he [Yamonhdeyi] said to him then.

"Héé, łekón lonh. **Héé, dene dzont'e, héé, ługe**
"Hey, tasty it must be. Hey, people bad, hey, fish

łekón lonh," **éhdi.**
tasty it must be," he [boy eagle] said.

I **wots'inh éhsán, dih** **úh, chi úh, łínt'ónh**
There from there then, grouse and, duck and, all

eghon, eghon, eghon. Áán, ehdacho. Eyóon xá'at'in.
he kills, he kills, he kills. Yes, bald eagle. There he does that.

Eyóon duh eghon yéh Behchon úh, diín-a ługe
There now even there Bistcho Lake and, where fish

wónlin ehsíin, **mbet'oh dahathe'on,** **ługe kasudedih.**
exist even, its nest scattered around, fish hunt for.

Úh łíé ju i gáa, eyi t'á **onlá éhsán**
And one also that yes, that wing feather he did then

k'ahju, "Diín-a wots'inh ndetá **tl'a, tth'éh**
again, "Where from your father well, sinew

t'á **eht'o k'eh elin tl'unh. Tth'éh,**
wing feather/arrow feather arrow on it is string. Sinew,

xedatth'éhé ét'i diín-a wots'ính ndetá andayeh'inh,"
moose sinew like where from your father gets it from,"

sóon yéhdi. **Úh éhsán**
then he said [Yamonhdeyi asked]. And then

noja.
he [Yamonhdeyi] came back.

"Te'e, kaa, ehdacho t'áé **níanilá."**
"Father, well, bald eagle wing feather he brought back." [she said].

"Éé, setúé kaa, łínt'ónh ndahxendéh gudeleh
"Hey, my daughter well, all our earth taking away

úh á'at'in. Mbet'adzin ghida íin   i   ju, mbets'ín
and he is.   Depending on living before that too, to him

nidé'in éh'ondíh. Gáa, łíónh xúle," éhdi   úh.
gone   seems like. Yes, all   gone," he [her father] said and.

  "Tth'éh diín-a ndetá   andayeh'in?"
  "Sinew where your father he gets it from?" [Yamonhdeyi asked].

  "Yéh," sóon yéhdi.
  "There," then she [the girl] said to him.

  Goin sóon déhya.   Éé, eyiá wonlin nechi cho
  There then he went. Hey, there animal big   horribly big

thetin. Thetin   éhsán. Dunhze   jon mbetthít'eh
sleeping. It was sleeping then.   Yellowlegs here on top of its head

éhsán. Dunhze   dahthekón   úh éhsán. I   sóon
then.   Yellowlegs nesting   and then.   That then

nda'edhéhtth'on   édé, adi   édé
anything making a noise then, it [yellowlegs] makes a noise then

edawodíh.   "Dunh, dunh, dunh, dunh," ke'ính
he [monster] knows.   [Sound of yellowlegs]   he sees it

ínyá "dunh, dunh, dunh, dunh," xéyínlá   ínyá.
then   [sound of yellowlegs]   he did like that   then.

  Edu wodeh   úh sóon. "Mbetth'ené gheleh,
  Not making a sound and then.   "Its legs   thin,

edzatth'ené gheleh, yíí dédeh'in?" yéhdi
legs   thin,   what you saw?"   he [monster] said to him

éhsán.
then.

  "Tl'o, tl'o sendayeh edéhts'i," sóon yéhdi.
  "Grass, grass in my view blew,"   then he [yellowlegs] said.

Wots'i úh sóon.
He lied and then.

  Xóhén sóon tl'o tah nige   úh sóon.
  Close then grass in he [Yamonhdeyi] crawled and then.

"Héé! dluen lonh   sóon   ndáwotl'á,"
"Hey! mouse wish for upon me run into,"

kudi.   Yewonh ndáetl'a. "Mbets'ín segha
he [Yamonhdeyi] thought. Upon him he ran.   "To it   for me

wodinhxath," yéhdi.   "Se'e mbedzeé k'ih,
clear away,"   he [Yamonhdeyi] said. "Really his heart on,

i   mbeghá xanehxáh," yéhdi.   "Édé
that its fur gnawed away," he [Yamonhdeyi] said. "Then

ndetsáhndi   igha,"   yéhdi.   Xéyínlá.
I'll help you   [future]," he [Yamonhdeyi] said. He did like that.

Úh   éhsán   i   jon   dluen   jon,   "Yegha   seghá
And   then   that here   mouse   here,   "What for   my fur

xanedzéh?"
nibbling away?" [the monster said to the mouse].

"Héé,   ndetthua   eyi   ts'ídoa   mbegóhdli   úh
"Hey,   your relatives   those children   they're cold   and

á'ahin,"   éhdi.
I'm doing it," he [the mouse] said.

I   éhsán   se'e,   i   éhsán   edeghádéh   yedzeé   kin
That   then   really,   that then   really hard   his heart   on

yéht'a.   Éé,   i   tthindádí'é.   "Éé,
he [Yamonhdeyi] shot [arrow]. Hey,   that struggling in death. "Hey,

edzatth'ené   wozé   'tl'o   sendayeh   e'edéhts'i,'   dindi.
legs   twiglike 'grass   my view   blew in front of,'   you said.

Héé!   héé!"   dejá.
Agh!   Agh!"   he [the monster] started to say.

I   dhéhxin   úh   beeh   t'áh   yetth'éhé   i   éhsán
That   he killed   and   knife   with   its sinew   that   then

xáint'ath.   Se'e   detsáli   cho   sóon   onlá.   Gáa,   i   ju
he cut out.   Really   clean/white   lots   then   he did.   Yes,   that   too

dhéhxin.
he killed.

Sóon   ndadéhja   úh,   gáa,   noja   éhsán.   K'ahju
Then   he came back   and,   yes,   he came back   then.   Again

eht'olonh   ele,   tl'a,   Nóghe   wú   ét'i   i
arrowhead   it is,   well,   Wolverine tooth [arrowhead] like   that

tthee,   dundáa   ets'edi.   I   éhsán,   "Diín-a
stone,   large game arrow   it's called. That   then,   "Where

wots'inh   dundáa   anda'inh?"   yéhdi.
from   arrow   you get them from?" he [Yamonhdeyi] said.

Ech'unts'ínguh,   "Yéh,"   éhdi.
Another direction,   "There,"   she [the girl] said.

Goin   éhsán   ajá.   Éé,   tthee   ét'i   denít'eh   on la
There   then   he went. Hey,   stone   same as black   but

"tl'eng, tl'eng, tl'eng, tl'eng, tl'eng, tl'eng, tl'eng,"
[sound of arrowheads flying around]

xádat'in.   Diín-a   náikin   ehsíin   sóon
they're doing that. Where   landed   wherever   then

niyedínlá.   Gáa, i   ju   eyi   níayénila   úh
he picked them up.   Yes, that too   that he brought it back   and

éhsán.
then.

"Éé, setúé   kaa, ndahxa ndéh go'edeleh.
"Hey, my daughter   well, for us   world he is taking away.

Ndahxa ndéh go'edeleh   úh at'in. Mbegha sah
For us   world he is taking away and he is.   For him   bear

nelin edeh. Eyi dundáa ele, heé dechin eht'olonh, i
you be then.   That arrow   not, just wood   arrowhead,   that

t'áh sah ts'edi   ndáwots'eyeh igha,"   éhdi
with bear it is called play   [future],"   he [the old man] said

éhsán.
then.

Mbetúé   sóon k'éyedheh, i   dedhóo
His daughter   then chases him,   that man [Yamonhdeyi]

ndádíhthon.   Gáa, łínt'ónh k'éyedheh úh sóon.
she started chasing. Yes, kept on   chasing him and then.

Xoní   hé   sah. K'ele   ayíleh   úh sóon. Mbetá,
Suddenly just bear. Almost she does and then.   Her father,

ts'íyoan   ju   éhsán aghet'in. Eyi ts'éu éhsán
old woman   also then   they were. That girl   then

k'ékedheh   úh éhsán i   dundáa éhsán.
she was chasing him around   and then   that arrow   then.

Se'e   újon eyi ketáyedeh'e úh sóon se'e újon adlá
Really well that he attached it and then really well he made

úh éhsán. Jon   sah at'in   i   éhsán theht'a.
and then.   Here bear he was   there then   he shot it.

Yedhéhxin. Yedhéhxin úh éhsán.
He killed it.   He killed it   and then.

"Éé, setúé   elin k'awu ndadhéhxin   úúú!"
"Hey, my daughter   it is again he's killed again [crying out]!"

éhdi   éhsán. Ts'íyoan,   kólaa ju éhsán.
he said then.   Old woman,   old man also then.

Sóon k'ékeghedhéh,   k'ékeghedhéh úh   éhsán.
Then they chased him around, they chased him and   then.

I   k'eyedhéh   i   dene   k'íadheh
That they chased him that person [Yamonhdeyi]   they chased around

úh sóon. Tsátu   tu   netlon i   éhsán. I   sóon
and then.   Beaver pond   water lots   that then.   That then

ługe ajá éhsán. "Jidínhin!" tétl'a. I
fish he became then. "Splash!" he went into the water. That

sóon ts'íyoan guxúle úh, i edu guch'á
then old woman gone and, that not away from them

ajá úh yéh éhsán ługáa elin i éhsán
happened and there then small fish he was that then.

I tontsa ets'edi eyi, ónket'i ndudélin
That pelican it's called that, two land

kudi. I kólaa éhsíin i éhsán diáa tu
he [old man] wanted. That old man whatever that then this water

edon, jon łíónh tu xúle úh onlá. Dechináa yue
he drinks, here all water gone and he did. Small wood under

tuáa éhsán ługáa dahghebeh úh.
little water then small fish he was treading water and.

I ts'íyoan éhsán tu tadienh ts'ín
That old woman then water middle to

ndághenitá úh tuáa édé, tehtsán egóh édé,
they were searching and little water then, insects if then,

yeghon. "Ni zonh guneyon, éé? Ni zonh
she kills. "You only you are smart, hunh? You only

guneyon, éé!" ghedi. Tehtsán eghón, łíónh
you are smart, hunh!" they said. Insects even, all

gheghon éhsán.
they killed then.

Éé, i di ługáa, "Set'uze egon tu xúle. Eyi
Hey, that that small fish, "My skin drying water gone. That

tontsa cho mbedhee, mbedhee, níenihkah,"
pelican big his throat, his throat, pouch you poked through,"

dunhze ts'ín éhdi éhsán.
yellowlegs to he [Yamonhdeyi] said then.

Dunhze sóon éhdi ínyá, "Edatth'ené woze
Yellowlegs then he [pelican] said then, "Legs spindly

sedheébé náihda ehsóon," yéhdi éhsán.
my pouch you move might," he said to it [yellowlegs] then.

"Tehtsán, tehtsán tthíth'ené eyi
"Insects, insect skulls that

k'ándehta."
I'm looking for" [the yellowlegs said].

[The end of the story is missing from the tape.]

Storyteller's Commentary

Dene la xattheeh se'e xattheeh dígeh auts'indla éhsíin.
Person first really first earth made before.

Got'ónh dene mo̲ndeji, tl'a, wonlinghedi łínt'ónh dene
Long ago people dangerous, well, animals all people

ét'e, ts'edi. I t'áh eyi daúh wodih tl'a
the same as, it is said. That because of that how stories and

dene, Dene Dháa dene éé, tl'a, héé, egeyah
people, Ordinary People people hey, well, just, white man

xónht'i ju. Eyi deneghadih xónht'i édé eghasuts'eli
like that too. That priest like that then pray

édé gáa, i ju ónht'e ehłéh. Dene ele jon
then yes, that also like that he used to be. People are here

Alexis keghá eghasulin ejin. Eyi ju gáa,
Alexis Seniantha for someone he prays he sings. That also yes,

k'onht'ónh ts'edi. Áán, eyi ónht'e úh. Wonlin
from the beginning it was said. Yes, that is it and. Something

édé da'úh awót'in ehsíin se'e łonts'edi.
then how is happening that is really they tell the truth.

Eyi yídét'ónh wodih. Edu duhddhenéh wots'inh onht'e
That old time story. Not modern day from it is

on, dene k'ondhi la edulin edayedíh tl'a, ni ewon
but, people modern nothing they know well, you even

néhwoghedeh édé. Edulin edaghedíh. Yídét'ónh wodené
they talk to you then. Nothing they know. Long ago people

deti ehsíin kehwodeh eyi la. Duh ts'ín edulin
elders that were they talked to someone that. Now up to nothing

edéhtl'éh edats'edíh úh hé edéhtl'éhkúan ju xúle úh,
paper they knew and just school also gone and,

hé dechintah woghedi, wonlinghedi ets'int'e úh, gáa,
just in the bush animals, animals the same as and, yes,

godaháa kasuts'ededi ets'etthi gah úh xónht'i
a little of something search for to eat rabbit and like that

zonh. I t'áh dene da'úh wonlindah wok'ándeta
only. Therefore people how same way look for

wok'áneta úh da'úh gheda k'ehé wogha, dá'uh tsáttheh
look for and how to live way for, how drifting

éhsín eyi gha got'ónh wodihé wónlin.
maybe that for long ago stories exist.

Kéhwots'edeh   édé i   dene moṇdeji ju ts'edi.
Talking to someone then those people dangerous also it is said.

Dene keghon   ju ts'edi úh i   xónht'i édé.
People kill someone also it is said and that like that then.

Ts'eṇdetéh   édé mbedah ke'ets'edindhe kindí t'áh,
When going to sleep then about think   mind with,

kuts'edi tl'a, tahdah   kindí   netlon   ts'inlin
they think well, sometimes their mind lots [worry] being

ats'int'e. Eyi gáa, eyi wodih kólaa   ehsíin
you are. That yes, that stories old man whichever

kéhwodeh édé i   k'éhén, i   k'éhén, i   k'éhén,
they talk/tell then that that way, that that way, that that way,

i   k'éhén.
that that way.

10 The Man Who Received a Vision in Old Age

Aan, yidét'ónh ts'ído ehłin, Ehtsun séhwohdeh
Yes, long ago child I was, Grandmother told to me

i la.
that.

   Aan, dene łígé eht'o t'áh zonh ats'et'in ehłéh
Yes, person one arrow with only uses always

ts'edi. Dene łígé ehkegu, wonlin deyah xadíh
it is said. Person one young man, somewhere go in a hurry

xetl'int'ónh úh et'ádhi xá'at'ai mbedhé elin. "Eyi
in the morning and hide piece it is like his belt it is. "That

sedhé onht'e," kudi úh niyedínla. Mo wolin-aleh
my belt it is," he thought and he took. Mother working

úh sóon edu yek'ándehta. Gáa, dedondhé sóon
and then not looking at him. Yes, his mother's belt then

nidínla úh jon ededhonah xéyínlá.
he took and here he put around himself he did like that.

   Jon xodehtthi wots'ín mo ya'in sóon. "Éé,
Here up to here up to mother she saw him then. "Well,

sechuen sedhé a'onht'e" sóon yayính. Edu wodeh.
my son my belt it is," then he threw them. Not he talks.

   Eyion dene, ts'ído elin t'ónh óon ajá, óon
That person, child he was before then it happened, then

wok'endadedah. Edu mba'awodi wónjon deti
he wanders around. Not sounding [vision] for him really older

adadih. Gáa sahgáa k'edínya sóon, "Tu
he was becoming. Already little creek he went to then, "Water

uhdon," kudi úh tehdendet'on. Ínyá, ínyá
I will drink," he wanted and he stooped to drink. Only, only

mbedonh, mbedonhghácho wónlin úh mbadzahdáwonht'e.
his beard, his big beard was and he was unhappy.

"Edu, edu segha k'íodeke i t'áh endádla.
"Not, not for me appears [vision] that because of impossible.

He edu k'a ghehda.   Xédé se'eghodade, edonh."
Just not use I'm living.   Just   I'm eaten alive, so what."

(Wónjonh sedhahtth'on ts'ído.)
(Really   listen to me   children.)

K'íadah   i   mbedonghá ndéhyon úh, edu
He was walking around that his beard   it grew   and, not

k'a mendayeh   wodeké   úh sóon. Sahgéh
yet in front of his eyes appears [vision] and then.   River

taméh   wonlin,   kek'ali   úh wonlin   tene.
river bank something, white packed trail and something tracks/trail.

I   sóon, "Hé se'eghodade edonh.   Edu
That then,   "Just I'm eaten alive so what.   Not

sendayeh   wodeké úh ínhk'e,"   éhsán
in front of my eyes [vision] appears and I don't care," then

ndéhtin.
he went to sleep.

Gáa   tonht'in ghinté, se'e   xetl'ee tahdin
Already long   sleep,   exactly night   middle

wonlindaháa, wots'edeh   edhin.   Edu dene
about,   somebody talking sound coming. Not people

núdlin   onht'e. Ets'edahxoh edhin   ts'adel úh,
not expected it is.   Chattering   sound coming coming   and,

inhłéh   ya'ats'íde, edhin.   Gáa   mbets'ín
to each other talking,   sound coming. Already toward him

audadih úh.
coming and.

"Ínhk'e   edu sa'awodi   di   sedonghá
"I don't care not sounds for me [vision] this my beard

ndéhyon on, edu edu sendayeh   wodekéh.
grew   but,   not not in front of my eyes [vision] appears.

Ínhk'e   adi   ehsíin   sade   edonh.
I don't care sounding whatever it is I'm eaten so what.

Sets'edhéhxin   edonh. Edulin onht'e sóon."
Something kills me so what. Nothing it is   then."

Xoniá   éé,   dene   xéde ehkegu   tah   wonighahi
Suddenly hey, people just   young men amongst arrayed

cho   sóon monhndats'indeli! Gidhonah k'íadah. Kólaa
many then came upon him!   Around him they walk. Old man

mbetthíghá inhtah   theli,   kólaacho,   guk'éh
his hair   mixed together is there, big old man,   after them

gheyah. Úh eyi ehkegu   łínt'ónh k'édhonghedadél úh,
he goes.   And that young men all   walking around him and,

gáa, edauts'edíh   úh sóon. Edu wots'edeh.
yes,   he felt their presence and and so. Not speaking.

Óon ke kekélah zonh aghet'in,   edu keteh ju
Then foot at the foot only they were there, not over also

aghet'in   kekélah.
they were there at the foot.

Kólaacho   gutah   theya ínyá, "Sechuen yundíe
Big old man among them he came then, "My sons   behind

ndetáa,   ndetáa   yundíe at'in. Tl'a, di dene
your uncle, your uncle behind he is. Well, this person

etundét'ine óon, edu ahthídleha   k'ehe wónlin.
poor   then, not able to do something with way exists.

Ekozína i   kónht'i la dzá'agúht'e éhsín keh
That one that like that   bad things   maybe with

kehwolin-aleh godahthi," éhdi. Úh sóon yéh
work with   somewhere," he said. And then there

mbech'ahín ts'edéde úh sóon.
away from him they went and then.

Dets'edédé   xónla   i   kek'éh wok'ándehta,
They went away he did like that that after   looking,

ínyá ts'íyuné yets'inh óné   ts'inh wahtheh
then wolf   from him other way from   they all were running

úh. I   kólaacho i   ts'iyuné yoan,   i
and. That big old man that wolf   old/small, that

mbewuk'adhe ewon edulin. Gáa, etth'ené kín
canine teeth but   nothing. Yes, bone   on

yayedinhadli, ghonha   kek'éh ghegoh. Gáa, detahín
gnawing,   that's why following he went. Yes, in the bush

nídé'in tl'onh, gáa   tonht'in   ghoin'a.
he went after,   already after quite a while duration.

K'ahju dene adi   gheyah edhin.   Jon xódéhthah
Again   person sound going   sounding. Here this far

i la dene wots'ín nídé'in íin   éhdi, ts'aya
that person to there he's gone before he said, someone's coming

edhin.   Ínyá dene   chinehé cho
sound coming. Then person [said to be Wolverine] stocky large

kets'ín ghetl'eh. Ehsóon   thetin,   yets'ín aughayal
toward   walking.   Must have been sleeping, toward   walking

úh   sóon.
and   then.

Yedhonah   tl'ónda'inh,   "Xáhton,   jon dónendíh   úh
Around   circling,   "Stranger,   here how are you and

anet'in?"   sóon yéhdi.   Edu yets'ín   wodeh.
you are?"   then   he said to him. Not toward him he speaks.

"Etunénet'ine   ni'ítl'adá,"   yéhdi.   "Ni'íya! Ni'íya!"
"You are pitiful get up,"   he said to him. "Get up!   Get up!"

úh   sóon yedhon   theya   úh. "Sech'onahéh   úh
and   then   around him   he went and. "Facing away from me and

nínitl'a,"   éhdi.   Úh jon xónht'i óon, yek'eh níndét'on
you stand,"   he said. And here like that then, on him   sucked on

edu xónde   éhsín.   "Se'e   sek'ánihta,"   jon yek'eh
not   never will   maybe.   "Really   look at me,"   here on him

níndét'on   ínyá,   ínyá   mo   dhé ts'égia
he put his mouth on then,   and so mother's   belt dirty

dahdínla   lóon.   "Di   ghonhón edu   nendayeh
he picked up then.   "This because of not   before your eyes [vision]

godek'éh   a'onht'e,"   yéhdi.   "Edu   dáut'e,"
happens   it is,"   he said to him. "Not   what about this,"

yéhdi   ínyá.
he [Wolverine] said to him   then.

"Aneleh   éhsín, aneleh,"   yéhdi.
"Do [what you want] maybe,   do [what you want]," he [the man] said.

Edeghonh ts'ekédat'in   úh yek'ándehta   úh yéh
For himself he cried and cried and he was looking at him and there

déhtl'a.
he [Wolverine] ran off.

Úh   kek'éh níndé'in.   Gáa   k'íadah,
And   after   he was gone.   Already he [the man] was walking,

édé wots'inh sóon yáhthetin, k'íadah.   K'ahju'á
then from   then   he slept,   he walked. Again

yahk'eh   k'íadah   ínyá. Héé, ghonzen sóon
on the snow he walked around then. Hey, darkness   then

kóan   déhk'on úh sóon, eyi   edu   wodeh.
small fire   he started and then,   there   not   sounding [sparking].

Héé, i   sóon thetin, thetin.
Hey, that then   sleep,   sleep.

K'ahju'á mbets'ín   ets'edahxoh edhin.
Again   toward him chattering   sound coming.

Goka   wok'ándehta,   k'ahju'á dene.   Xattheeh
For something he was looking for, again   people. Before

ya'in íin   edu onht'e, ech'une. Héé, dene   yaújon
seen   before not it is,   different. Hey, people   nice

xédé, edu mendat'éné kónk'é   ewon mbek'eh wónlin.
just, not clothing   spark marks even on it   was.

Xédé dene   mbet'áedínbái, onk'et'ine ketthet'ónh
Just person fancy/elegant,   two people before the rest

yonhnáit'adzi. K'éhá k'ahju dene   yonhnáide.
came upon him. After again   people came upon him.

Gidhonah, gidhonah k'éghothe   sóon.
Around,   around   they ran around then.

K'ahju'á kólaacho kek'éh   gheyał.   "Sechuen, di
Again   big old man after them he was walking.   "My son,   this

dene etundét'ine, dedéndíe edulin ek'ah. Dih   dhaxin
man   he is pitiful,   he is hungry nothing eat.   Grouse   killed

édé mbádahtsi. Godahthiaa yi   gha jon aat'in?"
then feed him.   Go on   what   for here are you?"

mbetá   guyéhdi.
their father he said to them.

"Ts'iyuné adi," kudi.   Ínyá denecho   tahghónigha,
"Wolf   called," he thought. Then big person tall,

yéh thihła k'udéhde úh sóon. Ah,   ah   t'áh
there across they went and then. Snowshoes, snowshoes with

ghadéh. I   kólaacho, gutá   éhsán.
they walk. That big old man, their father must be.

Óon kólaacho konhnáinya   kónt'e úh, "Guk'éh
Then big old man came upon them like that and, "After them

dut'áh   sa'anedeh," yéhdi.   Úh sóon yek'éh,
we two walk   come with me," he said to him. And then   after him,

yek'éh gheyah.   Edin ju mbe'ahé   t'áh yek'éh
after him he was walking. Him also his snowshoes with after him

gheyah.
he was walking.

Jon'á edu tonht'ina xeda, xeda k'íagoi
Here   not   far   moose, moose roaming around

lonh.   Eyi tah xédé ahk'é   xéwónht'e.
must have been. It among just snowshoe tracks like that.

Dúhden'á xeda tadéhtl'a lonh. Anáh!
This way moose run must have been. Oh my!

Gadzondéh lonh óon dechin tahdahádendaghelin.
This high must be then tree among crisscrossing [windfalls].

I t'eeht'ónh wots'inh óon yéh dáudéhtha wots'ín
That before then from then far really far from there

óon. Ah inhdeh thela úh ts'it'ené cho
then. Snowshoes in front of each other was and dirt lots

náiyu úh. Xeda tadéhtl'i k'éh. Ah t'áh
thrown there and. Moose that ran off after. Snowshoes with

xáats'inhthe.
everyone ran out from.

Edu tonht'in ínyá yídahúh, yídahúh xáuts'edéhk'ón, úh
Not far then up, up camp, and

inhtadanh ghonjonh ets'ehda. Kólaa etthii
across from each other pleasantly they were eating. Old man in front

kendatthe gheyah. Ts'iyuné xáughinhthedi
in front of someone he was walking. Wolf everyone ran away

lóon onht'e, "Di'á kegha la hé ts'iyuné tsóné
must have been that was, "This for one just wolf droppings

yahthela. Kegha sechuen gu'eht'oné kahinh," éhdi úh.
were there. For my son their arrows I do that," he said and.

Ts'iyuné tsóné ahkahle eyeh úh sóon, kek'éh
Wolf droppings pocket put them and then, after them

ghat'áh. Ínyá ets'ehda konhndaghint'a úh sóon,
they were walking. Then eating they both meet them and then,

gáa, eghedin ju kegáh etthén ghedet'ééh. . . .
yes, them also with them meat cooked. . . .

Káa, ts'endetéh tonht'in winédé diín sóon? Hé
Yes, go to sleep long while time elapsed where then? Just

wolingháé ts'édé adadli, t'áh sóon dene
animal fur blanket made from, with then people

inhtadáinh thete úh. Kólaacho kedáméh mé
across from each other sleeping and. Big old man on the side wall

degáh sóon ndéhtin úh. "Jon nitéh,"
on the edge then he slept and. "Here you sleep,"

yéhdi. Yekagáh ndéhtin sóon, gáa
he said to him [the man]. Alongside him he slept then, already

ndetéh igha éhsán.
he slept was must have been.

"Ndechee wonlin łínt'ónh agheleh ehłéh.
"Your brothers things all they use usually.

Ndá'edegints'edí yudahúh gua dahonchu, yudahúh
Your share of food up a bit put some, up

wonlin dahthe'on. Tl'a, edu nigedí'ahi a'onht'e."
something put something up. Well, not take that was."

Ndetéh igha sóon de'etthénaa yídahúh degeze
He slept for then his small portion of meat up between

yedinhdi, úh sóon ndéhtin.
stuffed it, and then he went to sleep.

Gáa tonht'in ghinté úh gáa ndaudágah
Already long slept and already morning

inhkahdehk'ale. Xoniá mbegóhdli endádla,
whiteness upon the sky [dawn]. Suddenly he was cold really,

mbegóhdli úh sóon. Gáa ndáidah, ndáidah dah sóon,
he was cold and then. Already move, move every then,

yah tené ndádhetth'eni mbakeghonht'e. Úh gáa
snow packed trail sounding seemed like to him. And already

újon k'íodát'inh úh sóon, ts'enidhe úh ts'édé
good enough light to see and then, he woke up and blanket

edek'eh xónla.
on himself he did like that.

Jon-a ts'iyuné adi, edhin xe. Etth'ené egón
Here wolf sounded, sounded just. Bone knee

ghada'eghéhadli, etth'ené k'ahe ghada'eghéhadli. Édé
chewed pieces, bone bare eaten pieces [scraps]. Then

ts'iyuné tsóné dahghodendít'ehi cho taha thetin. Di
wolf droppings black everywhere lots amidst he slept. This

etthén dahthe'oin i zonh, edulin.
meat he put up that only, nothing.

Yeha ts'íyuné ghodéhtthe úh, "Jon dáuhde
Over there wolf ran off and, "Here what will I do

igha onht'e?" kudi. De'etth'ené náin'on sóon
[future] be?" he thought. His piece of meat took down then

yahoneh. Inkélu k'édze onhde sóon, xáughinkin úh
over there. Path frozen other side then, clear out and

kón déhk'on sóon. I etthén ghetthé. I se'e deti
fire he made fire then. That meat he ate. That really old

edu dene elin se'e ndahxét'e t'ónh wots'ín sóon,
not people be really just like us ago since then,

dechin tah at'in   lonh.   Edu mendayeh wodekéh edu
bush   in   he was   must be.   Not vision   appears   not

mba'awodi   ínyá. Ajíi   wots'inh wohte
sounds for him [vision] then. Happened since   really

edadíh,   úh adadíi.
he knows, and he is becoming.

Úh   gáa   mbctú   sóon dághejá élính
And already his father then where   don't know

wok'endadedah.   Yahk'eh awódeh   édé   ah
always thinking about it. Winter   when it is then snowshoes

adídleh   úh   i   t'áh k'íadah. Wok'endadedah,
makes himself   and that with walk.   Thinking about it always,

dets'ín mbeti   at'in,   mo   úh, mbetá   úh, aghet'in
where   his parents they are,   mother and, his father and, they were

edaghodíhí sóon. Netlon ghedé ajá   sóon, gáa,
that he knows then. Many   years passed then, yes,

xode   goin   dene,   mbetá   wots'ín nighede'in
finally there person, his father toward   they had gone to

edaghodi   wodadeh nandeta   ínyá. Ts'íyoan   kólaa   ju,
he knew of around   looking   then. Old woman old man   too,

ónket'ine, (mendayeh   yéh   wok'ánehta). Memo
two,   (in front of him there he looked).   His mother

ets'inhin   wot'in,   ek'eda'ehyidli ets'inhin,   eghedéhyidl
left-handed she was,   chopped brush   left-handed, chopped brush

úh.   Ts'enit'a,   kek'éh   sóon, keink'élu
and. Same two previously passed   after them then,   someone's path

ndat'inh   úh   kek'éh   aghet'in.
he checks   and after them they were.

Ínyá   kólaa,   ts'íyoan   ju   ndaghedéhi,   gughon
Then   old man, old woman   also   that were living, on them

náinya.   Edu yendadíh. "Éé,   sechuen gulon sechuen
came to.   Not remember. "Hey, my son   wish   my son

a'ot'in sóon!" éhdi,   kólaa.   Dets'édé   ts'inh   dadinlá
be   then!" he said, old man. His blanket   outside   hang

sóon, gugáh   kuinya   se'e   kek'onditah óon   edu kets'ín
then, with them   entered really glancing   then not to them

ghodeh   ghedi.
he talks they said.

"Ené,   gáa   sian aht'in úh. Seghot'ene
"Mother, already me   I am   and. My clothes

dáahłá?"
what did you all do?"

"Héé, sechuen, gáa ndegot'eni k'eíyeh,
"Hey, my son, already your clothing carried around,

k'eíyeh. Gáa łínt'ónh thu'a'it'e i
carried around. Already all couldn't wait anymore that

t'áh kíi mbets'endéhthídleh."
because of just left them behind."

Edu ghodeh éhsán mbadzahdáts'edi. K'ahju dechin tah
Not he talked then he didn't like that. Again bush in

níadé'in. Hé xáníode'in. Eyi óon dene gáa,
gone again. Just he was long gone. There then person yes,

ehkegu ajá, gáa kúan theda níghóntth'ed úh.
young man became, already married about that time and.

Dene wonh náinya. Ínyá, "Séhndázíi nelin," kéhdi,
Person upon meet. Then, "My son-in-law be," he said,

kólaa líin yéhdi. Mbetthíloh, i mbetúé
old man he was he said to him. At the head, that his daughter

yetadáanh ndadehi, mbetthíloh, eli tah egháddhé
across from that lives there, at the head, spruce amongst shavings

thela. On, "Séhndázíi nelin," kéhdi.
were. But, "My son-in-law you be," he said to me.

Edu kudi. "Dónht'it'áh i ts'uu gutadáinh
Not he wanted to. "How come that girl across from

ndádehi mbedádeh, elin tah egháddhé wónlin?"
the one living around her, spruce amongst shavings were?"

kudi sóon. Héé, ts'inh mbeghelé tahthe'on. Kaa
he thought then. Hey, outside his pack was. For

ndetéh igha, nighotth'e úh sóon. "Ehtsíe
he sleeps [future], at that time and then. "Father-in-law

ndegáh nduhté ekon, kíi godah nduhté. Nde'oh
with you I'll sleep but, just somewhere I'll sleep. Close by

nduhté éhsín." Ts'inhin déhya úh tonht'i sóon,
I will sleep maybe." Outside he went and far then,

dechintah dahyedintíi éhsán, kúan audindla, ghinté.
bush opening then, house made, he slept.

I dedhóo, i mbetúé, dedhóo yegáh at'in.
That man, that his girl, man with him he was.

Yedhéhxin ka yek'éh déhya lonh. Edaghodíh, xetl'ee
To kill him for after him he went then. He knew, night

edaghodíh, ts'edhehxei   igha   edaghodíh.   I
he knew,   someone would kill him [future] he knew.   That

t'áh   ndéhtin   ké'edídlá.   Edu ndeteh, sóon hé
because of   he went to sleep pretended to. Not he sleeps, then just

mbets'édé áuhla   úh.   Ts'édé yueh xadéhtl'a
his blanket left in place and.   Blanket under he jumped out

ts'iyuné ajá   tadéhtl'a.   Úh hé   i   mbets'édé sóon
wolf   became   he ran away.   And just that his blanket then

edulin. Wotl'onh ts'inh   sóon tonht'in ghodéhdhe
nothing. After   from there   then   far   after a long time

éhsín eyi   ghodadeh nandeta.   Edulin dene.   Thún
maybe that around   he was looking. Nothing person. Couldn't

óon minka ats'eji.   I   t'áh   i   kónk'é zonh
then for him happened to be. That because of that firepit only

ghoh'on, úh mbets'édé ju   xúle, úh ts'iyuné
was there, and his blanket also gone, and wolf

k'ínhín   tadéhtl'a.
way [like a wolf] he ran off.

Ghotl'onh ts'inh sóon k'ahju k'íadah.   Edu dene
After   from   then   again   he walked.   Not person

núdlin,   hé   dechin tah   xoniá   ts'uhya,
he expected, just trees among   suddenly someone passed,

ts'uhya   lonh. Kek'é   ndáiya   sóon. Yi
someone passed then. Someone's place he came upon then.   What

ka yek'éh   aut'in? Kekeeh   ndaghot'inh
for following him he was? Someone's tracks he passes once in a while

úh sóon dechinah   gha'oni'á olah. Yekeeh
and then on the side of the tree this trail   every. His footprint

nóndadáha   wotthínlé édé ju,   dechin
he comes after passing [checking] clearing   then also, bush

k'ínhín xáat'in.   I   dene úhya íin,   se'e
way   he's like that. That person passed before, really

mbek'eghónht'e sóon, sah yek'éh uhged   úh.
doing like him   then,   bear after him he crashed through and.

I   t'áh dene nda'úhja   úh, sah ju   kek'éh
That with person he already passed and, bear also after him

nídé'in   úh. I   t'áh   sóon, yekeeh   nóndadah
away he went and. That because of that then,   his tracks he passes

úh. Yek'éh,   gheyah duméh   ge   tah,   dene   thetin
and. After him, he went at the edge spruce among, person he slept

líin.
must have been.

Tthíóné   zonh   yets'ín   úhgé,   sah   yets'ín
Away from   only   from him   he crashed,   bear   from him

úhgéd   úh.   Aut'in   úh   sóon   yek'éh   ndáitl'a
he crashed   and.   He was still   and   then   on him   it [the bear] jumped

úh,   yedhéhxin   lonh   úh   yatthé   lonh.   Yuúh
and,   it [the bear] killed him   then   and   it ate him   then.   There

ge   tah   ts'ín   dahyohdhe   tahín   eyondígo   úh.
spruce   among   toward   snow on trees   in it   he wanders around   and.

yetl'onh   sóon   xáhgáhín   sóon,   yetl'onh   níniya   úh.
After that   then   evening   then,   after it   he arrived   and.

Se'e   k'éyehdeh'inh.   Dene   ghetthed   enúdlin.
Really   he was looking around.   Person   he ate   maybe.

Ke'ahé   ehdah   ndadáthe'a,
Someone's snowshoes   too   were standing propped,

ke'eht'o   ju   thela.   "Dene   ghetthéd   enúdlin,"
someone's arrows   also   were there.   "Person   he ate   maybe,"

kudi.
he thought.

Néji,   ndéjid   úh   awójá.   Úh   gáa,   "Sin
He was afraid,   he was afraid   and   it happened.   And   already,   "Me

ju   xásíleh   igha   éhsín,   úh   endádla,"   kudi
also   he will do that   [future]   maybe,   and   tired/exhausted,"   he thought

úh. Ah   gáhdéhya   sóon,   déhya   ts'ín   sóon
and. Snowshoes   he took off   then,   he went   toward   then

edek'éh.   Dahyohddhé   ch'ada'ehxe   hé   "di-di-di"
after himself.   Fluffy snow on trees   he knocks off   just   "di-di-di"

wodi.   K'íadah.   Tl'a,   gáa   ghozen   úh   audadih
it sounds.   He walked along.   Well,   already   darkness   and   happening

úh   sóon.   Duméháa   k'inhín   sóon   uhya.
and   then.   On the edge of the muskeg   way   then   he went.

I   t'ah,   se'e   dechin   tah   dahyehdít'í   i   éhsán.
That   because of,   really   trees   among   clearing   that   then.

Úhya,   dek'agáhí   wots'inh   detah   niya.
He walked,   beside   from   in the bush   he went.

Dahyedínt'i   íin   sóon   kúan   ddhenéh   tah   yidáanh,
Clearing   before   then   shelter   day   in   across,

eli   ónket'in   xónht'e   náintthi   úh.   Yídính   sóon
spruce   two   like that   he placed standing   and.   Behind   then

nái'a, **woyon,** **yéh** **get** **ndadéhya** **ts'ín**
standing, he's smart, there spruce they were standing toward

déhya. **Úh ts'ibe** **k'eh** **elin,** **ge** **dádzie**
he went. And swamp/muskeg on there was, spruce cones

dzedze **xónht'i,** **niyedíinla** **éhsán.** **Eyi dátthie**
bunched like that, he picked it up then. That spruce boughs

k'enihshídli **sóon.** **I** **mbe'ehtin** **sóon, se'e**
he cut something off then. There his sleeping place then, really

ts'ehtin **keyínlá** **úh.** **Yídáanh ts'ín** **eli**
sleeping did to look like that and. Behind toward spruce branches

det'ohthe **cho ónket'i xónht'e.** **Gáa** **tonht'i déhxe**
springy lots two like that. Already long evening time

úh **sóon** **ye'ín'eh** **sóon.** **De'ahé** **inhdeh**
and then behind it then. His snowshoes one ahead of the other

nínila **goin de'eht'oé níadínlá.** **Eyi** **yegáh**
he placed them there his arrows he took. That with it

wodéhshídli **gáa** **ts'edehxál eyóon adedhe úh,**
he trimmed it already size there that long and,

inhxondeh **ts'íhchud** **eyonht'i** **sóon dahghetinh.**
each like that gripped able to then he was holding.

Mbedátthie **ghadaghehyídlí, edegáh** **ndái'á sóon éhda.**
Its branches cut in half, beside him put up then also.

Gáa **tonht'e woin'a, tonht'e déhxedl.** **Úhya**
Already long time, long late into the night. He passed

ínyá **mbek'éh** **wonlin** **ódat'in. Gáa, i** **sah** **at'in**
then after him something appeared. Yes, that bear he was

kudi. **Duméh** **detah** **niyi** **sóon.** **Kón**
he thought. Along the edge bush passed and then. Fire

lónedeleh. **kóan** **kedindinh a̱ndawotih.** **He**
feed [put into from side] small fire barely see again and again. Just

uhshiné **dihdinla.** **Mbets'ín**
stump [standing dead tree] he threw in the fire. Toward him

ghego **xónhén, két'e sóon. Tindehge úh**
he was crawling close, just like then. Detoured and

inhts'in tthidíndzih **sóon.**
wind off the trails then.

Yets'ín **gáa,** **ghego.** **Sah yetadáanh wots'inh**
Toward him yes, he crawled. Bear across from around there

edetadáanh **wots'inh** **sóon yek'á̱ndehta.**
across from each other around there then he was looking for him.

Úh   i   dátthíe   cho se'e dene thetin k'inhín
And those spruce boughs lots really person sleeps way

onlíi. I   sóon yech'a'etthi úh ndá'edahi. Se'e mé
he did. That then he was poking and moving.   Really lean-to

xónht'i, wots'inh sóon deké   éhndádhe   úh,
like that, from   then his feet he was standing up   and,

yek'ándehta,   sah. Edu wondédah sóon, i
he was looking at him bear. Not long after   then,   those

dátthíe   ech'aetthih,   kón tse   yueh. Yek'éh
spruce boughs he was poking at, fire firewood under. On him

ndaítl'a sóon. Dátthíe   cho k'ade'áh, sah. Jon
he jumped then. Spruce boughs lots chewing,   bear. Here

yegáh mbédhe gáh ndada'e   sóon, dátthíe
with it lean-to   beside he stopped then,   spruce branch

k'ade'áhli sóon.
chewing   then.

  Se'e   yetthíchien   éhsán,
  Really his back of neck cavity must have been,

ndáyedéhxe.   Edu ndáidah wots'ín sóon. Yexenihxel
clubbed him with stick. Not moving   until   then.   He killed him

yéh   yedéhtin   úh. Yechon'enit'a ndaudiga,   ts'ína
over there he carried him and. He gutted him   next morning, then

dene   tthíghá   mbebé   t'á thela úh. Yinlá   k'énit'ai
person hair   his stomach in was and. Its paw he cut off

sóon. "He i   zonhan at'in," kudi   úh
then.   "Just that that's all he was," he thought and

ndéhtin.
he went to sleep.

  Gáa   ndaudagah úh sóon, diín wots'inh at'in
  Already at daybreak and then, where from   he was

síin?   I   dene wots'inh at'in   wowoh'in kudi,
[question]? That person from   he was to see   he wants,

sóon goin. Ek'enáiyai   k'íodehtha sóon déhya.
then   there. He came to the main trail that distance   then   he went.

Gots'inh et'eh dene   úhya   at'in   łodéhtha   yekeeh
From   still   person passed he was time and again his tracks

nondadah. Gáa   yet'áh, gáa   tonhtin ínyá. Dene
he checks. Already with it, already far   then.   Person

ndadeh úh wónlin ínyá. Dechin méné yi'ónéh
living   and there was then.   Log   lean-to the other way

ndadéhja   sóon.   "Xáhgáhts'ín édé, wozen édé mbets'ín
he went back then.   "Evening   then, dark   then to him

duhshíin,"   kudi.
I'll go,"   he thought.

Yéh na_nde'íin   i   t'áh sóon detahahín, gáa,
There he was hiding that with then   in the bush,   yes,

wozené úh audadih úh sóon kets'ín déhya. Sah inlá
dark   and becoming and then   to some   he went. Bear paw

detah theh'on. Sah dexethéhé eyi sóon kuehghinya.
in   he put it. Bear his pack   that then   he went in.

Kólaa   ts'íyoan   ghehke.   "Éé, xahton! Dene
Old man   old woman   they were sitting. "Hey, stranger! Person

dáké'útlegi?   At'in sechuen yéh, 'Dih
how is it that he's walking around? He is   my son   there, 'Grouse

ka k'eohtleghi,'   ndi.   Úh déhtl'a íin,   kaa, duh
for I'll walk around,' he said. And he went before, yes, now

ta'i dehxel úh xúle. Woden ts'inh sóon ts'uhtl'a.
three evenings and gone. Where from   then   he passed by.

Sechuen dajá   úh onht'e?" éhdi úh.
My son   where is he and he is?"   he said and.

On edu yets'ín wodeh. "I lonh   onht'e,"
But not to him   he spoke. "That must have been he is,"

kudi.
he thought.

"Gáa, tonht'i netéh   igha   niwontth'e úh sóon,"
"Yes, far   he sleeps [future] he came to   and then,"

kólaa yéhdi.
old man he said to him.

I   tl'onh éhsán xondéhja   íin,   eyi sah inlá
That after   then   he went back out before, that bear paw

xái'on sóon. "Ehtsie, dáduhsi?   Ndéhgondeh
he took out then.   "Grandfather, what can I say? I'll talk to you

di'a gondih aleh igha,"   yéhdi.   Kólaa gáh,
this news   it makes [future]," he said to him. Old man by,

eli   k'ih ní'éni'on. Kólaa ts'ekeghedetéh
spruce branches on   he placed it. Old man they were crying

ts'edi.
it is said.

Gúhyéh   óon deti éhdi.
That's how then elder he said.

PART TWO

DENE TEXTS

Accounts of the Prophet Nógha

11 Nógha's Song

(Edanmó   yéh   ndáidah.)
(Edanmó   by means of she's living.)

Hee di   dígeh elin.
Hey this   land   it is.

Hee hee hi-a hi-a.
Hey hey hia hia.

Ndahetá dígeh elin.
God   land   it is.

Hee hee hi-a hi-a.
Hey hey hia hia.

Ane   la hia hi-a hi-a.
Mother   la hia hia hia.

Setá la dígeh elin.
My father land   it is.

Ane la dígeh elin.
Mother land   it is.

Hee   hee hi-a hi-a.
Hey   hey hia hia.

Sctá   dígeh elin-a.
My father land   it is.

Ha ha hi-a hi-a.
Ha ha hi-a hi-a.

Hee hee hee.
Hey hey hey.

Setá la dígeh elin.
My father land   it is.

Heya haa hia hia.
Heya haa hia hia.

Ane la dígeh elin.
Mother land   it is.

Hee hi-a.
Hey hia.

Hee hee hee.
Hey hey hey.

Setá la   dígeh elin.
My father land   it is.

Semó la   dígeh elin.
My mother land   it is.

Haa hi-a hi-a hi-a.
Haa hia hia hia.

Setá la hi-a dígeh elin.
My father hia land   it is.

Ane la dígeh elin.
Mother land   it is.

Hee hio hee.
Hey hio hey.

12 Nógha's Teachings

I   k'oh dígeh, i   wonlin   yeya'ítl'a
That cloud land, that something he [Weasel] jumped up to

ayínlá.   I   t'áh óon k'oh   dzelonh ehłeh ts'edi.
he made. That's why then clouds very top usually they say.

Xák'ewótthe   t'áh   xéwót'e   Ndawotá kudi.
That's what happened because of it's like that God   he wants.

Got'ónh zonh óon dene   xónht'e. Wa ah'i gáa kaa
Long ago only then people like that. Carrying on still

duh, xónht'i t'áh   éhsán eghasuts'eli. Dene
now, like that because of must be they pray.   People

ehsíin, deneghadi ju eghasuli. Dene Dháa   ju
which are, priests also pray.   People Ordinary also

yú'únéh edu   xónht'e óon, di   dene   ndadehi
away   not like that   then, these people living

eghasuli. I   ndát'in ghinlíi k'íoghinleh.
pray.   Those prophets that were appear to them.

   Eyi Ts'u K'edhe   ts'edi.
   That Girls Attached To [July Lake, British Columbia] they say.

Dene dháh la Ts'u K'edhe   wóye.   Tonhtét'ónh
Dene language Girls Attached To it's called. Long ago

ts'egu ónk'et'i, ts'egu gáa   nechi, ónk'et'i yahk'i
girls two,   girls already big,   two   winter

ghádé, kaa gheda.   March k'eh wóhkón úh gáa kaa
long, still they're living. March time warm and still

ehłeh.   Eyi ndátin ghinlíi, t'ándéhtthe. "Jon
continuously. That prophet he was, he died.   "Here

ndátin theda,"   séhdi,   setá.   Eyóon xattheet'ónh
prophet is sitting," he said to me, my dad. There's first

ndátin ghinlíi.
prophet he was.

   Eyóon mbedinzí, Gochee,   Gochee, yéh
   That's his name, Someone's Brother, Gochee, there

Fort Nelson wo'ónéh ts'inh. Gochee,   mbetá.
Fort Nelson around from.   Someone's Brother, his father.

Gochee úye, mbetá éhdi, eyóon onht'e.
Someone's Brother he's called, his dad he said, that it is.

Det'ónh— Edu dene dahé yídééht'ónh tl'a, got'ónh
When— Not people some long ago well, long ago

ndahthet'ónh, dene dahé mbetth'ené ju xúle úh héé,
before us, people some his legs also gone and hey,

tinthene. Xónht'i óon k'éts'ege, wohdludhi t'áh
pitiful. Like that but even so they pack him, toboggan with

k'éts'ege. Et'onlééh édé ju k'éts'ege, mbechonh
they pack him. Summer then also they pack around, while asleep

xédónht'i łínt'ónh ndats'edeh. Mbechonh edu dene
like that all living. While he's asleep not person

náidéh tonht'ónh, Tahchee aghejá. I xónht'i
living long ago, Meander River it happened. That like that

yídééht'ónh. Ts'égu ónket'i, Ts'u K'edhe, ts'egu,
long ago. Girls two, Girls Attached To, girls,

gáa, i Carol echo, éhsán mbetá
yes, that Carol same size [small girl], must be their father

ma'eṇdádla úh. Edulin ts'ehda, édé tínts'indeh úh
he's weak and. Nothing they eat, then they moved and

gigáh at'in. Edulin ju dedhóo.
with them he is. Nothing also boys.

Eyóon mbetá wohteh dedih úh ajá. Guch'a
That her father really sick and it happened. From them

dzahdajá. Kúan aghinlá. Ługe, ługe wonh
something bad happened. Shelter they made. Fish, fish for

da'eghe'ah i t'áh óon yahk'i ghádé ługetthén
they fished that why then winter all during fish meat

dahgheła. Mé xónht'e aghinlá. Xóndacho . . . kue
they took out. Lean-to like that they made. That big . . . inside

kón ghedéhk'ón. Ługetthén ghetthi. Ługetthén zonh
fire they started fire. Fish meat they eat. Fish meat only

sóon ghetthi.
then they eat.

Héé, óon March k'eh, gaa xódé łíé dene
Hey, then March on, then well, already one person

edaguyedíh. Guinka ajíi níaguedínla. Ghincha
he knew about them. For them he went he took them. They got big

aghejá.	Edulin	aghejá.		Eyóon	Ts'u	Kedhe
they became.	Nothing	happened to them.	That's	Girls	Attached To

woye.	Eyóon	se'ehdzoi	tene.	Ghinlé	setá	éhdi
it's called.	That's	my trapline	trail.	It was	my father	he said

ndahxewodeh.
he talks to us.

Úh	wotl'onháa,	Bo		mbetá,	Mbek'ádhi
And	a little later,	Paul Metchooyeah	his father,	Mbek'ádhi

úye,	eyi	ndátin	ghinlé.	I	ju	kahju	wotl'oanh
he's called,	that one	prophet	he was.	That	also	again	later

Nógha,	di	t'áh	dint'e.	Dint'e la.	Gochee	mbetá,	i
Wolverine,	this	with	four.	Four.	Gochee	his father,	that

Yahtl'unhi	mo,	góon	edanedíh?	I	mbetá	onht'e.
Yahtl'unhi's	mother,	[question]	you know?	That	her father	he is.

I	ju	ndátin	ghinlé.
That	also	prophet	he was.

Chatien	óné,	Tthatúé,	Tsátin
Fort Nelson people	other side,	Beaver people,	Beaver

dháh	wodeh,	i	ju.	I	ju	ndátin	ghinlé,
language	he speaks,	that	also.	That	also	prophet	he was,

gots'inh	ju	łígé	ndátin	woghinlé	a'onht'e,	Chatien
from	also	one	prophet	was	he was,	Ft Nelson Slave

wogha.	Jon	Rainbow Lake	wo'óné	tlincho	t'áh	i
for.	Here	Rainbow Lake	around there	horses	with	that

ghon	ndats'adah,	Dawots'ethe	ehłeh.	Eyi	Tthatúé
for	they went,	Tea Dance	usually.	Those	Beaver people

héé,	újon	ejin.	Dali,	Zamai	mbetá	yéhdi.	Héé,
hey,	well	he sings.	Talley,	Jean Marie	his father	he said.	Hey,

újon	ejin.	Inhts'ághedi	ghinlé	got'ónh.
well	he sings.	They help each other	they were	long ago.

Harry	Dahdóné,	mbetá,	i	ju	ndátin	ts'andi,	i
Harry	Dahdona,	his father,	that	also	prophet	he helps,	that

ju	ndátin	ghinlé.	Dali	ju.	I	ju	Yahtl'unhi
also	prophet	he was.	Talley	also.	That	also	Yahtl'unhi's

mo	ju	mbetá,	eyi	ju.	I	xónht'e	Talley
mother	also	her father,	him	too.	That	like that	Talley

yets'ándi,	Nógha	eyi	xónht'i.	Xónht'e	t'áh
he helps him,	Wolverine	that	like that.	Like that	because of

óon	eghasugheli.
then	they pray.

Gáa,   łonghedi.   Łonghedi.   Got'ónh
Yes,   they tell the truth.   They tell the truth.   Long ago

ndahxéwoghedeh, wónjonh k'ésín edu awójá.   "Dígeh
they talked to us,   just   way   not   it will happen.   "Land

la edulin awódeh,"   éhdi.
nothing   will happen,"   he said.

  "Éé,   ink'eh łígé dene zonh édéghón   da'etl'eh
  "Hey,   that time one   person only   even though   he dances

édéghón   gáa mbegha ts'ejin! Edu, edu endádla
even though still   for him   they sing!   Not,   not   tired

kudahdi,   łígé zonh dene edeghon   gáa mbegha
you all think,   one   only   person even though still   for him

ts'ejin   da'etl'eh. I   wots'ín dáahde   ehsíin
they sing   he dances.   That   up to   what you all do   whatever

wots'ín   di   dígeh, di   dígeh Ndawotá ayínlíi
up to there   this   land,   this   land   God   that He made

dáde   ehsíin. I   kón k'eh edek'ée níts'in'a la,
what He does   whatever.   That   fire   on   tobacco   placed in,

edu mbets'endáhłeh ínle! Yídeeh   édé ndahgha
not   you all throw it away not!   In the future   then   for us

élính   wolé   éhsín. Men ndátin elin úh   ndahgha
confused   it will be   maybe.   Who   prophet he is and   for us

élính   kéwót'e   éhsín,   óon   ndahdasi,"
confused   it will be like that   maybe,   and so   I told you all,"

éhdi.   Héé, tonht'e ts'ín kehkewodeh
he [prophet Nógha] said.   Hey,   long ago to   he talks about people

lonh,   Nógha íin,   seda   kéhwodeh.
must be,   Wolverine   before,   before me   he talked to people.

  "Deyi   Shin Dené elin ejin   ehsíin   edu endádla
  "Whoever   Song   Person he is   he sings   whatever   not   hard

kudi,   kaa eyi eghasuts'elik'é ts'ín mbeda'awot'in
he thinks,   still   that   praying place   to   before him appears

ehsíin.   K'éh ts'ín k'ahju kólaa   ajá   édé,
whatever maybe.   After   to   again   old man   he becomes   then,

ech'u,   ech'u   dene k'ondi   ehsíin. Gáa gots'ín k'éh
different,   different   person new   that is.   Still   to there   after

ts'ín   gáa kaa. Dáwódeh   ehsíin i   kón k'eh edek'ée
to   still.   What happens   that is   that   fire   on   tobacco

níndah'á   úh, Dahwots'ethe gha eghasuahłi la   edu
you all place it   and, Tea Dance   for   you all pray   not

deghahtsi," éhdi. **"Édé zonh** **újon aghaht'e** **éhsín.**
you all let go," he said. "Then only good you all will be maybe.

Edu xónht'e édé, di **dígeh nechi onht'e, edulin**
Not like that then, this land big it is, nothing

ak'ehé la adeh, **edulin ak'ehé la adeh,** **nekínle**
on it it happens, nothing on it it happens, it's heavy

onht'e," éhdi **"Ewon di** **mbek'eh inhts'in úh**
it is," he said [Nógha] "But this on it wind and

xónht'i dahé **ndátset. Eghasuahłi úh se'e újon**
like that something strong. You all pray and really well

eghasuahłi úh se'e ndahts'ín újon édé, edu ndahts'ín
you all pray and really to you all well then, not to you all

awódeh **éhsín. Wonlin ndahts'ín adadil** **édé,**
it will happen maybe. Something to us will be happening then,

endádla édé. Wónjon eghasuahłi édé edin zonh edu
hard then. Well you all pray then him only not

ndahts'ín awódeh **éhsín. Éhsín yídeeh** **édé**
to us it will happen maybe. Maybe in the future then

udhahtthon," éhdi. Éhdi **kéhwodeh** **kaa,**
you all listen," he said. He said he talked to them well,

udhéehtthon, kaa, wohshon, kaa, necha gua úh óon
I listened, well, I'm wise, well, bigger a little and then

kéhwodeh.
he lectures people.

Xehtl'ah, "Ndeteghelé, gáa, edéhtl'éh ónket'i thela,"
Last, "Your drum, yes, drawings two on it,"

Nógha **ewon.**
Wolverine [prophet] even.

Edu edats'edíh i **edéhtl'éh. Héé, got'ónh, dene**
Not known that paper. Hey, long ago, people

edéhtl'éh edadíh lonh édé, degúh sóon xónht'i ehsíin
paper they know must be then, that way then like that that is

edats'edíh wóde **éhsín. Mbeteghelé tah** **edéhtl'éh**
they know will happen maybe. His drum in with paper

ónk'et'i thela **dawodígá.**
two there were getting dawn.

Héé, dene wónjon łondi **úh, Ndawotá ts'ín**
Hey, people good he tells the truth and, God to

adi, i tl'onh xónht'i di ndátin onht'e. "Di
he talked, that after like that this prophet he is. "This

óon ndahgha dádhed; gha di, sin la gáa gulaa,
then for us standing; [future] this, me already done,

Ndawotá sughedi," éhdi. Ínyá dádi ehsíin.
God he wants me," he said. Then what he said whatever.

Alekesi, sechuen ét'i onht'e setl'oan deyah igha.
Alexis, my son he's like he is after me he's going [future].

"Óon dene kondi xónht'i ghá, xónht'i adeh úh,
"Then people modern like that will be, like that happen and,

dahé endádla gutsonde úh gutthí ndátse. Xónht'e
some hard you help them and their head hard. Like that

ju edulin guedeh wots'ín ghedeya dawoghethedh úh,
also not quickly to there they go they're dancing and,

xónht'e eghasugheli édé, ihtthi zonh łíé ndahxónht'i
like that they pray then, straight only one for us like that

éhsín. Éhsín óon ndahxin shin dene ídlin óon,
maybe. Maybe then us song person we are then,

'yeghonh xá'at'in,' kudídi úh. Wónjon mbek'eh ts'ín
'why like that it is,' we think and. Well on it to

a'ahthít'in, dahé thetin t'áh níntin édé
we are, some sleeping because of you go to sleep then

ndáten. Héé, shin édé menanedíh, gáa, méhnejin
he dreams. Hey, song then you remember it, yes, you sing with it

i xónht'e óon duh shin onht'e." (Gáa, łondi lon.)
that like that then now song it is." (Yes, true.)

"Shin dené ehsíin yets'andi ehsíi, wonts'edle
"Song person whichever he/she helps him whichever, a little

wondehde lonh." I xónht'i t'áh óon łondi kuhdi
winning must be." That like that because of then true I think

t'áh.
because of.

"Di mbetá teghelé. Ni mbek'eh anet'in édé újon.
"This his father's drum. You on it you are then good.

Tadeke gha endádla. Dene łínt'ónh edu újon, ni
Loosing for hard/difficult. People all not good, you

mbek'eh anet'in édé újon, saújon," seghedi
on it you are then good, I like you," they are saying to me

úh nígiyéniton. Tinthene kuhdi, edu ats'inh ehjin.
and he put it here [drum]. Pitiful I think, not before I sang.

Ínyá gits'ín séhdi t'áh gáa duh la se'e
Then to it he said to me because of still now really

guyéhjá.
I turned out to be like them.

Újon ju shin edahdíh úh
Well also song I know and

wontsédle ju xónht'e eghasuhłi ndéetin édé.
a little also like that I pray I'm falling asleep then.

Wontsédle gáa, wónlin ndáhten. Gáa, łonghedi
A little yes, there is I dream. Yes, they told the truth

lonh. I t'áh i di k'éts'ín sin sandáwotsed,
must be. That because this this way me hard for me,

gáa, i k'ésín ahjá. Inhk'eh dene netlon lon
yes, that way I became. Following after people lots then

xónht'e.
like that.

Tl'a, dene dahé yídééht'ónh detah at'in. I
Well, people some long ago in the bush they were. That

ét'i ts'ído, ndátin ka, yú ju xúle úh
the same children, prophet for, medicine also nothing and

eduline. Ndátin ka, wonlin ndáhteni édón ndátl'eh
nobody. Prophet for, something thunder no matter hits

ehsíin, edanedíh, dechin ya'ihch'i. I xónht'e óon
whatever, you know, tree it splits. That like that then

ts'ehtin. Ketá kéhdi, eyi ts'ín ts'endeteh úh,
they sleep. Their father he told them, there to they sleep and,

xónht'i t'áh wonlin edats'edíh kéét'e. Eyóon
like that because of something they know like that. That's

dahé ndáwotset. I t'áh dene endádla
something strong. That because of person difficult

édón, gáa wonlin ahk'ehe ats'inle édé, újon
no matter, still something way there is then, well

adeh. Eyi xónht'e edawodíh i t'áh.
he becomes. That like that he will know that because of.

Xónht'e yúdené elin dahé yúdené ét'i ka
Like that doctor he was some doctor the same as for

kughedi t'áh. Xá edahdíh, dene dahé
they think because of. Like that I know, people some

yídééht'ónh elin dzahdadeh.
long ago he was became very sick.

Ka, újon agiyíleh, ghinlé. Duh i łínt'ónh
Well, well they make them, they were. Now those all

k'ewoghindhe úh, duh ts'ído yándíyeh dahé edu
wasted and, now children growing some not

xónht'e. Edu ndáwoteh kudi. Eyi zonha
like that. Not dream they want. Those only

dzahdonht'e. Dahé ndáten édé újon.
they're bad. Some dream then good.

"Ech'u dene óon Dene Dháa úh łéét'e, i ju
"Other people then People Ordinary and the same, those also

dahé ech'u dene óon ndáten édé wohteh
some other people then they dream then really

mbet'auwode'áh éhsín. I k'ínhín kudi édé
he's useful maybe. This way he wants then

xónht'e édé, se'e endádla wots'ín ni'iyah xónht'e
like that then, really hard to he can go like that

ju dene ts'inli," éhdi, setá.
also people you are," he said, my dad.

Úh łínt'ónh andét'í ndahxéwodeh. "Ts'egu ju edu
And all anything he talked to us. "Women also not

újon at'in. Detah, detah zonh ats'etin újon.
good she is. In the bush, in the bush only they are good.

Łínt'ónh ts'egu k'áts'endeta édé, eyi ju edu újon,
All women look for then, that also not good,

mbéh xeda ju edu ts'edhéhxin úh. Wonlin
with it moose also not they kill and. Animals

kets'eehdene," ndahxéhdi. Łínt'ónh andéét'i t'áh
don't like you," he told us like that. All lots of things with

ndahxewodeh. Dá'úh yídíinh dene ghinli.
he talked to us about. How long ago people they were.

"Dahwots'ethe édé dient'e dene guin gáa,
"Tea Dance then four people there yes,

tinihxel édé, héé, újon ts'ejin. I la Ndawotá
start drumming then, hey, good one sings. That God

ghádéh. I ghádéh meyawondhe," éhdi.
way. That way you will be able to tell," he said.

"Ndawotá edagedíh, ínhk'é élính
"God He knows them, following after He doesn't know

kudahdi edon, ndahxódat'in i ét'i onht'e.
you all think so what, you will appear to Him that the same it is.

Łínt'ónh, edanahedíh di díeh k'eh. Edin dene
All, He knows us all this land on. He people

akinlá onht'e úh, donht'e ehsíin, łínt'ónh
He made it is and, how is it whichever one, all

edandahedíh. **'Gulóon** **ndahtsáundí** **endádla,'** **kudahdi**
He knows us all. 'Hopefully He will help us really,' you all want

édé, **tat'enegúh** **i** **dene,** **łígé** **zonh** **kudi** **úh,**
then, three times that person, one only he wants and,

edek'ée **kón** **k'eh** **níts'eni'a.** **Édé** **úhzonh** **li** **detah**
tobacco fire on he placed. Just anywhere in the bush

ts'endehtéh **edon,** **endádla** **kuts'edi** **édé,** **edek'ée** **kón**
one sleeps no matter, hard one thinks then, tobacco fire

k'eh **níts'eni'on.** **Se'e** **eghasuts'eli** **ts'endéhtin** **édé.**
on one places. Really one praying one sleeping then.

I **awónht'e** **gáa** **ndets'áudendi,** **ndets'áudendi** **edu**
That it is really you will be helped, you will be helped not

edu **wodeeh** **ts'ín** **awódeh,"** **éhdi.** **Łondi** **lonh.**
not future to it will happen," he said. He was right must be.

"Tsádhéh **ewon** **kudahdi** **édé** **edeek'éc** **kón** **k'eh.**
"Beaver fur even you all want then tobacco fire on.

'Gulón, **guedeh** **sayú'áh,'** **kudi,** **guedeh**
'Hopefully, quickly He will give it to me,' he thinks, quickly

netlon **ats'eleh** **i** **tsá** **úh** **łínt'ónh** **łéét'e,"** **éhdi.**
lots one makes that beaver and all the same," he said.

Ndahxéhwodeh, **"Dedih** **edon** **ndatse** **édé**
He [Nógha] spoke to us, "Sick no matter strong then

eghasuahłi. **Gulón** **łígé** **k'íhín** **tat'eneguh** **eghasuli** **úh**
you all pray. Hopefully one way three times he prays and

xónht'e **aht'in** **édé,** **mbek'audeghah'in** **éhsín,"** **éhdi.**
like that you all are then, try it maybe," he said.

"Ewon **yídeeh** **édé** **ndahgha** **élính.** **Deguh**
"Even so in the future then for us confused. Which way

xéwót'e **ndahxa** **élính** **úh,** **awoje** **edon,**
it will be like for us confused and, if it happens no matter,

awode **edon.** **Eyi** **edu** **medidahá** **eyi.** **Eghasuahłi**
if it happens no matter. That not ignore it that. You all pray

edu **ededahdhi.** **Gáa,** **endádla** **wots'ín,** **edulin.** **Se'e**
not you all quit. Yes, hard to, nothing. Really

ełat'in **zonh** **dene** **ndadhed** **úh,** **da'etl'eh** **édón,**
one only person stands [to dance] and, dance no matter,

i **wots'ín** **mbéhghasuahłi** **gha,"** **éhdi,** **óon**
that to you all will pray with it [future]," he said, then

kets'ín **wodeh.**
to them he talked.

"I   ju'úh, Deshine yiné, Deshine yiné ets'edi
"That also,   Cree   song, Cree   song it is called

júh,   ónket'i. Tegheli netsédle," yéhdi.
also, two.   Drum   small,"   he said.

Sedain   yets'ín wodeh.
In front of me [he actually saw him speak] then   he spoke.

"Tegheli netsédle úh   di la mbéh   ndátin   ehxeli   onht'e.
"Drum   small   and this   with it prophet he drums   it is.

Di la Deshine yiné, tegheli netsédle. Ónkét'i la edu
This   Cree   song, drum   small.   Two   not

deghahtsi,   ndats'e'íi júh.   I   júh, xádeh   edu
you all let go, hand games also. That too, he does that not

deghahtsi,   dets'ín ndáhwonts'ín   ndá'á.
you all let go, where   they tire of playing you all play hand games.

Díin   kudahdi   ehsíin   ndá'á.   Dene
Where you all want to whatever maybe play hand games. People

ndahk'andehta i   edu mbets'endahłeh."
watching us   that not you all let it go."

    Ndátin   kewoghinde   ndéehsin, gáa, i   k'ésín.
    Prophet he talked to them I told you, yes, that way.

"Yídeeh   édé   xéwot'e   éhsín," éhdi.   Edu
"In the future then it will be like that maybe," he said. Not

edawodíh   got'ónh,   kóntúé   éhsán   yéhdi.   "Á
he knows   long ago, liquor   must have been he said to him. "Fog

ét'i   xá'ajá,"   éhdi.   "Edu k'íodat'in kéét'e.
the same as it became like that," he said. "Not able to see like.

Xódéhthah dah, edele wónlin,"   éhdi.   "Ye   ghon
How long   for, blood there is," he said. "What for

onht'i, edu edawohdíh.   Edahtth'e   édé,"   éhdi.   "Úh
it is,   not I will know. You all listen then," he said. "And

kudahdi   ndahdzie   t'áh   udhahtthon!"
you all think   our ears   with   you all listen!"

    "Ye   ghon adi,"   kudídi   íin.   Netlon éhsán
    "What for he's saying," we thought before. Lots   must be

kudi   éhsín, duh ts'ín, "Kóntúé ts'edon,   he
he thought   maybe, now to,   "Liquor they drink, just

ka'élính   úh. Dahé ghohdludhi yeghon,   edele wónlin."
they're crazy   and. Some vehicles   kill them, blood there is."

Edayedíh   gots'ín   xódéhthah óon   wok'ándehta,
He knows   to there   that far   then he sees [into the future],

héé, tonht'e. Úh xoni, xoni edin zonh, "'Ye
hey, it's far. And suddenly, suddenly him only, "'What

ghon ats'edi,' kuts'edi, dene xót'in éhsín,"
for how they are,' they think, people they're like that maybe,"

éhdi. "Eghasuts'eli ghon. Ye ghon eyi dene
he said. "Praying for. What for that person

eghasuts'eli, ye ghon ets'et'in?" éhdi, tónht'etónh
praying, what for it is?" he said, long ago

ts'ín. "Edu dene edahdíh xót'in éhsín,"
to. "Not people you all know who are like that maybe,"

éhdi óon. Duh níoni'on. Gáa, edahdíh, eyóon
he said then. Now it's happening. Yes, I know, that's it

ayéhdi, tónht'etónh ts'ín eghasuts'eli.
he talked about it, long time ago to praying.

"Nekinhle óon gáa, Ndahwotá edulin awódeh óon.
"Heavy [huge] then yes, God nothing will happen then.

Mbekeeh tahdah ech'á awónht'e.
On it [the surface of the earth] sometimes different/unusual it is.

Dzah dzah dek'íodekeh, kaa, xónht'e. Ewon kín
Bad bad are happening, well, it's like that. Even depending

dene újon ts'inlé, xede edulin onht'e. Edu
person good you are, just nothing it is. Not

mindihts'edíh'a," éhdi ehłéh. "Gáa, tahdah ihts'i
worry about it," he said all the time. "Yes, sometimes wind

ju neche enúdlin tonht'e ts'ín," xéwodeh. "I
also it's big must be for to," he says like that. "That

xónht'i ch'a éhsán at'in. Łígé zonh gha ju
like that avoiding must be he is. One only for also

ats'et'in, eghasuts'eli," éhdi. "Jon zonh
they do, he prays," he said. "Here only

ndahxa'eghasuídli kudídi gha. Di díeh necha.
we pray for them we think [future]. This land is big.

Dígeh wok'eh ehsíin xódacho, łínt'ónh wogha
Land all over whatever there is that big, all for

dídi," éhdi.
we talk," he said.

"Del'ayah édé, metesée
"We were to go in [in the fence at Tea Dance] then, [Tea Dance] fence

t'ayah edé, wónjon eghasuídlin. Héé, denadihi
they go in then, just we pray. Hey, priest

mbedhats'e'áhi kehwónht'e. Edu wots'edeh tonht'e
communion seems like that. Not they talk far in the future

ts'ín óon wónjon Ndahwotá guedíe. Di dígeh ehsíin.
to then just God their land. This land that is.

Gulón ndahtsáundi," éhdi óon. Kón k'eh
Hopefully He [God] will help you all," he said then. Fire on

edeek'ée ni'ah. Tth'á, tth'á wónjon dets'ali, xeda
tobacco he put. Cup, cup just clean, moose

tlehé nechi ju, ju kón ghenihchu.
fat big also, also fire he gave some.

Gáa gulaa édé tl'o, tl'o ats'inle édé, łínt'ónh
Already finished then hay, hay they made then, all

edulini ndadeh. Yéh Zama ts'ín úh Johaa,
no one living. There Zama toward and George Kolay,

Mogi tene ts'ín úh, sahgeh Diyuo,
Simon Kolay trail toward and, river Mega River,

Rainbow Lake ts'ín úh, Echinchah, łínt'ónh tínts'inde.
Rainbow Lake to and, Chinchaga River, all they move.

Kénét'i dene, kénét'i dene, tlincho ya'edegheh. Tl'o
Ten people, ten people, horses they went with. Hay

ats'inleh wots'ín gáa, xónht'e detah dah. September
they made around yes, like that the bush in. September

k'eh óon níatsinde. I wots'ín
on then they came back [to Hay Lakes]. That to around them

k'éts'edeh.
they walk.

Héé, fah xeda ka, etthén ats'edídleh. I éhsán
Hey, far moose for, meat we make. That then

yahk'eh mbet'á ts'ín. Łígé úh ónk'et'i ts'edhéhxe édé
winter inside to. One and two they kill then

gáa, netlon etthén xónht'i. Níats'indeédé la gáa tse
well, lots meat like that. They come home then firewood

ats'edídleh. Úh wotl'éh kodle t'áh wots'eleh kúan,
they make. And mud muddy with they paint house,

wotl'éh kodle t'ah wots'eleh. K'ahju ét'i kón,
mud muddy with they paint. Again the same fire,

wotl'eh kodle t'áh. Héé, dekónhín xúle. Kón
mud muddy with. Hey, lamps nothing. Fire

déhthene, kón édé héé, wóhtahle.
you light, fire then hey, bright.

Etthén   ju   ts'edet'eh ehteh, ndats'edeh. Úh la xónht'e
Meat   also they cook   usually, they're living. And   like that

ehteh. Héé, duh xónht'e ndegha ahteh édón.
usually. Hey, now like that for you I do   no matter.

Sa'awonteh éhsín xónht'i wotl'éh kodle nái'a, yídééh
I'll do for you maybe like that mud   muddy put up, long ago

kúan netsédle ahteh édón   sa'awonteh, xónht'i.
fire   small   I do   no matter I'll do for you, like that.

Wok'ándehteh   ehteh.
Hc watchcs   usually.

Héé, gáa, i   xónht'e édé yídínht'ónh wóh'on!
Hey, yes, that like that then in the past   appeared [vision]!

Gáa, duhddheneh wots'ín ndahxéhwodeh.   Ghinlé,
Yes,   today   to   he spoke to us like that. He was,

héé, mbewodihé endádla ehtéh,
hey,   his stories   lots   usually,

Ahkimnatchie.   Yídééht'ónh, dandet'i t'ónh
Ahkimnatchie [his adopted father]. Long ago,   how many ago

yeh   Yahti Kúan   ts'edi,   gots'ín óon
there Priest House [Fort Providence] they call it, to there then

ah   t'áh, Mbehcho   wots'ín kóntah
snowshoes with,   Big Knife [Bistcho Lake] to   visiting

ehteh. Yídééht'ónh wowodihé ju. Mbetá   ehsíin
usually. Long ago   stories   also. His father that was

at'in. Łínt'ónh edawodíh. Ndahxéhwodeh,   xéwónht'e
he was. All   he knows. He spoke to us like that, it is like that

mbéhwodeh   kéhwodi   ghinlé yídééht'ónh łínt'ónh
he talks to him he spoke to them before   long ago   all

edawodíh.
he knows.

Eyi   ndetá
That   your father's [Margaret Ahkimnatchie's father, Fred Didzena]

teghelé la góon   mbek'eh edéhtl'éh?   Ye   sóon
drum   [question] on it   writing/drawing? What   then

mbek'eh déhtl'éh? I   ju   gáa, yéhwodeh.   Nógha
on it   drawn?   That also well, he talked about it. Nógha

inhgah   eghasuli mbetá.   Eyóon   mbetegheli
together   he prayed her father. That is   his [Fred Didzena's] drum

dahtheton. Ye   sóon mbek'eh edéhtl'éh? I   ét'i
hanging.   What then on it   drawn?   That   the same

et'on ju onht'e, i la gheh'in, kúan ju gáa, kúan
leaf also it is, that I saw, house also yes, house

ju enúdlin. Héé, újon mbetegheli . . . Thén
also must have been. Hey, good his [Nógha's] drum . . . Star

dahtheli i ét'i mbek'eh the'on. I xédónht'i
on it that the same on it was. That like that

mbek'eh yathela ts'et'oen ju, xónht'e gáa, i
on it were on it leaves also, like that well, that

kudi yek'eh ní'yínleh gáa, eyi eghasuts'eli.
he wants on it he put on yes, that he prays.

Éhdi, "Edeek'ée la andéét'i t'áh mbetáudééh'a,"
He said, "Tobacco how many with useful,"

yéhdi "Dene 'eghasuauhti,' kudi, edeek'ée
he said to him. "Person 'I will pray,' he thinks, tobacco

et'o. Łínt'ónh díeh wok'eh lidí ju ónket'i dene
he smokes. All land on it tea also two people

yendéleh. Eghasuts'eli ats'eleh ts'endehtéh
he leaves it [tea]. They pray they do they're going to sleep

i ghádé, ets'int'odi tl'oanh kedzee yełani'a
that ready, smoking after someone's heart he crossed

ats'inlá. Ts'endéhtin, édé kechonh, ts'endéhtin
they did. They go to sleep, then while sleeping, they go to sleep

kechonh ewon. Wohteh mbéhkets'audedi.
while they're sleeping even though. Really one is helped.

I la ndahte édé. Yídeeh édé mendahdíh,"
That you all sleep then. In the future then you all remember,"

ndahéhdi. "Edeek'éé, dene ehsíin yendéleh onht'e.
he said to us. "Tobacco, people that are leaves it it is.

Kón ghets'inchu, łéét'e," éhdi. "Kinzoh ats'et'in
Fire you feed it, it is the same," he said. "Alone one is

édón."
no matter."

"Deneghadih k'ohsele ju edu ts'edetsi.
"Priest necklace [rosary] also not let it go.

Úts'eton!" éhdi. "Édé gulóon mbotsinadi ehsíin
Hold tight!" he said. "Then hopefully that which happens that are

sets'audundi," ts'edi. I denadihi k'ohsele
you will help me," they say. That priest necklace [rosary]

eghasuts'eli. Łatani'i xónht'i ts'endéhtin édón,
one prays with. Cross like that one goes to sleep no matter,

i kíonejid ehsíin edu kets'ín xonhen adeh, edu
that dangerous that is not to them near comes, not

kets'ín adeh. Yídeeh édé wok'ándahtah éhsín. I
to there comes. In the future then you will all see maybe. That

udháhtthon." Ketahín xá'at'in wodeh óon, gáa, i
you all heard." In a crowd he was he spoke then, well, that

yéhdi, "Dech gua ech'uin." Kéhwodeh. Gáa,
he said, "Further a little another way." He lectured people. Yes,

udhéehtthon ehłeh.
I listened all the time.

"Tth'á tsené ats'elehi ju. Mbet'audeh'a," éhdi.
"Dishes dirty one makes also. They are useful," he said.

"Tth'á tsené mbéhats'atthede édé, xónht'i tth'á tsené
"Dishes dirty you use to eat then, like that dishes dirty

edu ats'elá mbéhats'atthede édé. Gots'ín Ndahwotá gáh
not one did you use to eat then. To there God with

ketsen ats'eleh k'e wónlin. Nótónkets'edehxeli k'é
someone's dirt one makes way exists. Washing place

wónlin. I ndáts'int'e ehsíin edawots'edíh." I
exists. That the way you are however they will know." That

łínt'ónh ketthíteeh xáadeh ghádé, tahdah tsén,
all overhead it happens like way, sometimes dirt,

tsén mbetah i xáint'e, kenieh, kedhá.
dirt in it that he took out, someone's nose, someone's mouth.

Héé, eledzé ét'e. "I la tth'á xónht'i tsén t'áh
Hey, gunpowder the same. "That dish like that dirt with

atthedi onht'e. I ch'a tth'á nótóndehxeli
eating it is. That away from dish washed

ehsíin wohteh mbetsaundendi," éhdi. "Woteh
that was really you'll be helped," he said. "Really

mbetsaundendi úh. Udháhtthon!" éhdi. "Ndahkúan
you will be helped and. You all listen!" he said. "Our house

wónlin ehsíin tth'á edu tsén t'áh at'in le. I
exists that is dishes not dirt with it is not. That

t'áh dene andats'edle édé, héé, di díeh k'eh
with people reborn then, hey, this land on

'egeeyah mbetthíghá dedeli,' kudahdi. Újon
'white person his hair red,' you all think. Good

mbódat'in łéét'e, édé ju dene k'ésín kódat'in. Tu
he appears the same, then too people way appears. Water

ét'i ketthíteeh   xája   édé wónjonh, egeeyah
it is overhead   it happens then just,   white person

ets'int'e,   dene   andats'edleh. Guin óon xónht'e?
he is like him,   person reborn.   There then it's like that?

Eyóon dene,   'edu kuendahshah,' éhdi,   'kuehshah
That is person, 'not I'm going in,' he said, 'I'm going in

igha.   Edu xónht'e.   Edu ka,'   sets'edi,   edu
[future].   Not like that. Not yet,'   they said to me, not

kúets'eyah,   óon kek'ándehta," éhdi.
you go in,   but one watches," he said.

Eyóon i Nógha   ets'edi   ndátin ghinlíi. Nógha
That is that Wolverine they call him prophet he was. Wolverine

úye,   ehtée éhdi. Nógha   úye.   Ya'at'in,
he's called, uncle he said. Wolverine he's called. He was with him,

Ahkinatchee yegáh   thedee.   Mbedéedze óon gáh
Ahkimnatchie with him married. His sister then with

theda,   inhłechidle   aghint'e,   Ahkinachee. I
he's married, brothers-in-law   they were,   Ahkimnatchie. That

Nógha   íin   mbets'iyuen, Dóamo,   edanedíh
Wolverine before his wife,   Suzanna Providence, you know

éhsín. Eyi mbedéédze óon setá   yegáh theda. Úh
maybe. That his sister then my dad married.   And

inhłechidle   i   t'áh,   edayedíh
each other's brothers [married to sisters] that because of, he knows

łint'ónh yá'atin.
all   they are together.

Nóghe   héé, woyon.   Wonlin   mbech'a
Wolverine [the animal] hey, he's smart. Something while sleeping

níts'enéneh'ín   édón,   edu edayedíh édón   níyedíya,
you hide something no matter, not he knows no matter he takes it,

éhdi. I   dene héé, woyon.   I   Nóghe   edadíh
he said. That person hey, he's smart. That Wolverine he knows

i   t'áh.   I   t'áh   óon Nógha   úye.
that because of. That because of then Wolverine he's called.

Se'e   edayedíh. Xónht'i t'áh   yídééht'ónh
Really he knows. Like that because of long ago

mbets'ínleh.
it happened to him.

K'uen,   een, i   wolin   edu ehda.
Woodchuck, yes, that something not he eats.

Nógha   úye.   Nóghe   edadíh.
Wolverine [prophet]   he's called.   Wolverine [animal]   he knows.

Héé, wonlin   ehsíin   edawodíh!   Nóghe
Hey,   something   that may be   he will know!   Wolverine [animal]

dzahdonht'e   onht'e.   Eyi   edadíh   úh   k'uen   ju
he's bad   he is.   That   he knows   and   woodchuck   also

xónht'e   ehsíin,   ehsíin   godahi   edu   etthi   enúdlin.
like that   whatever,   whatever   something   not   he eats   must be.

Eyi   t'ah   atthéé   t'áh   aja   enúdlin.
That   with   he ate   because of   it happened   it must have been.

Dene   xónht'i   tl'a   wonlin   edu   etthi   édé   ts'edi
Person   like that   well   something   not   he eats   then   they say

édé,   héé,   móndeji,   endádla.   Xónht'e   yatthee   édé.
then,   hey,   it is dangerous,   really.   Like that   he ate it   then.

T'andéhtthe.   Xá'adeh. . . .
He died.   That's what happened. . . .

  Tl'a,   Nóghe   onht'e,   i   t'áh
  Well,   Wolverine [animal]   it is,   that   because of

Nógha   úye   éhdi.   Héé,   ka,   gáa,
Wolverine [prophet]   he's called   he said.   Hey,   well,   yes,

endádíndla   ewon,   mbedzonh   wodedíh   i   t'áh   la
he was energetic   but,   his chest   sick   that   because of

aja   enúdlin   kuhdi.   Aan,   tl'a,   Nógha
it happened   must be   I think.   Yes,   well,   Wolverine [prophet]

mbedzonh   wodedíh,   úh   aja   enúdlin   t'áh
his chest   sick,   and   it happened   must be   because of

ajá.   "Yéh   Behchon   la   ts'ín   sa'at'in,"
it happened.   "There far   Bistcho Lake   to   come with me,"

yéhdi.   Héé,   újon,   dene   újon   elin.
he said [to my dad].   Hey,   he is good,   person   he is good   he is.

  Xálónh   nda'edlo   ehtin   dene.   Úh   jon   onht'e   úh
  Really   he laughs   I am   person.   And   here   he is   and

kegha   ju   eghasuli.   He   keyah   wodeh   úh   ehxel
for someone   also   he prays.   Just   with you   he talks   and   he drums

édé,   gúh,   "Xáaht'in,"   éhdi.   "Metesíi   óinhdé,
then,   then,   "I'm like that,"   he said.   "[Tea Dance] Fence   other side,

edulin   onht'e,   tonht'e   wots'ín   metesíi   óinhdé   tínt'ónh
nothing   it is,   far   to   fence   other side   all

ndáwots'eyeh   the'on.   'Ndáwóye,'   kudahdi   édé
play   it's at.   'We play,'   you all want   then

ndáwahye úh edu kets'elehe onht'e. Edu
you all play and not evil/strange it is.   Not

dahwohtl'eh   kudi   ehsíi   ju   ndádhed édé gáa,
he wants to dance he wants whoever also he stands then yes,

he   da'etl'eh. Duhddheneh gáa, xónht'e gha niwontth'e
just he dances. Today   yes, like that for it came

onht'e. Dándéhtháh kudahdi gáa gulaa sedadi,"
it is.   How far   you all think that's enough tell me,"

éhdi óon.
he said then.

　"Héé, újon,   gáa gulaa édé, gáa gulaa,"
　"Hey, it's good, that's enough then, that's enough,"

ats'edi gha. . . .
they say [future]. . . .

　Héé, újon. I   duh i   éti   ndátin ju, újon,
　Hey, good. That now that the same prophet also, good,

da'edlo úh, eyi ét'e   łeghent'e.   I   duh, i
he laughs and, that like that they're the same. That now,   that

at'in k'ésín. Gáa ka edu tats'ede'áh. Jon xéhtláh la
he is   way.   Still not one loses it.   Here last one

eghasuinli la, Hatl'o dúhdín elin   k'e   xónht'e
he prayed,   Habay   this way there is willow like that

ayeh'in. Eyin kuhdi eghasuinlé kuhdi. Jon xéhtlah la
he had.   There I think he prayed   I think. Here last one

eghasuinli. Yéh   Danais Zahéh wodúhdín
he prayed.   There Danais Creek this way

ehda   tl'o   wónlin. Di   ét'i
land bounded by bend in river grass [hayfield] it is.   This the same

ehda   tl'oe.   Héé, újon.
land bounded by bend in river grass[hayfield]. Hey, good.

　"Gáa   gulaa   Ndahwotá seghededi.   Łahts'et'i
　"Already finished God   he is telling me. Five

ddheneh zonh seghedi   íin.   Gáa   gula kuhdi,
days   only he is telling me before. Already the end I think,

gáa   gula,"   éhdi. "Gáa   sa'endadla.   Edu deguh
already the end," he said. "Already I am exhausted. Not more

éhsín.   Gáa   gula kughedi," éhdi. Úh   xóon
maybe. Already the end they think," he said. And so

ndéhtin.   Nógha   ets'edi.   Héé, dene   újon.
he went to sleep. Wolverine he is called. Hey, person good.

13 Nógha's Prophecies

Aan, setá   mbewodihé   wo'inle'á,   thedhe,
Yes,   my father   his message   that was,   mother's brother,

mbechidle. Se'e   xattheeh   ech'ulon   mbeteghelé
her brother.   Really   before   another   his drum

auleh   úh.   I   mbeteghelé   edu   xattheehi   yeh
he was making   and.   That   his drum   not   that was at first   there

at'in   íin   dene   ju.   Mbegha   gu'ats'inlá   úh   yek'eh
he was   before   person   also.   For him   made   and   on it

dintl'eh   ínyá.   Yihda   ju   mbek'eh   the'on.   Sa   ju
he wrote   then.   North star   also   on it   placed.   Sun   also

mbek'eh   the'on.   Ye ghonh   gúhyeh   mbegha   k'íodatian
on it   placed.   Why   that way   for him   it appeared

kéhé?   Edéhtl'éh   k'ih   ní'eni'on   mbedinzí   k'ih.   Kúan
that way?   Paper   on   he put   his name   on.   House

ju   mbek'eh   wóh'on.   Eyi la   Ndahxetá   ets'edi.
also   on   put on.   That   God   it is called.

"Sedígeh   awónht'e,"   éhdi.   I la   mbedígeh   mbek'eh
"My land   that is,"   he said.   That   his world   on it

ndáídéhi   yídeeh   dáodehíl   óon   ndahxedadl.
we live   ahead   how it will happen   then   he told us about.

"I la   mbedígeh   mbek'eh   xónht'e   dene   nendúé úh,
"That   his world   on it   like that   person   nothing   and,

ónket'lne   zonh   édé ghon.   Lígé   ejin   úh   lígé   yegha
two people   only   then even.   Once   sings   and   one   for him

da'etl'eh   igha.   I   wots'ín   di   shin   edu   shon
dances   [future].   That   until   this   song   not   old

ayileh   úh   k'onddhi   júh   łéét'e,"   éhdi.   Gáa   eyi
he does   and   new   too   the same,"   he said.   Already   that

setá,   thedhe   mbechidle,   Ndahxetá
my father,   mother's brother   her brother,   God

mbéhedawodíhí   gáa k'aa   mbedhá   wok'eh   wolinahłeh.
with him he knows   still   his words   the same way   I live.

Éhdi la, "**Yídeeh édé wowon'ín egoh éhsín,**"
He said, "Ahead then you will see might maybe,"

séhdi. "**Ech'un dene edéhtl'éh eh ndahxene'ah**
he said to me. "Different people paper with they lie to us

igha," **séhdi.** "**Yídeeh édé di edéhtl'éh t'áh**
[future]," he said to me. "Ahead then this paper with

ndahxets'ende'ahi la. Edéhtl'éh dendítl'edzi,
they will lie to us. Paper yellow,

mbéhndahxets'endi'a, édíi la di ndahxets'ído edu
the one they fooled you with, whichever this our children not

mbedenaghahdi éhsín," **éhdi óon dúhddhenéh**
you all will remember them maybe," he said but then today

on awónht'e. "**Wowon'ín egóhó endúé egóhó,**" **séhdi**
but it is. "You will see maybe not maybe," he told me

íin. I la Ndahxetá wodihé eh séhwodeh ínyá. Edu
past. That God's story about he told me that. Not

sin zonh dene andet'e eh wodeh. Gúhyeh óon
me only people many about it he told. That way then

éhdi íin. Ahán, i la di emohts'ededlin ts'edi úh
he said before. Yes, that this this advice was said and

di eghasuts'elin inhtthi'omeh wots'edehi segha
this praying side by side talking about it for me

łéét'e.
the same.

Di ndahxedígeh mbek'eh ndáídehi yídeeh
This our land on it we live ahead

dáodehi óon. Ndahxedadí íin. "Eyi
what will happen then. He told us before. "That

eghasu'ahłin mbeduindahdíh édé ndahxedígeh enłát'in
you all praying if you forget then our land one

sa k'íodadedhe wots'ín edulin sa éhsín," **éhdi.**
month that long until nothing sun maybe," he said.

Eyi la wodihé, gáa eghasuinli dígeh wodih a'onht'e.
That story, already prayer land story it is.

I mbeghadeh dígeh wóh'on. Xetlint'ónh sa xáiyał
That same land put. Morning sun rising

ínyá óndaginsa ju úh inhda'ende'ah.
then moon also and passing each other [eclipse].

Ddheníighadeh ddhenéh tadindzinh níni'on édé,
All day day middle [noon] put there then,

wolindah łíé sadzee wots'ín inhłahde at'in gha
about one hour to there same spot it is [future]

éhsín. "Ye ghonh gúhyeh xájá édé sa
maybe. "What for that way happen like that then sun

nda'ah i łíé ke'ejade. I wots'ín enłak'ehe at'in
sets that one did the same. That to there together he was

édé. Eyi'a wozen ighá," éhdi a'adi. Eyi'a
then. That darkness will be," he said he told. That

mbewodihé a'onht'e. I la dáhthít'e di ghádéh, jon
his story was. That how we are this way, here

xódéhteh edu wonejid úh ndahxehwodeh eyóon. I
many not frightened and he told us like that. That

t'ah edu sin sewodihé onht'e. Setá
because of not me my story it is. My father [uncle]

ndatín ghinlí i sedadi. I dene łínt'ónh
prophet he was this he told me. Those people all

edawodíh i a'onht'e.
know this is.

"Wok'endeghehta, wok'endeghehta i ghedi zonh
"I'm always watching, I'm always watching that live only

k'eghendehta," séhdi, úh edu káh. Tonht'etónh,
watching," he said to me, and not yet. Long ago,

wolindah łahts'et'iet'i xet wónlin éhsín, kuhdi got'ónh
about fifty years it is maybe, I think back

óon setá mbek'ewoghindhe. T'ónh gáa k'aa mbedhá
then my father he died. Before still his words

ekendahdíh, i ghonh óon adehsi. Edu ju edéhtl'éh
I remember, that is why then I speak. Not also paper

k'ih the'on. Óon sindí t'áh mendahdíh i ghonha
on placed. Then my mind with I remember it that is why

ahsi. Gughedhótthon łínt'ónh enłak'éhé. Wonlin
I'm saying. Let's listen to them all together. Something

łets'enítl'e úh, tthihtheti úh, edu mbelonh k'íodat'in łii
stick together and, pulled out and, not its end see

guhyeh lon xót'e. Yídeeh wogha ndahxets'ído.
that way let's be like that. Ahead [future] for our children.

Eyi la dene łínt'ónh lon edutth'e gúh. Dene
Those people all desire will listen then. People

mbets'ído wónlin ehsíin lonh. Gulon eyi setá
their children are that are must be. I wish that my uncle's

dhá   kendawodih.   Kuhdi ghonh   óon
words they will remember. I want for that reason then

ahsi.   Gáa   setá   dhá   wotlondih'a wonlin
I'm saying.   Already my uncle's words many times   something

sedadi   ínyá. Xodéhtheh wots'ín wolindah dahsi
he told me then. That's all   to there about   I say,

sendajine,   mahsi.
my brothers, thank you.

14 The Dene Prophets

Mbek'ádhi   ets'edi,   semo   mbetá   onht'e.
Paul Metchooyeah's father he's called, my mother her father it is.

Semo   mbetá.   Eyóon gáa kaa mbetene újon. Tónht'e
My mother   her father. There still   his trail good. Long ago

ts'ín onht'e. Gúhyeh xéwodeh   éhsín. Łígé ghedé
to   it is.   Like that he spoke like that maybe. One   year

gha, łígé ghedé gha eghasuli, łínt'ónh dene łéndahde
for, one   year for he prays, all   people they gathered

édé eghasuli. Anéh, mbetá,   ndátin   ghinłíi, éhdi.
then he prayed. Mom, her father, prophet he was,   she said.

"Wónlin nodúé di   dígeh wok'eh wónlin, wónlin
"There   nothing this land   on it   there is, there is

nedúé. Duh éhsín gah   nedúé,   gah   nedúé úh chi
nothing. Now maybe rabbits nothing, rabbits nothing and ducks

zonh wónlin." Iíh gáa, dene   gha eghasuli. Łígé
only there are." And well, people for he prays. One

ghedé gha. Gáa, et'ontl'onh dechin t'ahin, dechin
year   for. Well, in the fall   bush   in,   bush

t'ahin ats'edeh, igha   tínts'endeh,   igha   édé
in   they go,   [future] they move away,   [future] then

et'ontl'onh eghasuli. Mendajiné   gha eghasuli. "Gúhyeh
in the fall   he prays. His relatives for he prays. "That way

xéwót'e   éhsín. Gúhyeh di   ghedé la   gúhyeh
it will be like maybe. That way this year   that way

xéwót'e   éhsín," éhdi   édé. "Se'e   gúhyeh," adin.
it will be like maybe," he said then. "Really that was," he said.

Eghasughinle édé gáa, Dawots'ethe k'é   awóndli
He prays   then well, Tea Dance   place they made

eghasuts'eli édé. Gáa, dawodigáa édé   dechin dek'ali
they pray   then. Well, dawn   then pole white

alehi; ndáttheh   ehgasuts'eli k'é.   "Dígeh wots'ín
he did; he put it up prayer   place. "Land   to

edahats'eleh   igha,"   éhdi.   I   dechiné   nái'i   i
one buys   [future]," he said. That pole   standing that

ét'i   sunibani onlíi,   dek'ali   mbéhts'endehtl'únh
the same   ribbon   he made,   white   he ties it

wónjonh dígeh wots'ín ndá'ol.   "Dígeh   wots'ín
well   land   to   floating down. "Land   to

edahats'eleh. Dígeh   wots'ín edahathídleh.   Di   ghedé
one buys.   Land   to   we buy/make.   This   year

dá'áh mbeteeh díkeeh gogha ndéh wots'ín dahatthídleh
during over it   we fall for   land to   we buy/make

gha," éhdi.   I   ét'i   línt'ónh dene   ehsíin
for," he said. That the same all   people that were

déyendétl'únh.   I   ghedé   xónht'e   dechintahín
they tied [ribbon on pole]. That year   like that in the bush

edaghejá   édé.   Édé ju   donge   ghendetez
if they went [into bush]   then. Then also hunger they will become

úh.   Edu ju wo'ónéh   ts'ín don   aguyíleh.   Edu
and. Not also from around to   hunger they will become. Not

wo'ónéh ts'ín dedíh   aguyíleh.   Edu ju   wo'ónéh
around   to   sickness they will become. Not also around

ts'ín wóhdli ehléh.   Eyóon Mbek'ádhi
to   cold   usually. That is Paul Metchooyeah's father

úye,   semo   mbetá.   "Wonlin   xúle endahthe
he is called, my mother her father. "Something gone you all think

édón.   Di   ghedé   wonlin   endaudeh   egoéhsín,"
no matter. This year   something might happen maybe,"

éhdi   édé.   "I   yahk'e édé,"   yéhdi,   andawodeh.
he said then. "This winter then," he said, it will happen.

Úh   Dahdon'e íin   ju,   Dahdon'e íin   ju
And Dahdona   before also, Dahdona   before also

semo   mbedéédzé óon gáh ghinda.   Ínyá
my mother   her sister then with he lived [married]. That

a'onht'e. I   ju   yetloanh ndátin ghinlé, úh Nógha
it is.   That also after   prophet he was, and Nógha

íin.   Eyi xálonh   at'in. Dahdon'e yek'éh   úh
before. That first/leading he is. Dahdona   after him and

xónht'e óon dene   eghasugheli.
like that then people they prayed.

Eyi   Yahtl'unh ets'edi memo,   eyi mbetá,   eyóon
That Yahtl'unh called   his mother, that her father, that

ju   eghasuinlín.   Kón   ghinhchudi   gha.   Eyi la   jon
also   he prayed.   Fire   he gave some to   for.   That   here

xónht'i   xeda   ónket'i   mbetegheli   k'eh   ndádéh,   k'eh
like that   moose   two   his drum   on   standing,   on

ndádéh,   eyi   etthídinh'á   ndádéh.   Mbetegheli
standing,   that   antlers together/hitting heads   standing.   His drum

k'eh   déhtl'éh   ehłéh.   Eyóon   kón   ghinchudi   ghinlé.
on   written   usually.   That is   fire   he gave some to   before.

Wonlin   kegha   udeké   ghedi,   kegha   udeké   di.
Something   for   he asks   they say,   for   he asks   he says.

Dechintahín   ats'éde   igha   kón   ghenichud   úh
In the bush   they go   [future]   fire   they give some to   and

kegha   eghasuinle   édé,   dechintahín   ts'ín   ats'ejá   édé.
for something   he prayed   then,   in the bush   to   they go   then.

Kíi   wonlin   kíodeni   ts'eghon   ehłéh.   Eyóon   kón
Just   something   appears   someone kills   all the time.   That is   fire

ghinhchudi   ghinlé.   Sin la   eyóon   mbeyiné   ghasuhdehłi.
he gave some to   he was.   Me   that   his song   I pray.

Mbeyiné   ghasuhłi.   Ddheníi   tah   kéét'e   óon   mbeyiné
His song   I pray.   Day   during   the same   then   his song

ghasuhłi.   I   kón   ghinchudi,   mbeyiné   woghinlíi
I pray.   That   fire   he gave it some,   his song   it was

ghasuhłi.
I pray.

Úh   eyi   Nógha   ets'edi   eyi,   Mbek'ádhi
And   that   Nógha   he is called   that,   Paul Metchooyeah's father

tloanh   di   dígeh   eghasuinlí.   Héé,   wohteh   dene
after   this   land   he prayed.   Hey,   really   person

újon   ehłéh.   Kets'ín   wodeh   édé   wónjon,
good   all the time.   To someone   he spoke   then   nicely,

se'e   kets'ín   wodeh.   "Yahk'e Wotiné,"   gúhyeh
really   to someone   he spoke.   "Angels,"   like that

ndéhdi   kéhdi,   kets'ín   wodeh   ehłéh.   Eyi
he said to you   he said to them,   to them   he talked   all the time.   That

mbek'ewoghindhed   úh   yetloanh   déhya   jon
he was wasted/died   and   after him   he went   here

ndahxáwonlinalch   i   óon.   Eyóon   ma'endádla   úh
for us he works   that   then.   That is   he tired/became sick   and

gáa,   dedíh   lonh.   Tulonh   níandehja.   Eyi   et'onlééh
well,   sick   and.   Zama   he came back to.   That   summer

óon Nógha úye xúle. Úh eyi seda
then Nógha he's called gone [died]. And that in front of me

aghet'in la lonh óon eyi ndáten ti wohteh dedíh.
they were must be then that prophet leader really he's sick.

Wohteh dedíh i t'áh Hátl'ode níats'eteh
Really he's sick that because of Habay they took him back to

ghats'edi eghedítthe t'áh. Settheeh got'ónh
they say they heard because of. Ahead of me before

kandaghejá lonh mbets'ín tíats'indeh. Úh sin,
they went with must be to him they moved back. And me,

sin eyi Hátl'ode, i Tulonh níandehja, edulin dene.
me that Habay, that Zama I came back to, nothing people.

Łínt'ónh edulin. Héé, sa'endádla, gáa, tl'o xádedhe
All nothing. Hey, I was tired, yes, grass that long

ketloanh ndehyon.
after then it grew.

  Di eyi ndátin ti, gáa, woteh dedíh.
  This that prophet head one, yes, really he was sick.

Ndádéhja, gáa, wozen níandehja. Edu ehtthe. "Ndechuen
He went back, yes, dark I came back. Not I ate. "Your son

sekauyá, sek'auyá." Damehtá yawodeh
he will visit me, he will visit me." Thomas' father he was talking about

úh, Shondi ju tat'i dene edu k'a. "Sek'auyá,
and, Shondi also three people not yet. "He will visit me,

nónje édé sek'auya ndéhdi," seghedi
he comes back then he will visit me he said to you," they told me

úh.
and.

  Eyi ndátin dedih ts'edi. Dehthíde tádit'e.
  That prophet he was sick they say. We went there three of us.

Sinlá uton úh sets'ín wodeh óon kendahdíh duh.
My hand he held and to me he spoke then I remember now.

"Yak'e yak'ín, Yak'é Wot'ine, Shondi ju,
"Angels [in]heaven, Angels, Shondi also,

Joe Dáidzené ju, ni ju úh, tadaht'e úh óon.
Joe Didzena also, you also and, three of you and then.

Ndahxin dinzí dek'eth Yak'e Wot'iné," ndahxewodeh.
Our names written Angels," he spoke to us.

"Goin daháa ts'ín nedinzí duk'ali edu
"There something to our names will be white not

et'ondin'a guk'ánduta ile," séhdi ehłéh,
bad things he will look for then not," he said to me usually,

ndátin. Eyi ghon gáa kaa éhdi, edu taudeh'á,
prophet. That for still he said, not I have made mistakes,

edu taude'on óon, gáa kaa. Eyóon mbegah
not I have made mistakes then, still. There with him

nindiya úh mbeghonh sadzahda'onht'e. Endádla.
I went and for him I was sad. It was hard.

Mbeghonh sendatú wónlin, ndasende'en.
For him my tears were, he told me to quit [crying].

"Azonh wonlin ahjá, édon, ye gha
"That's all something happens to me, no matter, why

sek'ede'á. Edu sek'ede'á," éhdi. "Gáa, kóntuh
you cry for me. Not you cry for me," he said. "Yes, like that

dahzeh, eghasuts'eli, ni sendahteh tloanh," éhsán
you all cry out, one prays, you put me there after," must be

sehwodeh. "Xehtlah di dígeh wogha xehtlah wots'ín
he spoke to me. "Finally this land for finally to

sewodihé ndahxandeh'áh igha," kéhdi.
my words I give it to you all [future]," he said to them.

"Ndáts'eudze," kéhdi. "Edulin xeda ts'edhéhxe
"One will go hunting," he told them. "Nothing moose one kills

óon xédónht'e níatsint'e. Yéh ndats'edze zonh edulin
then whatever they return. There one hunts only nothing

ts'edhéhxin, úh duhdzin sa da'ai ts'ín got'ónh
one kills, and this way sun comes up to back then

kadintl'eh. Ekoin dintl'a úh golon dhinxe édé,
you go for. There you go and moose you kill then,

eghasuts'elik'é detasets'ete gha ekoin
prayer place [Tea Dance circle] they put me in [future] there

dintl'a."
you go."

Dint'e goin dehthít'e. Úh eyi Łahxauwin'i wodih
Four there we went. And that [place name] ahead

yidadzinh tl'ok'é dahthít'e'a. Joan xeda wohteh
across hay place we went. Here moose really

tlincho ditadehthít'i. Tlincho dendehthitl'un. Tu
horses we tied up. Horses we tied up. Water

wónlin úh i eyídí tloanh. I dahín yídééh
there was and that we ate after. That both ways ahead

ts'inguh awodeh i duh goin inhxadeh aghejá.
direction it happened that now there at the same time they went.

Sin yídééh ts'ínguh yuhen dídeh k'iohdah goin
Me ahead direction over there in front of I will walk there

deya. Chek'ali kagáh mbek'ánehtanh. Yuhan xeda
I went. Poplar beside I was watching it. This way moose

sets'ín ghegoh, tsiya ónket'i yek'eh gheh'ah.
to me it was walking, yearling two after following.

Mbeda ni'endéhja úh jon mbeda chek'ali in-eh
For it I got ready and here for it poplar behind

ndahdhe. Úh jon teelah xáajíi.
standing. And here standing sideways it happened like.

Undihton, tagúh undihton. Mbeyadze ju ónkeh
I shot, three times I shot. Its young also twice

endiht'u, łahts'et'i úh i ya'inhkin úh óon.
I shot, five times and that they both fell over and then.

Se'e ddhenéh tadieh zonh wots'ín i xeda,
Really day middle only to that moose,

mbeyadze ju. Eyóon mbets'ín ndagodeehdli, sedzeek'é
its young also. There to him I kneeled, on my heart

mbets'ín.
to him.

Eyi níandíyi kíon eghasuts'eli det'á
That we brought back on that one prays inside

ts'intin. Eyóon ndátin ts'ín wodeh. Gáa,
he put him in [his body]. There prophet to he speaks. Yes,

łínt'ónh kón wots'ín ghinchud úh. Gáa, edin ju
all fire to they gave some and. Yes, him too

endadla óon, kegha ghejini tloanh kehwodeh
he was exhausted then, for them they sang after he lectured them

igha ts'edi. Deti ehsíin łínt'ónh yedhonah déhtth'i
[future] they say. Elders that were all around him they sat

óon kehwodeh. "Tat'i, di dígeh tat'i, díent'i
then he lectured them. "Three, this land three, four

edéhtl'éh, edéhtl'éh, díent'i, díent'i t'áh ndets'ende'ah,
papers, papers, four, four with one lies to you,

ndets'edi," yéhdi. Łígé dendíbeedzi auht'e
he says to you," he said to him. One blue it will be

úh, łígé dek'ali audeh úh, łígé dek'ali ajá édé
and, one white it will be and, one white happens then

łígé dendíbeedzi ajá   édé, łígé dendítledze adeh
one blue   happens then, one yellow   it will be

igha. Di łígé dídíl két'e adeh igha. Díent'i
[future]. This one pink the same it will be [future]. Four

edéhtl'éh ndets'ende'ah ndets'edi.
papers   he lies to you   one said to you.

Eyóon ts'inh i   wots'inh mbek'ewoghindhe ts'inh,
There from there from   he was wasted [died]   from,

łígé ghedé awójá.   Di   ghedé andawójá do'on, tsído
one year happens. This year happened spring, child

suniyé ts'edi   kats'eni'on, mbéhndaxets'eniá. Ndahdi
money they say they gave,   with it they lied to us.   Government

edéhtl'éhé, łígé dendíbeedzi kats'inla,   ndahdi
papers,   one blue   they gave out, government check

gha úh. Wotloanh i   gheda dek'ali ajá,   dek'ali
for and. Later that year white   it happened, white

ekéhatsinlá wotloanh i   ghedé dendítledze k'ehats'inlá.
on it one did later that year yellow on it one did.

"Eyóon ndets'endu'a   éhsín," éhdi óon. "Eyóon
"That they will lie to you maybe," he said then. "There

ech'u dene óon ndahxende'a   igha,"   ndahxéhdi.
different people then he will lie to you all [future]," he told us.

Óon wónjon gúhyi.   Níwóntth'e.
Then really it's like that. It happened.

"Di ndedígeh andéét'i, łínt'ónh, ndedígeh
"This your land how many, all,   your land

audendachoge woedéhtl'éhé adeh   igha. Łínt'ónh
it's big   map   will happen [future]. All

di dígeh, ndedígeh woedéhtl'éh ajed i   tloanh,
this land, your land map   happened that after,

i wotsinh edu wondeedhi, ndaxiendi nindahke
that from not long   you people huddled together

éhsín," ndahxéhdi óon. Duhddhenéh óon mbek'eh
maybe," he said to us then. Today   then on it

ahthít'in.
we are.

Ndahxets'ído ehsíin guyendeji   ets'edon,
Our children that are we were afraid of them drinking,

t'áh dene endiji. Eyóon got'ónh ndátin k'ewoghindhe.
with people afraid of. That is long ago prophet wasted [died].

Óon   ndátin   wots'ín   wodeh   óon   duhddhenéh   onht'e.
Then   prophet to   he spoke   then   today   it is.

15 The Death Of Nógha

Eyi Nógha, ndátin ghinlé la, xalonh újon. Dawots'ethe
That Nógha, prophet he was, really good. TeaDance

yawots'inla xónht'e, łínt'ónh kuets'edeh édé. Edu
they made like that, all came in then. Not

ju ketlonh déhya duh. I shin mbek'eh edatl'ehi
also after he came now. That song on it written

łínt'ónh mbeyiné, łínt'ónh. I ts'ídoa shin detl'ehi
all his songs, all. That children song written

k'ánitah i xónht'i. Goin níniya éhsán i k'éh,
you look at that like. There it arrived then that after,

yek'éh ejini t'ah adehsi yeh. Úh edu ju gots'i
after he sang with I say there. And not also he lied

dadehsi le. Ka, se'e mbek'ánehta. Edu edéhtl'éh kúan
I say not. Well, really you look at it. Not school

ait'in óon mbekendehjin.
he was at then he sang it.

"Eyáa onht'e ndahxa di díeh k'eh wok'ándahta. Ínyá
"That it is for us this land on watching us. Then

k'eh wogha shin ndahgha ats'inla. Wonlin
on for song for us was made. Something

mbéhwots'edeh keduh wonlin thun ats'clch édé, tth'á,
talk to with something slowly one does then, plate,

ketth'ee, mbek'ehetthetthi tth'ákahli
someone's plate, one eats on it plate

mbek'andats'ídleh. Úh se'e ndat'eni dets'ali
one cleans it. And really cloth white

manitets'enika. I k'eh tth'á níts'enikon
you place it down for him. That on plate one places it there

gots'ín edelé wolíi ledah. Mbek'eh edelé édé kaa,
to there blood lots there were. On it blood then well,

mbats'edintse a'onht'e," kéhdi úh.
one gave to him it is," he told them and.

Úh   thun   ndats'ededzé   édé   eyi   yéhdi   t'áh.   Ts'ejin
And   slowly   one goes hunting   then   that   he said   with.   One sings

édé   gáa.   Xahgahin   ke   edu   teeh   awodeh.   I   úh
then   well.   Evening   just   not   quiet   it will happen.   That   and

ju   gohkoni   yiné   yéhdi   t'áh,   ju   ayeh'in.
also   hot   song   he said to him   with,   also   he has.

Ts'ídoa   yiné   ju   ayeh'in.   Úh   kemo   yiné   ju
Children's   song   also   he has.   And   mother's   song   also

ayeh'in.   Úh   héé,   újon.   Kíi   ndahts'ín   dha   újon
he has.   And   hey,   good.   Just   to us   words   good

nandi'on   édé   edu   mbehats'ut'in   éhsín   edu   k'ah.   Gáa,
he gave   then   not   one uses it   maybe   not   yet.   Well,

wontlonh   sets'edi   úh   ni   xédé   néhwohdeh
later   one says to me   and   you   then   I will talk to you

úh. . . .
and. . . .

"Úh   yídeeh   édé   duhde   óon,"   konhwodeh   íin.
"And   in the future   then   this way   then,"   he tells about   before.

"I   shíh   i   ndahk'inhin   kónt'i   wonlin   dendéht'ehzi
"That   hill   that   our way   like that   something   black

ndahk'eh   ndahchun,   ajá   édé   i   tl'a,   endadla
on us   it rains,   it happens   then   that   well,   difficult

igha.   I   kíi   ndahlin   edon   jon   ndahugez
will be.   That   just   our dogs   no matter   here   it hangs on [biting]

úh   yeh   nindahxonisu.   Tíndahxongha   dedéhdin'e.
and   there   it drags us.   It starts growling   it drags off.

Ndahgáh   egóhó   ndahlin   ndahgon   dagujá   édé,
With you all   maybe   our dogs   in front of us   it happens   then,

dáaht'e?   Etundaht'ine   éhsín.   Eyi   adehsi
what will you all do?   You are all pitiful   maybe.   That   I say

ndahk'éh   ká'ajá   édé."
after us   it happened   then."

"Héé,   diga   kawots'edéh'on   awónht'e.   Eyi
"Hey,   pale   people are headed for   it is.   That

tin-ets'edon   t'áh.   I   t'áh   dene   ju
they started drinking   because of.   That   because of   people   also

dzahdahehłídleh   i   t'áh   ju   ats'et'in   t'áh.
we do bad things   that   because of   also   people are   because of.

I   la   endádla,"   éhdi.   "Dene   yahk'eh   wogha   kíondeji
That   difficult,"   he said.   "People   winter   for   dangerous

úh, úh ju at'in. Úh eyi shíh ju, xeṇdet'in
and, and also it is. And that hill also, this much

onht'e," éhdi. "Ndahxats'eni'on," éhdi. Úh ju,
it is," he said. "They gave to us," he said. And also,

eghadasuinlin ndah la.
they pray us.

Jon la edu eghasuilln. Jon di díeh la edu mbegha
Here not they pray. Here this land not for him

dawots'ethe k'é awots'indlai. I lonh ju, Tulonh
dance place they made. That must be also, Zama Lake

ju mbadawots'ethe úh, Chi Kúen ju mbadawots'ethe
also they dance for him and, Duck House also they dance for him

úh, Dehthi Zahéh ju, K'e Zahéh ju. Úh xóṇdeht'i
and, Straight River also, Willow River also. And that much

díeh xóon mbegha dawots'ethe ka kets'adeh úh.
land then for him they dance for they walked around and.

Úh gáa, tlin dháa t'áh ewon. Tlin dháa t'áh
And yes, dogs regular with even so. Dogs regular with

edon ka ts'ídoa ehdah łínt'ónh dek'eh mbetá
no matter for children also all on their father

dek'eh ni'inleh úh. Detl'a di ts'ededa édé kaa.
on it he puts them and. In the back this one sits then good.

"Gonh tlin," ts'eṇdeyu ka i dawots'ethe
"Ready dog," one tells dog to go for that dances

ehsíın łuhtl'ah tlin níts'enéniyú.
that were entrance dog the dogs were taken there.

Se'e dzene tanieh wots'ín konde'a awots'indleh.
Really day middle to door they made.

"Úh duhdei ts'inguh, dedhóo at'in. Duhdei sa
"And this way direction, boy he is. This way sun

ka'a, ts'egua at'in. Kónt'u dehtth'i gha ju,"
sets [west], girl she is. Like that they sat for also,"

éhdi ndi.
he said it is said.

Úh se'e ekúh ju gots'i le. Katl'odi jon ndaídeh
And really then also he lies not. Habay here we lived

íin ju. I ju kaa, mbegha Dawots'ethe.
before also. That also well, for him Tea Dance.

"Úh se'e agot'é éhsín łínt'ónh yundahéh
"And really it will happen maybe all ahead

dagot'é   **éhsín. Edu mbek'ínhín satsóné netlon**
what will happen   maybe. Not his way   metal   lots

ajá   **édé. Edu eyi at'in le onht'e. I**   **tlin**
happen   then. Not that he is not it is.   That dog

kayeh   **úh dene úh, tlin dháa úh. Andet'i**
he went to get   and person and, dog regular and. How many

inhtah mbekayeh'a at'in onht'e. I   **dzonht'e. Edu**
mixed   he went to get he was it is.   This it's bad.   Not

jon kúededah aaht'in le. Di yeh eghasulin
here you go in   you all be not. This for one prays

ndadahde.   **Eghasuts'elin ndadahde**   **úh. Onkede**
you all will live.   One prays   you all will live   and. Two

kún łahde kúen mbets'ído   **netlon, łahde kúen zonh**
house five house their children   lots,   five   house only

edon.   **Edulin onht'e úh." I**   **kaa ndahdongha. "Di**
no matter. Nothing it is   and." That for   he told us.   "This

ndéh la edu gok'eh ndaht'a."
land   not   on it   you all live."

    Mbedenáa xalonh jon nitthe di k'é, jon
    His wife   first   here she came this place, here

ats'ejá.   **I tl'a, i Dóamo.**   **Inyá xattheeh**
it happened. That well, that Dóa's mother. Then   first

jon-a. I   **edéhtl'éh kúan i móaa**
here. That school   that little mother [Dóamo's mother]

mbetth'ené dzonht'e t'áh   **edu edu editl'eh. I**
her legs   were bad because of not not she goes. That

t'áh   **theda. Tl'a, kaa, eyi yundahéh dagodehsi.**
because of she sits. Well, yes, that in the future what I say.

   Jon setthít'ah   **dehdi,**   **jon setthí jon.**
   Here behind my head he put his hand, here my head here.

Seh jon thetin. Jon mbegáh thida. Jon mbedené
With me here he slept. Here with him I sat. Here his wife

theda. Mbegáh inhłah thetin.   **Kaa, łodehthah**
she sat. With her together he was sleeping. Well, that long

ndadeji,   **łodehthah. "Kadzaht'e**   **igha."**
he breathed, that long. "I'm going to die [future]."

Setthít'ah   **dehdi úh, xoni minlá ka'ajá.**
Behind my head he put and, suddenly his hand it happened like.

Gáa, łiniji.   **Úh se'e dagot'e**   **ehsíin**
Yes, he stopped breathing. And really what happened that was

i   gáa,   łínt'ónh   na'endadeh.
that well,   all   that happened.

"I   ets'edon la edu   újon onht'e," ndi.   "Úh
"That drinking   not good it is,"   he said. "And

ekúhye wolin-ahłá édé ká'edah'in újon ni   aaht'e
like that I worked   then that's why   good you you all are

egoéhsín. Duhdeín tl'a, edu ka'aht'in le,"   éhdi   óon
maybe.   This way well, not you all be   not," he said then

mbek'ioghindhe   óon.
he wasted away [died] then.

Dek'ehtheda, dek'ehtheda ju.   I   ju   ayeh'in,
Picture,   picture   also. That also he had,

mbéédedih ju   ayeh'in. Shin la wónlin, dek'ali xáicho
soap   also he had. Song   there was, white   this big

tlehi   eyi ju ayeh'in. I   ju   detah. I   ju úh.
[moose] fat that also he had. That also in.   That also and.

Úh Ndawotá ts'inh a'onht'e. Tleh   ju,   tleh
And God   from   it is.   [Moose] fat also, [moose] fat

ju xácho ayeh'in úh. Dek'ehtheda i   ju   jon
also that big he had and. Picture   that also here

wots'ín dek'eh. I   sóon dágiyínlá?   Edu k'ah
to   on it.   That then   what did they do? Not yet

agiyeh'in éhsín   detahagot'e.
they have   must be   in the bush.

"Eyi edéhtl'éh, úh ju," éhdi. Káa kaa duh ts'ídoa
"That paper,   and also," he said. Still   now children

du   kats'edeye t'áh   óon. Ekónt'e óon. Ndátin
not tax   because of then. Like that then. Prophet

ajá   i   ghonh óon. Edéhtl'éh wóntsédle mbedatihli
he became that's why   then. Paper   a little   window

dewóntsédle dek'eh the'on. Ndahxats'eni'on duh do'on
a little   on it   it was.   He gave us some   now spring

ech'u   suniyah jon nits'eni'on. Eyi lonh
different money   here they give out. That must be

ayéhdi   kuhdi. "Mahsi Ndawotá, kudahdi   i
he was telling about I think. "Thanks God,   you all think that

a'ahch'u. Ech'u onht'e edon   ahch'u,   Ndawotá
you all grab. Another it is   no matter you all grab, God

kudahdi," ju   éhdi. Eyi suniyah edéhtl'éh.
you all think," also he said. That money   paper.

Mbeteghelé gáa, mbek'ánehta. Gáa, eh'inh óon.
His drum   well, I saw it.   Yes, I saw   then.

Tth'ih   dahthetthu   mbek'eh   nínte.   Gáa, ats'eleh
Mosquitos   hanging   on it   he put it up.   Well, one does

mbedechiné   łínats'eleh   úh.   Edéhtl'éhtú   t'áh   mbechinah
its drumstick   one stops   and.   Pen   with   its edge

ju   ats'inlá   úh   ts'ínhín   dahthetin.   Ttheeh   thetin   úh.
also   he did   and   out   he put it out.   Ahead   he slept   and.

Etleha   di   edhin   guyéhdi   níayediton   édé
Night   this   noise   he said to them   if he takes it back   then

mbek'eh   ni'on   k'eh.   Eghon   ét'i la   edu   eh'in   i
on it   it is   on.   Even   the same   not   I saw   that's

ghonh.   Tl'a,   wodéhtth'ed   ehsíin.   I   mbetegheli   k'eh
why.   Well,   it happened   that was.   That   his drum   on

ninige.
they bit it [mosquitoes].

  Gáa, eyi ju.   Gáa, mbekúen   kuehajá.
  Yes,   that also.   Yes,   his house   inside it happened.

Kíi   ts'inh   edhéh   nái'ai   ju   ayeh'in.   Ekóntuh   edulin
Just   outside   tipi   also   they had.   Like that   nothing

di   kónt'i   ats'eh'in   edulin.   Edhéh   zonh.
this   like   they have   nothing [referring to house].   Tent   only.

Edhéh   nái'ai   edanedíh?   Kónt'i   et'ontlonh   t'ónh.
Tipi   you know?   Like that   fall   after.

Níts'enilá   edhéh,   edzo   ats'elehi la.   Nits'enida   edhéh
They put up   tent,   traps   they do.   They moved   tent

ndats'ege   úh,   mbechinah   kodéhthadzé   tl'o   t'áh   łínt'ónh
they put up   and,   its edge   piled   hay   with   all

mbechinah   awots'ileh   úh.   Łé   ts'ín   mbetah   netlon
its edge   they made   and.   Smoke   to   inside   lots

dúyé   kaa,   kónt'i   egóhó   mbeyueh   ts'edéhtin.
really   well,   like that   or   under it   camped.

Edhéh   nái'ai   tah   ats'eh'in.   Úh   eyi   kíi   tth'ih   tl'a.
Tipi   in   they had.   And   that   just   mosquitoes   well.

I   yéh   Hátl'ode   wots'ín   yéh   wodeh'ai
That   over there   Habay   to   over there   goes that way

highway   nandet'a   egóhó   got'ats'ín.   Jon   tl'unhdené
highway   landing strip   or   beyond.   Here   forestry

kúen   godahi   gua   aheh'in.   Eyi   eyi   kúncho
building   something   a little   he had.   That   that   big building

ndadáin'ín eyóon onht'e. (Yandileh íin eyóon
standing up that's how it is. (Messed up before like that

sin ndahdeh wots'ín. Ndettheeh gua ju,
I live to. Down the river bank a little also,

Alikmo settheeh ndadeh.)
Alec's mother down the river bank from me she lived.)

Sa déhdeli úh godah dechinah wodéhdele
Sun red and somewhere edge of the woods all getting red

i ju. I ju sin ká'e'á. I ju "'setsotl'ah,
that also. That also me he wants me. That also "'visit me,"

séhdi ," ghedi, mbets'ín dehtl'a. Sinlá edegúh
he told me," they said, to him I went. My hand he held

dedzeek'eh nisedenil úh. "Héé, ni zonh óon di
on his heart he put it [hand] and. "Hey, you only then this

ndéh gok'eh tsuneya úh theneda. Wonlin ju
land on you take pity on him and you stay. Something also

thaht'ónh sek'ah éhsín kaa, di ts'ek'ahi enedhen? Eyi
long ago he eats maybe well, this that's eaten you want? That

ju mbeké yaítl'a úh, mbejihé úh mbe'ah úh
too his moccasins ruined and, his mitts and his snowshoes and

ghaendade, edu mondinle mbegha ayunleh." Mbechoan
he watches, not mourn him for him you will do." His son

ts'ín Alec ts'indi, úh séhdi. "I kaa kaa
to Alexis you help him, and he said to me. "That for for

zonhán audéhdesi, kíi nendah łonníojih."
only I want to say to you, just in front of you I'll stop breathing."

Kaa, mbegáh theda kaa, eyi sa déhgoli. (Kaa, eyi
Well, with him he sat well, that sun set. (Well, that

chbcc ju dza'adeh.) Nótondéhthíghe úh se'e újon
auntie also dying.) We washed him and really well

ndat'eni k'ondi t'ayítin. Éé, kónt'uh la dechinxeeh
clothes new we put him in. Hey, like that coffin

edu kónt'uh. Di mbetsée eyi Harry Dahdon'e íin
not like that. This his son-in-law that Harry Dahdona before

kaguindeh. Dene dechinxeeh cho tats'ełeh. Edu
he called for. People coffin big he brought. Not

káyinlá lonh édé, edu kónt'e éhsín. Kozin
he did like that must be then, not like that maybe. Over there

i kaguinde úh, dechinxeeh dene mbetahtheda gha
that he called for and, coffin person placed in it for

ju ats'ule ndin t'áh. Se'e edu teyeh. . . .
also they make he said with. Really not quiet. . . .

Úh xattheeh tl'a, dene, dene kíi ts'inh
And before well, people, people just outside

kuindehtheda. Edhéh ju kaa, łiniji édé edhéh
inside they sit. Tent also well, he's dead then tent

mbek'ets'edeghal úh. I aint'inle de'oin goa
they take down and. That was there around the corner a little

ndats'eged úh dene ech'adehłíi ehsíin. Édé zonh
stand up and people different that were. Then only

ju ts'ído detáts'eteh. Úh duh níonidhedi
also children put in. And now everyone running around

kíi egeyah athíjá i t'áh. Dzahagúnht'e.
just white people we became that because of. It's bad.

Dzaheninditthe. Héé, dzahagúnht'e. Gulóon edu
They are in a bad position. Hey, it's bad. I wish not

kagot'e. Éé, gulóon unieht'e, daúdeh t'áh
it's like that. Hey, I wish they are slipping, what will we do with

k'inhín níawokeh. Di ét'ia mbets'ats'edeh edu
way be the same way. This the same we tell them not

editthe. Mbegha niguntthe édé ndátse. I t'áh
they listen. For him medicine trap then strong. That because of

eṇdadla. Sin ts'ído ehłin t'ónh wots'ính
it's difficult/hard. Me child I was before from [since then]

eyi mbetsun ju, gha'aht'in. Kaa,
that his grandmother also, I was with her. Well,

diká'echo éhsín. Jíe egóhó
this big [as big as an adolescent] maybe. Berries maybe

kauts'edhéhthile. Tthundleh úh kónt'i i ehdah.
we went for. Wild rhubarb and like that that also.

Jíe denidil édé ju jíe kaa ts'edeh. Kónt'ónh la
Berries red then also berries for we went. Long ago

kíi gha eṇdádla.
just for difficult.

Bibliography

Unpublished Sources

Census of Canada. Handwritten schedules from Fort Vermilion, N.W. Territories, 1891. Ottawa: Public Archives of Canada.

Clut, Isadore. Letters to Bishop Taché, 1861 to 1888. Typescripts of original letters. Isadore Clut Collection. Ottawa: Oblate Archives.

Jenness, Diamond. "Mythology of the Sekani Indians, Fort McLeod and Fort Grahame, British Columbia." Unpublished manuscript, 1924. Ottawa: Archives of the National Museum of Civilization.

Marten, Charles (Shall). Transcript of interview conducted in Fort Chipewyan, Alberta, August 1988. Edmonton: Boreal Institute for Northern Studies.

Marten, John J. Transcript of interview conducted in Fort Chipewyan, Alberta, August 1988. Edmonton: Boreal Institute for Northern Studies.

Peter, Louise. "Wolverine." Unpublished manuscript, 1976. Fairbanks: Alaska Native Language Center, University of Alaska.

Peter, Moses. "Wolverine and the Wolves." Unpublished manuscript, 1972. Fairbanks: Alaska Native Language Center, University of Alaska.

Preston, Richard. "Cree Narration." Ph.D. dissertation, University of North Carolina, 1971.

Trippe de Roches, Boniface. Transcript of interview conducted in Fort Chipewyan, Alberta, August 1988. Edmonton: Boreal Institute for Northern Studies.

Published Sources

Abel, Kerry. "Prophets, Priests and Preachers: Dene Shamans and Christian Missions in the Nineteenth Century." In *Historical Papers, Communications Historiques: A Selection from the Papers Presented at the Annual Meeting Held at Winnipeg 1986*, edited by Donald Avery, 211-24. Ottawa: Tanamac International, 1986.

Asch, Michael. *Kinship and the Drum Dance in a Northern Dene Community*. Edmonton: Boreal Institute for Northern Studies, 1988.

Farrand, Livingston. Traditions of the Chilcotin Indians. *Memoirs of the American Museum of Natural History* Jesup North Pacific Expedition, 4. New York, 1900.

Guédon, Marie-Françoise. "Upper Tanana River Potlatch." In *Handbook of North American Indians*, vol. 6, *Subarctic,* edited by June Helm, 577-81. Washington, D.C.: Smithsonian Institution, 1981.

Hearne, Samuel. *A Journey from Prince of Wales Fort in Hudson's Bay to the Northern Ocean.* Toronto: Champlain Society, 1911.

Honigman, John J. "Kaska." In *Handbook of North American Indians,* vol. 6, *Subarctic,* edited by June Helm, 442-50. Washington, D.C.: Smithsonian Institution, 1981.

Hymes, Dell. *"In Vain I Tried to Tell You": Essays in Native American Ethnopoetics.* Philadelphia: University of Pennsylvania Press, 1981.

Jenness, Diamond. "Myths of the Carrier Indians." *Journal of American Folklore* 47 (1934): 97-257.

Krott, Peter. *Demon of the North.* New York: Alfred A. Knopf, 1959.

Luckert, Karl. *Coyoteway: A Navajo Healing Ceremonial.* Tucson: University of Arizona Press, 1979.

McLean, John. *James Evans, Inventor of the Syllabic System of the Cree Language.* Toronto: Methodists Mission Rooms, 1890.

Mech, David L. *The Arctic Wolf: Living with the Pack.* Toronto: Key Porter Books, 1988.

Miller, Christopher. *Prophetic Worlds: Indians and Whites on the Columbia Plateau.* New Brunswick: Rutgers University Press, 1985.

Nelson, Richard. *Make Prayers to the Raven.* Chicago: University of Chicago Press, 1983.

Peterson, Jacqueline. "Review of *Prophetic Worlds: Indians and Whites on the Columbia Plateau.*" *Ethnohistory* 35 (1988): 191-96.

Petitot, Emile F. *Exploration de la Région du Grand Lac des Ours.* Paris: Tequi, 1893.

——· *Monograph of the Déné-Dinjíe Indians.* 1878. Translated by Douglas Brynner. Ottawa: Public Archives of Canada, Canadian Institute for Historical Microreproductions, 1980.

Rhodes, Richard A. and Evelyn M. Todd. "Subarctic Algonquian Languages." In *Handbook of North American Indians*, vol. 6, *Subarctic,* edited by June Helm, 52-66. Washington, D.C.:Smithsonian Institution, 1981.

Rice, Keren. *A Grammar of Slave (Dene).* The Hague: Mouton, 1989.

Ridington, Robin. *Swan People.* Ottawa: National Museums of Canada, 1978.

Slobodin, Richard. "Kutchin." In *Handbook of North American Indians*, vol. 6, *Subarctic,* edited by June Helm, 514-32. Washington, D.C.: Smithsonian Institution, 1981.

Spier, Leslie. *The Prophet Dance of the Northwest and Its Derivatives*. General Series in Anthropology 1. Menasha, Wisconsin: George Banta, 1935.

Tedlock, Dennis. *Finding the Center: Narrative Poetry of the Zuñi Indians*. Lincoln: University of Nebraska Press, 1978.

Teit, James. "Kaska Tales." *Journal of American Folklore* 30 (1917): 427-73.

——. "Tahltan Tales." *Journal of American Folklore* 32 (1919): 198-250.

Tobey, Margaret L. "Carrier." In *Handbook of North American Indians*, vol. 6, *Subarctic*, edited by June Helm, 413-32. Washington, D.C.: Smithsonian Institution, 1981.

Wyman, Leland C. *Blessingway*. Tucson: University of Arizona Press, 1970.